AA

ORDNANCE SURVEY
LEISURE GUIDE

O|S

NORTH
MOO

D0808645

Produced jointly by the Publishing Division of the
Automobile Association and the Ordnance Survey

Cover: one of the Low Bride Stones, near Grosmont
Back cover: unloading the catch at Scarborough
Title page: Wheeldale Moor
Contents page: Runswick Bay
Introductory page: Little Fryup Dale

Editors: Jean Heselden, Rebecca Snelling

Designer: Neil Roebuck

Consultant for the North York Moors National Park:
Ian Sampson, Information Officer

Editorial contributors: Dr R Brown (The Wildlife of
the Moors); John McDonnell (Christianity on the
Moors); Joan and Bill Spence (The Coast, Heather
Moorland and the Dales, Railways on the Moors and
the Gazetteer short features); Alan Staniforth (Walks);
Derek Statham (Man and the Landscape);
Peter N. Walker (A to Z Gazetteer)

Picture researcher: Wyn Voysey

Original photography: Rick Newton

Typeset by Avonset, Midsomer Norton, Bath.
Printed in Great Britain by Purnell Book Production
Limited. Member of the BPCC Group.

Maps extracted from the Ordnance Survey's 1:63,360
Tourist Series, 1:25,000 Pathfinder Series and
1:250,000 Routemaster Series, with the permission of
Her Majesty's Stationery Office.
Crown Copyright reserved.

Additions to the maps by the Cartographic Dept of the
Automobile Association and the Ordnance Survey.

Produced by the Publishing Division of the Automobile
Association.

Distributed in the United Kingdom by the Ordnance
Survey, Southampton, and the Publishing Division of
the Automobile Association, Fanum House,
Basingstoke, Hampshire RG21 2EA.

AA ISBN 0 86145 489 8 (hardback)
AA ISBN 0 86145 269 0 (softback)
OS ISBN 0 31900 107 5 (hardback)
OS ISBN 0 31900 106 7 (softback)

Published by the Automobile Association and the
Ordnance Survey.

AA ref: 57655 (hardback)
AA ref: 58735 (softback)

NORTH YORK MOORS

Contents

Using this Book 4

Introduction 5

Man and the Landscape 6

Christianity on the Moors 10

Heather Moorland and the Dales 14

The Wildlife of the Moors 19

The Coast 23

Railways on the Moors 27

A to Z Gazetteer 32

Directory 70

Atlas Legend 78 / Atlas 80

Motor Tours 96

Walks 102

Index 118

Using this Book

The entries in the Gazetteer have been carefully selected to reflect the interest and variety of the North York Moors although for reasons of space it has not been possible to include every community in the region. A number of small villages are described under the entry for a larger neighbour, and these can be found by using the index.

Each entry in the A to Z Gazetteer has the atlas page number on which the place can be found and its National Grid reference included under the heading. An explanation of how to use the National Grid is given on page 78.

Beneath many of the entries in the Gazetteer are listed AA-recommended hotels, guesthouses, camp sites, garages and self-catering accommodation in the immediate vicinity of the place described. Hotels and camp sites are also given an AA classification.

HOTELS

1-star	Good hotels and inns, generally of small scale and with good furnishings and facilities.
2-star	Hotels with a higher standard of accommodation. There should be 20% with private bathrooms or showers.
3-star	Well-appointed hotels. Two-thirds of the bedrooms should have private bathrooms or showers.
4-star	Exceptionally well-appointed hotels offering high standards of comfort and service. All bedrooms should have private bathrooms or showers.
5-star	Luxury hotels offering the highest international standards.

Hotels often satisfy *some* of the requirements for higher classifications than that awarded.

Red-star	Red stars denote hotels which are considered to be of outstanding merit within their classification.
Country House Hotel	A hotel where a relaxed informal atmosphere prevails. Some of the facilities may differ from those at urban hotels of the same classification.

SELF CATERING

These establishments, which are all inspected on a regular basis, have to meet minimum standards in accommodation, furniture, fixtures and fittings, services and linen.

Details are to be found in the AA *Holiday Homes, Cottages and Apartments in Britain* annual guide.

GUESTHOUSES

These are different from, but not necessarily inferior to, AA-appointed hotels, and they offer an alternative for those who prefer inexpensive and not too elaborate accommodation. They all provide clean, comfortable accommodation in homely surroundings. Each establishment must usually offer at least six bedrooms and there should be a general bathroom and a general toilet for every six bedrooms without private facilities.

Parking facilities should be reasonably close.

Other requirements include:
Well maintained exterior; clean and hygienic kitchens; good standard of furnishing; friendly and courteous service; access at reasonable times; the use of a telephone and full English breakfast.

CAMP SITES

1-pennant	Site licence; 10% of pitches for touring units; site density not more than 30 per acre; 2 separate toilets for each sex per 30 pitches; good quality tapwater; efficient waste disposal; regular cleaning of ablutions block; fire precautions; well-drained ground.
2-pennant	All one-pennant facilities plus: 2 washbasins with hot and cold water for each sex per 30 pitches in separate washrooms; warden available at certain times of the day.
3-pennant	All two-pennant facilities plus: one shower or bath for each sex per 30 pitches, with hot and cold water; electric shaver points and mirrors; all-night lighting of toilet blocks; deep sinks for washing clothes; facilities for buying milk, bread and gas; warden in attendance by day, on call by night.
4-pennant	All three-pennant facilities plus: a higher degree of organisation than one–three pennant sites; attention to landscaping; reception office; late-arrivals enclosure; first aid hut; shop; routes to essential facilities lit after dark; play area; bad weather shelter; hard standing for touring vans.
5-pennant	A comprehensive range of services and equipment; careful landscaping; automatic laundry; public telephone; indoor play facilities for children; extra facilities for recreation; warden in attendance 24 hours per day.

WALKS

The walks in this book have been carefully planned to suit families but a few need particular care if young children are in the party. Potential hazards are highlighted in the text.

It is always advisable to go well-equipped with suitable clothing and refreshment, and, as an extra precaution, a compass.

Please observe The Country Code at all times.

NORTH YORK MOORS

Introduction

Wide uninterrupted expanses of heather moorland, secluded farming dales and a dramatic coastline are just a few of the ingredients that make up the North York Moors. Discover here the ruins of great abbeys, a stretch of road built by the Romans and the places Captain James Cook knew as a boy. This book takes the visitor to stone-built market towns, traditional seaside resorts and romantic fishing villages redolent of smuggling and whaling tales. It contains tours and walks enabling exploration of the countryside, explains the legacies of the past and highlights the attractions that can be enjoyed today. Written by people who live in the North York Moors, and backed by the AA's expertise and the Ordnance Survey's mapping, this guide is as useful to those who return to the area year after year as it is to the first-time visitor.

Man and the Landscape

Walking across Glaisdale Moor in the heart of the North York Moors provides an experience of wilderness and solitude rarely found in the Britain of the 20th century. With only the haunting cry of the curlew, the harsh call of the grouse and the occasional bleating of sheep to break the peace, one's overwhelming impression is of a natural environment untouched by the hand of man. Nothing could be further from the truth. The upland moorland is a man-made landscape just like the familiar farming landscape of the lowlands.

A few miles to the south around Keldy is another man-made landscape of much more recent origin, the coniferous forest. Planted mainly during the inter-war period, these huge expanses of conifers have replaced belts of moorland and farmland along the southern fringe of the North York Moors. Dull and monotonous some of the more recent woodlands undoubtedly are, with their straight lines of pine or larch, but as the forests mature and more selective felling and replanting is carried out, a much more varied and attractive landscape results – so much so that these forest areas are fast becoming one of the main recreation zones of the Moors. The forest drive around Dalby, one of the first areas to be planted, attracts many visitors with its secluded car parks, picnic areas and viewpoints. Forest walks and trails are laid out for the rambler, often conveniently beginning and finishing at car parks. The remote

Glaisdale Moor above Great Fryup Dale. Inset: Cropton Forest. A 5½-mile forest drive starts at Levisham and has fine views of Newtondale

railway halt in Newtondale is also a starting point for forest walks.

Unlike the 20th-century forest, the farmlands of the National Parks are steeped in history. There are two main types. One is the sheep and dairy farming country of the main valleys, or dales as they are known in Yorkshire, which presents a well-tended farming landscape of stone walls, hedges, copses, small fields and neat stone-built farmhouses. Particularly unspoilt dales are Bransdale and Farndale.

The second type of farming landscape is found on the plateau surfaces of the Tabular Hills on the southern edge of the Park and along the coastal plain. Here are mixed farms with a varying proportion of arable land growing corn and root crops, interspersed with pasture grazed by cattle and sheep. The coastal plain is covered with a thick deposit of boulder clay laid down during the last Ice Age and this gives rise to more fertile soils than the sandstones and gritstones farther inland which were not covered with ice. As a result there is a farming belt around the moorland core, and only at Ravenscar above Robin Hood's Bay do the moors sweep down to the sea.

Man's first appearance

To begin the story of man's influence on the natural environment, we need to go back to the period when man first appeared in the area, shortly after the last Ice Age over 10,000 years ago. Although it has been known for some time now that man began to inhabit the area very early in this period hunting animals and gathering wild fruits and berries, only recently has it come to light that he appears to have learned how to manipulate the environment for his benefit. He realised that by burning, and thus opening up the lightly wooded canopy on the higher hills, the large animals on which he depended for food would be encouraged to breed and multiply. This deliberate burning marked the beginning of a long, but increasingly intensive, management of the land which continues today with modern technology.

Early farmers

Perhaps the greatest change in the prehistoric landscape of the Moors however, occurred around 3,000BC when agriculture was first practised. It is not known how it was brought to the area or by which people, but it spread rapidly on the

Hambleton Hills in the west of the area and on the
fertile soils of the Tabular Hills between Helmsley
and Scarborough in the south of the National
Park. Later, in the Bronze Age around 2,000BC, it
spread onto the higher plateaux of the Moors
where the remaining woodland was cleared away.
Apart from a few scattered remains of pottery and
primitive tools, these early farmers left little to
remind us of their long years of toil. However,
their burial places, or tumuli, are found everywhere
on the moors, often on the highest points. There
are over 3,000 of them, ranging from slight bumps
to mounds up to 20ft high and 100ft in diameter.
Good examples can be seen on the main moorland
divide, now followed by the route of the famous
Lyke Wake Walk. Loose Howe on Glaisdale
Moor, Shunner Howe on Rosedale Moor and
Wheeldale Howe on Wheeldale Moor mark the
site of Bronze Age tumuli. 'Howe' is an Old Norse
word meaning a grave mound. The chiefs and
leading members of Bronze Age tribes were
cremated and their remains placed in urns which
were buried under the barrows. In some cases,
such as the Bridestones on the ridge between
Bilsdale and Tripsdale, the burials were also marked
by stone circles. In other places the howes and
stones lie in long lines – right across Fylingdales
from the Bridestones to Maw Rigg above Langdale,
for example. Some well-marked settlement sites can
also be traced, with cemeteries of barrows, hollow
cattle-tracks, hut sites and the remains of small
fields.

Most of the North York Moors was settled
during this time and many of today's parish
boundaries probably follow the dividing lines
between Bronze Age clans. The communities were
self-sufficient and their territories planned to
contain water courses, pasture and woodland.
What is particularly significant, however, is that
the cultivation and grazing on the plateau surfaces
of the area rapidly exhausted the thin, infertile
soils. This made them acidic, encouraging the heath
and moorland so familiar today.

The Bronze Age gave way to the Iron Age
around 500BC when the climate took a turn for
the worse. Despite this, recent results from
advanced research techniques show that the
population increased and livestock and arable
farming were the dominant land uses. By this time,
the tribes were larger and organised well enough to
carry out warfare. Some evidence for this comes
from the construction of massive parallel dykes,
presumably defence works, at various sites around
the edges of the moorland area. The most well
known are the Scamridge and Levisham Dykes in
the Tabular Hills and the Cleave Dykes in the
Hambleton Hills.

The Roman occupation

The Romans left few physical reminders of their
occupation which was probably limited to military
control. There is a well-preserved 1¼-mile stretch
of road on the edge of Wheeldale Moor, called
Wade's Causeway (see page 43) and other Roman
remains include a fort at Lease Rigg near
Grosmont and coastal signal stations at several
places along the coast which warned of raids by
Saxon invaders. Perhaps the most exciting Roman
remains, however, are the military camps at
Cawthorn near Pickering. The camps are now
owned by the National Park Authority and will
shortly be opened up for inspection and study by
the public.

*Remains of a Roman coastal signal station on the Castle
Headland near Scarborough. Other signal station sites are
Kettleness, Saltburn and Ravenscar*

Invasion and settlement

The settlement of the area by Teutonic invaders
after the collapse of the Roman Empire produced
the pattern of villages and countryside we inherit
today. Angles and Saxons were followed by
Vikings and eventually by Normans after 1066.
Most place-names in the Moors are of Anglian or
Norse derivation. Villages ending in 'ham' or 'ton'
are Anglo-Saxon in origin, those ending in 'by' or
'dale' are Norse. Many names of landscape features
have a Norse 'hardening' such as rigg instead of
ridge, or beck instead of stream or brook. It is not
known in detail how the area fared during the
upheavals of invasion and settlement but certainly
the population seems to have declined from the
high point of the Roman occupation, and did not
recover until the Middle Ages.

The Middle Ages

During the Middle Ages the rural economy was
carefully geared to the natural resources available.
Each parish was largely self-sufficient but,
inevitably in an upland area, there were marked
differences between the fertile lands on the
limestone of the Tabular Hills and the acid
moorlands farther north. Bartering for corn and
livestock was commonplace and some livestock
were driven long distances to markets in the south.

The farming of the area was transformed in the
13th and 14th centuries by the monastic sheep
farmers who improved the wild and barren land,
first for sheep and later for arable or dairy produce.
These skilful husbandmen became large and
wealthy landowners operating from their strikingly
beautiful abbeys at Rievaulx, Byland and
Guisborough. With the dissolution of the abbeys
in the 16th century, an era of high farming was
brought to a close.

There was little in the way of agricultural
innovation until the 18th century but, nevertheless,
many new farms were established in the 17th
century when enclosure of common land occurred.
Reclamation of the moorland edge also intensified
as the population increased. During the late 17th
century a number of farmhouses were built on the
newly enclosed land using local stone.

The improvements in agricultural techniques in
the 18th century, especially the introduction of
root crops such as turnips and mangolds, led to an
intensification of farming which continued into the
mid-19th century as the population increased with
the growth of industry. Enclosure of the former
open fields of medieval times was completed and
much common grazing was also enclosed, especially
during the Napoleonic Wars in the 19th century.

Left: many of the houses in the former fishing village of Runswick Bay retain the traditional red-pantiled roofs of the area. Other unspoilt coastal villages are Staithes and Robin Hood's Bay
Above: an old alum quarry opposite Carlton Bank

Mining and quarrying

The Moors possess a great wealth of mineral resources which have been mined since prehistoric times, but the introduction of the railway to this isolated area in the early 19th century heralded a new industrial boom.

Of particular importance was iron ore, mined in the Cleveland Hills, Eskdale and Rosedale. Vast quantities of ore were extracted. There was an iron-smelting works at Grosmont, a smelting works and ore-export harbour at Port Mulgrave, as well as several smaller treatment plants and mineral railways, especially in Rosedale. The landscape at this time must have been a discordant mixture of moorland farming and heavy industry with expanding mining towns and villages in parts of Rosedale and the Esk Valley.

Other minerals mined include alum, used to 'fix' the coloured dyes in cloth and in paper making (see also page 24) and jet, a fossil carbon deposit much admired in Victorian England for its ornamental qualities (see page 26). The brown sandstones on the moorland above Whitby provided building stone for many famous buildings including the Houses of Parliament and Covent Garden but the quarries have now closed. Limestone is still quarried today but at one time the lime obtained by burning the stone was used as a fertiliser. Nearly every village and often individual farms had their own kilns, many of which can still be seen. Coal from deposits on the moors – albeit of poor quality – was used as fuel for the kilns and the open pit scars remain as evidence of this activity.

At one time the only volcanic rock found in the Moors was valuable for road construction. This rock, 'whinstone' as it is locally called, was formed from the hot lava which occupied a crack in the northern part of the moors stretching east from Great Ayton towards the coast at Ravenscar. Recent projects involve the mining of potash at Boulby and natural gas drilling at several places.

Villages

The villages of the Moors represent one of its greatest scenic assets. Their buildings are in local stone, a soft honey-coloured limestone around Helmsley merging to a grey limestone farther east and a rugged brown sandstone throughout the rest of the area. The red pantile is the traditional roofing material and the vernacular style is simple with clean-cut, robust lines. Some villages are completely unspoilt by modern additions but during the mining era of the 19th century different styles and materials, such as red brick and terracotta, were introduced in some areas.

The challenge of the 20th century

The creation of the National Park in 1952 does not mean that the area is publicly owned, but that the landscape is managed for its natural beauty and the enjoyment it gives to visitors. These objectives have to be married with the social and economic needs of the local population. The policies and projects of the National Park Authority are geared to these aims and of particular importance are the various grant aid schemes for such matters as tree planting, moorland management and maintenance of old buildings. As the need for primary food products from the area decreases in an era of surpluses, so the demand for an attractive outdoor environment for recreation increases. Thus in the 20th century the Moors are taking on another function in addition to the ancient activities of agriculture, forestry and mining.

Christianity on the Moors

In 657 King Oswy gave his daughter, Hilda, land to found a monastery after he was successful in battle against a pagan king: Whitby Abbey was the result

The windswept hulk of Whitby Abbey perched on its cliff above the harbour is an enduring reminder of the great monastic tradition in north-east Yorkshire. Yet the first stone of the building we see was laid less than 800 years ago. Almost 600 years earlier still the site had held the double monastery (for men and women) of 'Streoneshalch', ruled over by Abbess Hilda, kin of the Northumbrian royal house. The monastery numbered among its brethren the humble oxherd Caedmon who, with a little help from on high, achieved renown as England's first religious poet. The 8th-century historian, Bede, tells his story: 'It sometimes happened at a feast that all the guests in turn would be invited to sing; when he saw the harp coming his way, he would get up and go back to the stables. On one such occasion he settled down to sleep. Suddenly in a dream he saw a man standing beside him who called him by name. "Caedmon," he said, "sing me a song." "I don't know how to sing," he replied. "It is because I cannot sing that I left the feast." The man then said: "But you shall sing to me." "What should I sing about?" "Sing about the Creation of all things." And Caedmon immediately began to sing verses in praise of God the Creator that he had never heard before.' A 20ft-high sandstone cross near St Mary's Church on the cliff-top commemorates the story of Caedmon. On one side of the cross, erected in 1898, are the lines of his 'Song of Creation'.

Not only Whitby but the whole area is full of reminders of the Anglo-Saxon period of Christianity in England. There are parish churches dedicated to saints like Oswald, Hilda, and Gregory, quite a number of which preserve in their fabric fragments of pre-Norman stonework, notably re-used churchyard crosses. Bede and others have recorded the work of men like the brother saints Cedd and Chadd who established a monastery at Lastingham contemporary with St Hilda's foundation at Whitby. Despite the short-lived mission by the Roman-trained Paulinus who came from Kent to Northumbria in the early 7th century and baptised both the future St Hilda and her great-uncle King Edwin, the predominant Christianising influence came from St Columba's 6th-century foundation on Iona. Besides the controversies over the dating of Easter and the style of monastic tonsures (shaved heads), there were marked differences of missionary practice between the followers of St Augustine from Rome and the Celtic monks. The latter established their monasteries as focal preaching centres, from which members of the community (often ranked as 'bishops' but subordinate to an abbot) travelled out to preach the Word at stone crosses. These were set up as rallying points and often later became the site for the parish church. To this system is due, at least in part, the peculiar and durable tendency of churches like St Gregory's Minster at Kirkdale to be situated not in a settlement but at the strategic centre of an area of scattered hamlets. However, the clash between the Roman and Celtic factions in England was finally resolved at the Synod of Whitby in AD663, in favour of the Augustinians. Henceforward the date of Easter was standardised.

Devastation

Between them the Celtic and Roman missions Christianised most of pagan Yorkshire. But this 7th-century flowering of Christianity was soon to face new threats from other, fiercer pagans. The first assault by marauding Danes involved the sacking of St Cuthbert's sanctuary on Lindisfarne in Northumberland in 793. Two generations later came Yorkshire's turn. The monasteries of 'Streoneshalch' and 'Laestingau' (Lastingham) were ravaged by 870, and it was on subsequent occupation by Danish settlers that 'Streoneshalch' was renamed 'Witebi'. Danish invasions from the sea were followed by Irish-Norse settlers from across the Pennines in the following century, and a Norse kingdom was established at York. Christianity was securely rooted however. Despite the horror-stories associated with the Vikings the

Below: the ruins of Byland Abbey. Founded by the Cistercians in 1177, it was stripped of its treasures when Henry VIII dissolved the monasteries
Right: the Norman crypt of St Mary's, Lastingham

Danes were eventually converted when the whole Danelaw – the area of Danish settlement and rule in Eastern England – was absorbed into the English kingdom by the end of the 10th century.

Worse was yet to come however for north-east Yorkshire. The Norman Conquest brought in its train, in 1069, the appalling harrying of the North by William I. Domesday Book, compiled a few years later, shows parish after parish as laid waste and worthless. It was exceptional to find, as at Old Byland, a church recorded as still standing, and with a priest to serve it. Whitby was one of the very few centres to escape, largely, no doubt, because of its inaccessibility by land, but perhaps also because a new Benedictine community was even then erecting a successor to St Hilda's monastery. Its reprieve was brief, for 10 years later an attack by Danes drove the monks out. Some went to Hackness and Lastingham, but eventually returned in the following century to build the present abbey at Whitby, others went to York where they founded the separate house of St Mary's Abbey. For over half a century the few lay communities on and around the Moors had a struggle to survive and re-establish, and the clergy also had problems restoring its organisation.

Recovery: the age of the monasteries

Help for those in social, economic and spiritual straits arrived in the mid 12th century. Many Norman lords, unable to develop their new estates for lack of manpower, handed over portions of them to religious orders. These portions were often the remotest and least promising areas of an estate, and sometimes the new owners were monks invited from Normandy. In particular, new

Above and left: the most complete and beautiful survival of a medieval abbey in England, Cistercian Rievaulx has attracted admiring visitors for centuries. Of particular note are the 13th-century chancel and refectory – the main room of the south range

offshoots of the Benedictine tradition like the Cistercians, vigorous and intent on separating themselves from the world and its temptations, welcomed such grants, though in the interests of self-sufficiency they also made sure of getting benefits like mineral rights and fisheries. In 1131 Walter L'Espec, Lord of Helmsley, gave some land at Rievaulx to the Cistercians for the site of a new monastery which became the largest and finest Cistercian house in England. These orders were respected, and in a position to recruit willing hands. Within a generation great tracts of moorland and dale, especially in the western part of the Moors, were being successfully developed by the new abbeys at Byland and Rievaulx.

The Cistercians had one innovative feature which fitted them uniquely for large-scale reclamation of waste-land. Beside the core of priest-monks common to all communities following the Rule of St Benedict, whose presence was required in choir seven times a day and who could therefore spend little time working with their hands outside the cloister, the Cistercians developed a second tier of 'lay-brethren' or *conversi*, the 'bearded ones'. Often skilled farmers, masons or miners, these illiterate men were not ordained but joined the order in considerable numbers and wrought a remarkable transformation in the landscape. Rievaulx under the third abbot, St Aelred, for example, grew to a community of 650 men; 150 of them choir-monks, the other 500 laybrothers and abbey servants. Because the religious observances required of the *conversi* were much less time-consuming, it was even possible to establish groups of them at considerable distances from the

mother-house, from where they returned only for the major feasts. Thus most of Bilsdale, a few miles north of Rievaulx, was organised into a closely integrated set of 'granges' (farms) which ran huge flocks of sheep. At one time these contained over 14,000 sheep, the wool being sold to cloth merchants from Flanders, France and Italy. Iron was also mined and stone quarried for the abbey's new buildings. Further east, in the marshes below Pickering, other *conversi* teams drained the land (some channels are still called ' Friar's Ditch') and created more pasture with rich hay-meadows. Rievaulx even had a sea-fishing 'grange' at Teesmouth and a stud-farm in Upper Teesdale. Paradoxically, the Cistercian impulse to flee the world and tame the wilderness led to the creation of a major 'agribusiness' which put the Order, in areas like the Moors and the Cumbrian fells, among the foremost entrepreneurs of the age.

The success of the Cistercians encouraged older-established orders like the Augustinians of Kirkham and Guisborough, and the Benedictines of York and Whitby, to follow suit and develop large upland tracts for stock-farming and mineral extraction. Smaller religious houses also appeared in the heart of the Moors, like the Premonstratensian Priory of Grosmont, and small, often ill-endowed convents of nuns, as at Baysdale, Arden and Rosedale (this latter was a priory, not an abbey despite the modern name of the village). A late addition (c1400) to the roll of major monasteries was Mount Grace Priory. The most complete survival of a Carthusian house, with its pattern of 'hermit-cells', Mount Grace fully deserves a visit.

The Cistercians played little direct part in the cure of lay souls, since their rule forbade the acquisition of parish churches. The older orders, however, led the way in re-establishing parish organisations. From the 12th century onwards a majority of churches in the area were built, or rebuilt from whatever remnants the Harrying of the North had left. Lay lords of the manor followed suit, as on the estate of Pickering belonging to the royal Duchy of Lancaster.

The heyday of the *conversi* lasted less time than is generally realised. Well before the end of the 13th century their numbers dwindled, and then economic recession followed by the Black Death brought an end to the monasteries' period of growth. Their granges were generally broken up into family-sized farms and leased to a new class of independent husbandmen. Even the Cistercians joined the older orders in living off their rents instead of taking an active part in developing their estates. Nevertheless, in addition to the imposing ruins of the abbeys themselves the numbers of 'grange' and 'cote' farm-names on and around the moors are a memorial to monastic enterprise.

After the Reformation

The dissolution of the monasteries under Henry VIII brought about less disruption or indeed bloodshed in north-east Yorkshire than in some parts of the North, though moorsmen did march to join the Pilgrimage of Grace, the 1536 northern rebellion against Henry VIII. Although the abandoned monastic buildings inevitably decayed to the ruins we see today (Rievaulx was not only stripped of its treasures after its closure, but part of its fabric was used to provide building material for cottages in the village) the Reformation took a long time to achieve a final impact here, especially in areas protected by Catholic-inclined landowners like the Meynells and the Earls of Rutland. Indeed, Catholicism never entirely died out in some remote corners of the Moors. One of the last priests to die for his faith was Nicholas Postgate. Executed in York in 1679 at the age of 83, he was a native of Egton and had spent half a century serving the Catholics of the lower Esk Valley. His main base was at Ugthorpe, where the Old Hall contained a priest's hole.

Inexorably, though, deprived of its clergy, the old faith dwindled. Often its role was taken over not by the established church but by Nonconformists. Sir Thomas Hoby of Hackness was one Puritan squire who actively promoted Calvinist doctrines. Following the tour of Yorkshire by their founder, George Fox, in 1651 the Quakers established a vigorous presence in the area. The 18th-century Meeting House at Laskill, a stone's throw, as it happens, from the Rievaulx Abbey Woolhouse site, is one of the various relics of the Friends' great days.

Presbyterians, Congregationalists and eventually Methodists also came to play an important part in the area. A century after Fox, both John and Charles Wesley paid missionary visits to this part of Yorkshire. Rare is the moorland dale without at least one chapel in it, though some are now turned to more worldly uses. Castleton in Esk Dale, which grew from a handful of cottages at the end of the 18th century to a miniature market town by 1850, had acquired by then an iron-built Anglican church, a Quaker meeting house, and Wesleyan and Primitive Methodist chapels. There were increasingly clear social differences between those who adhered to the established church, mostly gentry and estate employees, and Nonconformists, who tended to be independent farmers and tradesmen. Even in Victorian times one senses bafflement and incomprehension, to say nothing of snobbery, in the Church of England's view of Nonconformists. One vicar complained at the 'wild sort of Methodists' who inhabited the fringe of his parish and who celebrated Good Friday with 'regular jollification, a fruit banquet, a series of races, and a concert'.

Two Victorian vicars

By Victoria's day the Church of England clergy had rediscovered a degree of fervour for converting others to their faith and there were a number of distinguished parsons in the area. Canon J C Atkinson of Danby, best known as a medieval scholar, also took his parish work seriously, and wrote that enchanting classic *Forty Years in a Moorland Parish* (recently abridged and published in paperback as *Countryman on the Moors*). On his arrival in Danby his churchwarden took him to inspect the church. Atkinson was startled to note that the man did not remove his hat on entering, and even more dismayed to see that the ragged green baize covering the altar was smothered in stale crumbs. His guide saw nothing odd in this: 'Why, it is the Sunday School teachers, they must get their meat somewhere, and they gets it here.' Essex-born gentleman though he was, Atkinson soon won the confidence of his flock by his obvious interest in their way of life and sympathy with their problems.

A different sort of parson was dominating Helmsley at about the same time. Vicar Gray had been known to use his fists to effect on a recalcitrant parishioner. A man of overflowing energy and generosity, he campaigned vigorously against lack of sanitation, unreasonable hours for apprentices, and the tight-lacing of stays, to mention but a few pet causes. He also indulged in often public arguments with his patron and lord of the manor, as well as with Methodists and Roman Catholics. Perhaps his most bitter attacks were against a 'Mr Burge', who was in fact Prior of the Benedictine monastery at Ampleforth.

Ampleforth – a modern monastic community

The monks had established themselves at Ampleforth in 1802, when the English community of St Lawrence, resident in France since the 17th century, was driven out by the French Revolution. With its famous Roman Catholic boys' school already developing, the Abbey was even then becoming an influential element in the district. It seems fitting to end this brief review of Christianity in north-east Yorkshire at the place where the Rule of St Benedict is once again kept by a monastic community, as it had been in the days of St Aelred and St Wilfrid.

The Quaker Meeting House at Laskill, completed in 1734, had a regular attendance of 20. Meetings were originally held in licensed private houses and between 1689 and 1708 there were eight of these in Bilsdale

Heather Moorland and the Dales

The North York Moors National Park covers an area of 553 square miles, 40 per cent of which is now open moorland. This is the largest expanse of heather moorland in England, a breaktaking sea of purple when it is blooming in all its glory during July, August and early September. In winter the moor takes on a dark and desolate air, well-deserving its old romantic title of 'Blackamore'. It seems hardly surprising that William the Conqueror and his retinue should have got lost in a blizzard up on the moors when he was inspecting his new kingdom after the Battle of Hastings.

The first tinges of colour appear in July when the ling (Scotch heather) with its tiny triangular leaves, begins to flower. There are two other types of heather to be found on these heights, the bell

Wheeldale Moor, the location of Wade's Causeway — a well-preserved stretch of Roman road
Inset: Young Ralph Cross, near the head of Rosedale

heather, which is a deeper purple, and the cross-leaved heath bearing large rose-pink flowers. Someone has calculated that three million flowers are produced by every square mile of moorland each year. During autumn the purple of the heather is edged with the rusty browns of the bracken, intermingled with green patches of bilberry.

The extensive moorland of the Park contrasts with intermittent dales. Some, such as Rye Dale and Riccal Dale, contain dappled-green oak and ash woods. Their warm south-facing slopes have areas of scrub, and sweet-smelling grassland is wedged between farmland and dark, shady conifer plantations. Farndale and Rosedale in the south, and the shorter valleys such as Danby, Fryup and Glaisdale in the north are a tapestry of small fields, rivers, hedges and woods.

Sheep farming on the moors

Heather, a hardy plant able to subsist on the poor

soil of the moors, is vital to the economic cycle related to sheep farming and the sport of red grouse shooting. The moors are still an essential part of farming in the area, although they once supported considerably more sheep than the 50,000 that are there today. Moorland grazing rights are valuable to farmers in the dales who keep their sheep on the moors for most of the year, bringing them to the lower ground as lambing time approaches. Though there were once many more sheep sales than there are now, they are still an important part of the farming life and attract buyers from a wide area. Critical eyes assess the sheep gathered in their pens before they come under the auctioneer's hammer at Goathland, Blakey, Rosedale, Castleton and Danby.

The most common sheep on the moors is the Swaledale, a hardy breed, easily recognisable by its black face, white muzzle and grey speckled legs. The ram's horns are massive and curly, whereas the ewe's, whose horn is valued by walking-stick makers, consists of a single curve. The Swaledale was introduced to the North York Moors in the 1920s and eventually took over from the Scottish Blackface as the most popular breed on the heights, although some Scottish Blackface are still kept on the moors. These do not have the white nose, they are broader in the back, and their wool is longer than the Swaledale's.

Sheep are said to be 'heafed' to the moor,

This view from Chimney Bank Top, Rosedale, is worth the climb up a 1-in-3 gradient from Rosedale Abbey

indicating that each flock knows its own territory. This knowledge is apparently passed down to the lambs by their mothers, but intermingling is inevitable as there are no fences on the moors. In order to avoid disputes of ownership the sheep are marked in various ways. A splash of colour near the shoulder or on the loin makes identification

easy from a distance, but ear notching, initials branded on the horns, and ear tags are also used.

These moorland sheep are extremely hardy as they have to withstand severe conditions on the wild, bleak heights. One of the greatest threats to their lives however is not the weather but the motor car. Sheep do not have much road sense and the motorist needs to be aware of them grazing by the roadside and drive with care. Losing an animal is costly to the farmer.

Grouse on the moors
The red grouse, dark reddish-brown in colour and about the size of a small chicken, is the 'moor bird', its low flight over the heather characterised by a whirring of wings followed by a glide. Its distinctive call may be described as 'go-bak, bak-bak-bak'. During the grouse shooting season, 12 August to 10 December, sportsmen stand in the shooting butts which are built of stone and topped with heather or bilberries so that they merge with the surrounding ground, while beaters work in a line across the moor, driving the birds to flight in the direction of the guns.

Controlled burning
The grouse is dependent on heather, needing the young, green shoots for food and older heather for nesting. With this in mind gamekeepers and farmers manage the moor by maintaining a patchwork of old and new heather. Controlled burning burns off the top, woody stems of the heather, encouraging the growth of new stems. A six-year rotation of areas burned, known as 'swizzens' or 'swiddens', ensures a continued supply of new growth. The burning is carefully carried out when the peat is damp, between 1 November and 31 March. At this time of year the fire will not penetrate the peat to smoulder for weeks or months and damage the heather roots.

A special licence is needed to burn the heather at other times of the year because of the permanent damage that can be caused. Wheeldale Moor and Glaisdale Moor still bear the scars of accidental fires which smouldered for months after the hot summer of 1976. Altogether four per cent of the heather moorland was destroyed. These areas may be covered by moss, lichen or rough grass by the year 2000, but before then it is more likely that wind and rain will have eroded the scarred areas

Top: red grouse on nest. The female scrapes out a hollow in the ground and lines it with grass or heather. Four to nine eggs are laid in April or May, and these have to be protected from the hooded crow. Above: a shooting butt

leaving a rocky, dusty desert.

If controlled burning did not take place the surrounding bracken would encroach more and more on the old, ailing heather, eventually taking over completely. Not only would the grouse disappear but a valuable source of late nectar for bees would go too. Hives are taken up to the moors by local beekeepers when the heather begins to flower and heather honey can be bought locally.

Routes across the moors
Trackways from many ages cross the moor, the oldest being the Roman road on Wheeldale Moor, known locally as Wade's Causeway (see page 43). There are also a considerable number of tracks from the days when packhorses and ponies were the only means of transport over the moors. These routes were often paved with flag-stones called 'trods' to allow the packhorses dry passage over the boggy moor. One very ancient route is the Hambleton Drove Road. This was used between the 17th and 19th centuries by Scottish drovers bringing their cattle south for sale at markets and fairs. A booklet on the road is available from the North York Moors National Park Authority. A good starting point from which to follow part of the route is Sheepwash, where the trackway crosses the beck. From here, where there are a number of car parks in an attractive moorland setting, the route passes the Chequers Inn on Osmotherley Moor before climbing 1,257ft Black Hambleton, with good views over the Vale of York. The route then splits, one way going southwards to York, the

A moorland track — part of the Hambleton section of an ancient drove road which ran from the south of England to Scotland. Inset: a Swaledale ewe

other turning eastwards to Malton.

The 93-mile Cleveland Way, the second long-distance footpath to be established by the Countryside Commission, was opened in 1969. This route, between Helmsley and Filey, is signposted and waymarked with the acorn symbol. It follows three-quarters of the perimeter of the National Park, encompassing the Hambleton Hills, the Cleveland Hills and the coast from Saltburn down to Scarborough, and takes 10 days to a fortnight to complete. In 1975 a 50-mile 'missing link' walk was devised between Crook Ness on the coast north of Scarborough and Helmsley.

The tough, 40-mile Lyke Wake Walk from Osmotherley to Ravenscar is a well-known walk across the moorland. The object of the walk is that it should be completed in under 24 hours, a feat which has been accomplished by over 80,000 people since the walk was established by Bill Cowley in 1955. Those who complete it can join the Lyke Wake Club, although you need to be reasonably fit and take sensible safety precautions before embarking on the entire walk. It has been necessary in recent years to dissuade large parties because of erosion along the path. 'Lyke' means corpse and 'wake' means the watching over of a corpse. The name of the walk is taken from the ancient 'Cleveland Lyke Wake Dirge' which suggests that after death the soul would make a journey over the moors.

Another long-distance walk is the 37-mile White Rose Walk linking the landmarks of Roseberry Topping and the White Horse at Kilburn. There is also the 54-mile North York Moors Crosses Walk which takes in 13 of the moorland crosses and starts and finishes at Goathland. An official walk of the route is held in July.

Stone crosses

The North York Moors contain hundreds of standing stones and crosses, probably Britain's largest assembly, and certainly unique in such a compact area. They include parish boundary markers, way markers, religious crosses and memorials and vary in shape from complete crosses to mere stumps. Some are of great antiquity and craftsmanship while others are rough blocks.

Over 30 of the moorland crosses have been given names. One of the most distinctive and best known is Ralph's Cross, or Young Ralph, used by the North York Moors National Park as its emblem. This 9ft-tall, slender stone cross stands prominently beside the road which crosses Blakey Rigg between Hutton-le-Hole and Castleton, near the crossroads to Westerdale and Rosedale on a site which affords marvellous views across the moors and into several dales. Its age is not known, but it is thought to be an 18th-century replica of an original highway marker. For centuries, it has been customary for travellers to place coins on the top, for the benefit of those less fortunate than themselves. This custom almost destroyed Young Ralph. In 1961, the slender stem broke as a man tried to recover some coins. The cross was carefully repaired, but in October 1984 vandals smashed the cross and it had to be repaired once again.

This medieval cross is Old Ralph, not to be confused with Young Ralph, a taller cross 200yds away. From Old Ralph there is a view of the sea

Old Ralph, only 5ft high, stands on the moor almost hidden by heather about 200 yards to the south-west of Young Ralph and along the road to Rosedale is Fat Betty, formally known as the White Cross. This has a separate round headstone sitting on top of the main 'body'. These are now cemented together because of vandalism, but coins also used to be left here under the top stone for poor travellers. The Margery Stone, sometimes called Old Margery, is also nearby and serves as a marker for the Lyke Wake Walk. A legend seeks to account for the presence of these stones. Ralph, an aged servant at a nunnery in Rosedale, escorted Sister Elizabeth to the moors to meet Sister Margery from Baysdale. The fog descended and they were lost, but had the sense to sit and wait until it cleared. Thus the rendezvous was eventually accomplished. Old Ralph is said to have marked the occasion by erecting these stones.

Lilla Cross on Fylingdales Moor may be the oldest Christian monument in the north of England. It is named after Lilla, a faithful servant who lost his life in AD626 saving King Edwin from an assassin's dagger. The cross is also a marker, standing near the crossroads of two ancient moorland roads.

The dales
The wide tracts of harsh moorland are cut by pastoral valleys where villages and isolated farms brighten the landscape with their red pantile roofs. The peace of many of these secluded dales has changed little since St Aeldred, the 12th-century third Abbot of Rievaulx, spoke of the tranquillity of Rye Dale: 'Everywhere peace, everywhere serenity and a marvellous freedom from the tumult of the world.' Roads use the pattern of moor and dale by following the riggs (ridges) between these features. The rigg roads give extensive views of heather moorland for often the valleys cannot be seen and the heather seems to stretch to the horizon without interruption.

Bilsdale, with easy access at both ends of the dale, carries a road from Helmsley to Teesside. There are only two tiny villages in the dale, Chop Gate and Fangdale Beck. This is one of the farming dales which was cultivated by the Cistercian monks of Rievaulx. Today there are about 1,300 farms throughout the North York Moors and in the dales they are primarily livestock concerns where sheep and cattle are reared. However, now that transportation of produce is easier, some of the farms are concentrating on dairy farming, as the milk tankers frequently seen on the roads testify. If the livestock farmer does not have enough land available for producing winter feed, the young animals are sold to be fattened or cross-bred on farms in lower areas.

Newtondale carries the North York Moors Railway but no motor road. This 12-mile long dale contrasts with the other dales, being formed when Ice Age lakes in Esk Dale and Wheeldale overflowed. The water rushed south towards Pickering, carving out a twisting, steep-sided valley as it did so. Sheer cliffs overlook nature holding sway far below.

On the north side of the Park, Westerdale, Danby Dale, Great Fryup Dale and Glaisdale are smaller than those to the south. These dales run into Esk Dale which runs west to east carrying the River Esk to the sea at Whitby. North of the Esk Valley the land rises to more expanses of moorland before dropping down towards the flatter land of Teesside beyond the borders of the Park. To the west the moors roll to the Hambleton Hills, where much moorland has been reclaimed for rich farmland. They end at the western escarpment with magnificent, often awe-inspiring views westwards across the Vale of York to the Pennines 20 miles away at such points as Roulston Scar, Sutton Bank and Whitestone Cliff. To the north are tree-studded hills and Lake Gormire, to the south Hood Hill.

Rising gently from the Vale of Pickering the land flattens to form a table-like top about 3 miles wide and about 25 miles long from east to west, giving it the name Tabular Hills. The northern side of the table ends suddenly and leaves a bold escarpment with a number of cliff-like promontories pointing northwards. One of the results of this is that the traveller, whether on foot, in the saddle or in a car comes across delightful surprise views which will make him stop and take in the breathtaking scenic panorama.

Lovely Little Fryup Dale is one of the numerous tributary dales of the Esk Valley. Walk 7 descends from the moors to pass along the dale to Danby

The Wildlife of the Moors

The unique, isolated upland block of the North York Moors is in many ways the meeting place for the north to south and east to west variation in our countryside and its wildlife. The combined influence of geology, weathering processes – including glaciation – and human management over thousands of years has given rise to a landscape which contains many interesting and unusual plant and animal communities. If you are patient you may be rewarded with the exciting sight of a merlin pursuing a meadow pipit, or a badger returning to its sett; a pine marten or a red squirrel; a rare bat, butterfly or orchid.

Moorland

The beautiful purples of the flowering heathers in August and September are an eye-catching sight and, occupying over 40 per cent of the National Park, moorland is a major wildlife and landscape resource. Man had managed it to create ideal conditions for the red grouse which is a permanent resident of the moor, totally dependent on the ling or common heather for its life cycle, and by encouraging more birds to breed for shooting man has also favoured visiting species. Waders such as the golden plover, curlew, the familiar lapwing, snipe and redshank overwinter at the coast, but breed on the open moor as do colonies of black-headed gulls. Britain's smallest bird of prey, the merlin, breeds in the older, woody banks of heather. Little bigger than a mistle-thrush, this rare member of the falcon family has been a symbol of the 'Watch over the National Parks' campaign. Meadow pipits and skylarks also nest in these old heather areas and the blue streak of a merlin pursuing a pipit as it rises vertically into the air from cover is not an uncommon sight. While most birds are summer visitors, the snow bunting comes south from Scandinavia to the relatively mild moors in winter.

In their turn the birds are all directly or indirectly dependent on the insect and other invertebrate life found on the wetter parts of the moors. Surface-living beetles, spiders and harvestmen swarm in great numbers in the spring, but their food source is a mystery. The beautiful emperor moth caterpillar is obvious on the heather, as is the northern eggar moth. The tipulid flies, or daddy-longlegs, larvae hatch from the peat in spring and are vital food sources to the pipits, curlews and visiting starlings, jackdaws and crows when they have young to feed. Red grouse chicks must have insect food in the first 10 days of their lives and even merlins make use of the larger moths for their chicks. This is why the wet and boggy areas are so vital to the overall ecology of the generally dry moors. In the floor of the deep, sinuous channel of Newtondale, thought to have been shaped by glacial meltwater, lies Fen Bog. This unique bog is a 40-acre nature reserve, but in places the peat is up to 59ft deep, and it is very dangerous to walk on its surface.

At the other extreme are the 'dry litter' areas on well-drained slopes. The soils here are peaty from a build-up of heather, leaves, sedges and mosses. They are covered in bracken, which poses an ever-increasing threat to the rest of the moor where it has started to invade the heather, pushing its underground rhizomes (root-like stems) forward by as much as 33ft a year. In the 'litter' lives the sheep tick, which feeds on the blood of mammals and birds and may seriously weaken or kill them through stress or disease.

Scavenging foxes, hares, common and pygmy shrews are found on the heather moor. On the bracken edges live the fast-flying whinchats, wheatears and brightly-coloured pheasants. Wood mice and bank voles are found feeding on the

Grey heron in flight. There are only about 4,000 pairs in the British Isles but there are several heronries in the North York Moors. Herons feed on fish, water-voles, beetles, frogs, moles and rats, ranging more than 12 miles in their search

bilberry at certain times of year on the drier slopes. Although rarely seen, these small mammals are important food sources for the birds of prey and the adder, which is often seen basking in the sun on old stone walls – also a favourite haunt for common lizards. The adder, with its zig-zag markings, is a timid creature which will not bite readily but should be left alone if found.

Short-eared owls breed and hunt over several moors and are sometimes seen gliding silently over the land in the day. Hen harriers, buzzards and rough-legged buzzards can sometimes be sighted flying over the moor seeking larger bird and mammal prey, while the magnificent peregrine occasionally passes through. Although ling is the dominant species of heather, other types are found too. These include the bell heather on dry banks, along with the very common bilberry, and cross-leaved heath on the wetter, peaty soils. This is one of the early flowering species. Cotton grass dominates the wetter blanket peat with its white carpets of flowers in the late spring, but the first green shoots are grazed heavily by sheep and hares. In the valley bogs insectivorous plants, such as the sundew and common butterwort, trap tiny flies to obtain the nitrogen they need for growth. The yellow spikes of the bog asphodel are frequently seen along with the rushes, but the bog bean is a much rarer find. Along stream sides the heathers are complemented by the fragrant bog myrtle and occasional juniper bushes, prized for making beer and gin respectively.

Woodland

Although deciduous woodland covers only five per cent of the land, much of it has been there a long time and some pre-dates the Norman Conquest. There is much variety in terms of tree species and ground flora but the two different types of underlying soil produce distinctive vegetation.

On the acid soils of the moorland fringes the main trees are sessile oak, birch, mountain ash, alder and Scots pine. The ground flora is poor on dry soils and is often stunted by heavy grazing from sheltering sheep. Wavy hair grass and bracken are widespread but on wetter soil species such as bluebells, and opposite- and alternate-leaved golden saxifrage indicate that the area has been wooded for a long time. These woods provide cover for many animals and birds, including short-eared, long-eared and tawny owls, the great-spotted and 'yaffling' green woodpeckers.

On basic and neutral soils more varied and extensive woods are found. These are often dominated by pedunculate, or lowland, oak and ash, with wych elm, field maple, alder by water and sometimes small-leaved lime. The shrub layer contains willow, hawthorn and honeysuckle. Hazel, often coppiced in the past, produces a valuable nut supply for birds and mammals. The Rye Valley contains large areas of such woods where the ground is covered with carpets of grasses, wild garlic, dog's mercury, ground ivy, wood anemone, wood sorrel, primrose and bluebell, to name but a few. The flora is particularly rich where sunlight breaks through the leafy canopy of the trees.

The networks of well-worn paths under the tall vegetation are not man-made, but long-established badger routes linking setts, latrines and feeding places. Of the 400 badger setts in the North York Moors over 250 are in woodland and another 80 in conifer plantations. Woodmice, grey squirrels and bank voles are common. Recently, the presence of the shy common, or hazel, dormouse has been confirmed. Stripped honeysuckle bark and neatly nibbled hazel nuts are often the only clues to this secretive creature's whereabouts. Over 50 species of bird have been recorded from the woods. These include woodpecker, tree creeper, wren, spotted and pied flycatcher, woodcock, reed and willow warbler, blackcap and woodcock. A common sign of the presence of thrushes are the snail shells left scattered around stones used as 'anvils'. In spring several traditional heronries are occupied by breeding birds. Groups of the great grey birds build their huge twig nests together in a few trees. The same pair often add to the same nest over the years, and noisy squabbles between neighbouring birds are common. Their favourite trees for nesting are old pines, but plantations of other tree species are also used.

Relict wood pasture, or parkland, is a unique feature at Duncombe Park, near Helmsley, as the variety of trees found here is more characteristic of ancient southern parkland. Ancient small-leaved lime and oak stand in grassland once grazed by cattle and deer and many types of rare beetle live under the bark on living and fallen wood.

Plantations

Although the coniferous plantations are largely the product of intensive planting by the Forestry Commission in the last 60 years, they have many similarities with the forests of northern Europe in terms of wildlife. In mature plantations the large blocks of spruce, fir, larch and pine have needle-covered floors, with few plants in their dark interiors, although wood ants are at home – as the large conical nests of needles show.

Cone-producing trees are a valuable source of food to birds and mammals. Squirrels, woodmice and woodpeckers strip the scales from pine and spruce cones in a distinctive way to reach the seeds inside. The little green crossbill uses its scissor-like bill to split the cone scales neatly. Areas of young plantation provide very important nesting and roosting sites for the nightjar.

There may still be a few pine martens left in some remote areas and the red squirrel, which had disappeared in the 1960s, has been recorded from forests in the south-west corner of the National Park, although it can be easily confused with a dark form of the grey squirrel from a distance. Roe deer had almost become extinct in England in the early part of this century, but man-made forests with their wide rides and clearings have encouraged an increase in the population. Fallow deer, either the dappled-brown or black form, may be seen crossing roads at dusk in the Hambleton area. Often it is only the rear end of a deer which is seen as the otherwise camouflaged animal retreats among the trees. The 'scut' or tail, is white in the roe deer and black-and-white in the larger fallow deer.

The variety of mammal and bird life on the edge of the forests resembles that of the broadleaved woodlands. Blue-winged jays, 'thieving' magpies, tiny goldcrests and firecrests, badgers, foxes and stoats are all found here.

The great crested grebe, nearly exterminated during the last century because its feathers were in demand for women's hats, breeds on Scaling Dam Reservoir. Their floating nests are anchored to reeds. Inset left: bell heather Inset right: Duke of Burgundy fritillary, the only European member of a family of tropical butterflies

A man-made environment

The wildlife found in the farming areas, in and around towns and villages, and along roadsides is broadly similar to that found in other parts of the country. However, the wetter meadows are home for some unusual butterflies such as the Duke of Burgundy and dark green fritillaries, the green and white letter hairstreaks and brown argus, and in some areas of scrub the rare fly, bee and greater butterfly orchids may be found. Barn owls are still common, compared with other parts of the country, and they are often seen gliding like silent ghosts at dusk. Their survival is partly due to the availability of food and suitable nesting sites in old barns and buildings. Buildings and old woodlands, along with a rich insect life, have also helped to maintain a healthy bat population. The moors area is a northern stronghold for bats and both the pipistrelle and brown long-eared bats are common. Their survival is helped by the existence of a series of limestone fissures, known as 'windypits', which are used as winter hibernating locations. The whiskered bat, Daubenton's bat, Natterer's bat and the brown long-eared bat have all been recorded in these caves. Signs of use by the very rare lesser horseshoe bat have also been found.

Marshes, rivers and reservoirs

Perhaps the best examples of freshwater marshes in the North York Moors are the banks of the River Dove in Farndale which are covered in yellow carpets of wild daffodils in the spring. There are still some fens in the Dalby Forest, and Ashberry Pasture is an interesting marsh, although modern drainage is drastically reducing this habitat type.

Freshwater lakes are scarce in the area, Scaling Dam reservoir being the largest. This is an overwintering and breeding site for birds such as the great crested grebe, with its prominent neck ruffs, little grebe, teal, wigeon, gadwell, tufted duck, pochard, goldeneye, Canada goose, mute swan and Bewick's swan. Fish-eating ospreys are occasionally seen hunting over small areas of water and trout ponds, which are also a favourite with herons as they pass through in spring and autumn.

There are long stretches of gently-meandering and fast-running unpolluted rivers and streams. The banks of many are wooded with alder, ash and willow. Unfortunately Dutch elm disease has taken its toll of the elm as the bare skeletons show. There

Unlike many other species, the whiskered bat is solitary. It is 3½ins long with a wingspan of 9ins

are populations of the bumbling water vole and the tiny black-and-white water shrew. The unpopular Canadian mink was introduced to Britain in 1929 and is present on most rivers in the area, taking fish and water fowl. There is even a small population of the now very rare and mischievous otter. The brilliant blue of a darting kingfisher is an exciting sight and the flicking tail of the dipper is sometimes to be seen on faster-flowing stretches of water. Small numbers of sand martins excavate nests in sandy banks on the Rivers Esk and Rye.

The coast

Much of the coast is designated as 'Heritage Coast' and long lengths of it are protected as Sites of Special Scientific Interest. On the cliffs maritime turf areas of sea pink and scurvy grass mix with farmland, small woods and old quarries. Hunt Cliff near Saltburn has colonies of fulmar, kittiwake, herring gull, cormorant and even house martin. Rarer visitors, such as Adouin's gull and red kite, have been seen passing through. Both the grey, or Atlantic, and common seal, are occasionally seen.

Enjoying the wildlife of the Moors

Much may be seen by driving the moorland roads, by walking short stretches of the 1,125 miles of public rights of way, by waiting quietly in the many rides of the Forestry Commission plantations or by following nature trails, such as that at Sutton Bank. The National Park contains over 20 Sites of Special Scientific Interest and there is a National Nature Reserve at Forge Valley and a Local Nature Reserve at Farndale. Eight nature reserves are managed by the Yorkshire Wildlife Trust and a permit to visit these may be obtained from 10 Toft Green, York YO1 1JT. Telephone (0904) 59570.

It is important to remember that many birds and mammals nest on the ground, especially on the open moor, so be ready to move away quickly if you come on them by accident. Leave wild flowers for others to enjoy and try to avoid damaging plants. It has taken hundreds, if not thousands, of years for the present variety of wildlife to develop and it is constantly under pressure. When looking at the wildlife adopt the approach of leaving only footprints and taking only photographs.

The Coast

Soaring cliffs, quiet bays, attractive beaches and picturesque villages combine in an endless variety of scenery to form the coastline of the North York Moors National Park. The word 'moors' does not readily conjure up a coastline, yet this boundary to the Park is as dramatic as the heather uplands, with the busy seaside towns of Whitby and Scarborough providing a contrast to the solitude and peace of the moorland.

To encourage the conservation of lengths of Britain's unspoilt coast, the Countryside Commission has designated certain sections, worthy of special protection, as Heritage Coasts. The coastline of the Park comes within the North Yorkshire and Cleveland Heritage Coast which stretches for 35 miles from Saltburn-by-the-Sea to Scalby Ness, Scarborough.

There is no better way to explore this coast than to use part of the Cleveland Way. A section of this 93-mile long-distance waymarked walk winds its way within sight and sound of the sea between Saltburn and Filey. There is no motor road which follows close to the shore so the motorist has to make short detours inland before exploring the next road leading down to the coast.

Boulby Cliffs

About a mile within the boundary of the Park, on its northern extremity, are Boulby Cliffs – at 666ft the highest point on England's east coast and England's second highest coastal cliff. Needless to say the cliff top commands a fine prospect of the coast and countryside.

The village of Staithes at the mouth of Roxby Beck. It is still the fifth lobster port in the country

Close by, deserted quarries and their adjacent tips recall the days when the chemical alum was obtained for the textile and leather industries, as well as for the manufacture of parchment and candles. Over 20 quarries were worked extensively for nearly 300 years but in the mid-19th century, overproduction and the high costs of a lengthy and complicated process of obtaining alum from shale started a decline in the industry. Closure was hastened by the development of a process which obtained alum by treating colliery waste with sulphuric acid and the last mine closed in 1871. In 1973, however, mining came back to Boulby with the opening of the first potash mine in Britain near Staithes.

Fishing villages

Until the arrival of the railway the handful of attractive fishing villages which huddle under the cliffs for protection against the onslaught of the sea were almost cut off from the rest of the world and consequently evolved their own character and traditions. Here the stalwart womenfolk cured the fish, repaired nets, collected bait and baited the lines and sold the fish brought back by their menfolk. The traditional haul was herring, but over-fishing in the North Sea has reduced stock considerably. Today the catch along the Yorkshire coast is mostly crabs, lobsters and white fish such as cod, plaice and haddock.

In the early 19th century cobles sailed out of the fishing harbours daily. Not exclusive to Yorkshire, this strong, sturdy, open boat is designed to cope with the harsh North Sea. Heavy in relation to size, it is flat-bottomed, a design which allows it to be launched from a beach. The boat was first introduced by the Vikings and its basic design remains unchanged, although inboard engines have replaced sails and oars. Dear to the heart of many fishermen, even though it needs skill in handling, the coble (pronounced 'cobble') is often painted in bright colours, with certain ones predominating in particular areas.

In Victorian days Staithes women would own several of these distinctive bonnets: white was for daily use

Women wearing Staithes bonnets were once a familiar sight in the village but even today this distinctive headwear can be seen. Made from nine pieces cut from a yard of material, the bonnets were designed to prevent water trickling down the fisher-wife's neck when she carried baskets of fish on her head. Different coloured bonnets were worn for differing occasions. Ganseys were worn by all the fishermen and the designs on these jumpers were a means of identification should a man be lost at sea.

Folklore and legends

In common with other remote places with close-knit, self-contained communities the coastal villages were riddled with folklore and superstition. Boats were burned after a sea tragedy and cats were sacrificed as the cobles returned from fishing trips to ensure a safe landing. To ward off bad weather, children would dance around fires on the cliff top as they sang, 'Souther, wind, souther; Blow father home to mother'.

The association of Robin Hood's Bay with the outlaw of that name are dubious, but romance is in this coast. According to one story, Sir Gurth of Ravenscar, a Saxon earl, sought Robin's aid when no Norman would help to repel raiding Norse pirates. Robin and his men successfully attacked when the pirates beached their vessel in the bay. Their victory saved the countryside from the ravages of the Norsemen. Another story is that whenever Robin was sorely pressed by his hunters in Sherwood Forest he would flee north to this quiet bay which served as a perfect retreat. He kept a fleet of boats in constant readiness, and used them to escape to sea until his pursuers had gone. One version maintains that he disguised himself as a fisherman. The ancient burial mounds behind the village known as Robin Hood's Butts were once thought to be a training ground for the outlaw.

Legends have also grown up around St Hilda, founder of Whitby Abbey, who was highly regarded by all those who knew her. One tale relates how she rid the area of snakes by cutting off their heads and turning them into stone. Support for this legend is seen in the coiled, snake-like stones found on the shore and cliffs. Those with less romantic ideas will tell us that these are fossilised ammonites, an extinct genus of shellfish belonging to the family of Cephalopoda. These multiplied here in great numbers in the early Lower Jurassic Period, 100 to 130 million years ago, when the area was under the sea. An extensive collection of the ammonites can be seen in the Whitby Museum.

Smuggling

Just as exciting as these legends, but soundly based on fact, are the tales of smugglers associated with much of this coastline. The houses huddle so close together up the cliff face at Robin Hood's Bay that it is said that contraband, mainly tobacco and spirits such as brandy, could be passed from one to another without appearing above ground. Some of the houses had secret rooms in which the smugglers could hide, and these still exist today. Another special feature of the houses is the landing windows through which coffins could be more easily removed than down the steep stairs.

Captain James Cook

James Cook, one of the greatest circumnavigators of the world, was born at Marton in Cleveland in

1728 – the son of a day labourer who rose to become the bailiff at a farm near Great Ayton, now on the edge of the National Park. Here Cook went to school before his apprenticeship with William Sanderson, a grocer and draper, in Staithes. This shop on the seafront where, as a boy of 17 Cook first smelled the sea and listened to mariners' tales, no longer exists having been washed away by the sea. However, Cook's Cottage incorporates some parts which were salvaged and bears a plaque unveiled in 1978 by His Royal Highness The Prince of Wales to mark the opening of the Cook Heritage Trail. This links places associated with Captain Cook: Marton; Great Ayton; Marske; Staithes and Whitby.

Before long Cook took the road to Whitby where he was apprenticed to John Walker, a Whitby shipowner and the house in Grape Lane where he lived with his master still stands today. Cook make his first voyage in 1747 on a collier (coalship), signed on as a seaman in 1750 and two years later became mate. He was offered command of a collier in 1755, but turned it down to join the Royal Navy. His navigational abilities were soon recognised and his work in helping to chart the St Lawrence River in Canada enabled General Wolfe's army to capture Quebec in 1759. Promotion came and with it command of an expedition to the Pacific (1768-1771) in the *Endeavour*, a Whitby-built ship. During the voyage he accurately charted the coasts of both Australia and New Zealand. Two more expeditions followed in the *Resolution* accompanied by the *Adventure* (1772-1775) and the *Discovery* (1776-1780), all Whitby-built ships. The first expedition, to find a new 'Southern Continent' in the South Pacific Ocean was unsuccessful, although Cook sailed the equivalent of three times the equatorial circumference of the earth. Cook never returned from his next expedition, which was to discover a new trading route to the East Indies around the top of North America. Tragically he was killed by natives of the Sandwich Islands (now known as Hawaii) in 1779.

Whaling
Close by Whitby Harbour a whale's jawbone commemorates the days when Whitby was a great

Scraping whalebone at Whitby in 1813, when the town was one of Britain's foremost whaling ports
Inset: William Scoresby Senior. A leading Whitby skipper, he earned today's equivalent of £70,000 a year

whaling port, sending 58 ships on a total of 557 whaling voyages to the Arctic between 1753 and 1835. Two well-known whaling captains from this period were the Scoresbys, both William, father and son. Local men would often accompany them on their voyages lasting six months or more.

The whaling ships hunted the Greenland whale in the Arctic to bring back blubber which was turned into oil for lighting, and whalebone – a thin horny substance from the whale's mouth – to make ladies' stays and hoops for dresses and sieves. The town's tryworks, brick constructions holding large metal pans in which the blubber from the whales was boiled to extract its oil, disappeared long ago.

The great days of fishing and whaling have gone but much of the atmosphere from that era remains in the old town. Modern harbour developments include a marina, which caters for sailing, and facilities enabling ships with timber and paper from Europe to use the port.

Lifeboats
The cliffs of this coast have been the graveyard of many ships, especially in the days when hundreds of colliers shipped coal from the Durham coalfield to London. There have been many daring deeds by lifeboatmen along this coast, but none more remarkable than that on 19 January 1881 when a vicious north-easterly gale with driving snow and hail lashed the Yorkshire coast and a ship was wrecked in Robin Hood's Bay, six miles south of Whitby. There was no chance of rowing the lifeboat through the open sea from Whitby so the men decided to take their boat overland, which meant a 500ft climb onto the wind-lashed moors, a battle with drifting snow, then a perilous descent into Robin Hood's Bay. Eighteen horses pulled the boat and 200 helpers cut through the drifts while villagers from Robin Hood's Bay made their way to meet them. Such was the effort that just two hours after receiving the call the boat was launched and although the lifeboat suffered severe damage in

A Yorkshire lifeboat goes to the rescue in 1860. The last rowing lifeboat was used at Whitby from 1947 to 1957

the treacherous seas, the rescuers managed to save the crew of six from the stricken vessel.

Whitby lifeboat crews have won more RNLI gold medals for gallantry than any other in Britain and Whitby has one of the best lifeboat museums in the country.

Whitby jet
Cook, the Scoresbys and other great seamen are recorded in the Pannett Park Museum at Whitby. Another aspect of the town's history traced in the museum is that of the jet industry. Jet, a glossy

Elaborate jet necklaces dating back to prehistoric times have been found in the Whitby area, but it was not until about 1850 that the industry boomed. There are now only one or two jet workers in the town

black fossilised wood, has been carved and polished to make jewellery since the Bronze Age. Nowhere else in England does it occur in such quantity or with such quality as at Whitby. It rose in popularity when Queen Victoria introduced it as a mark of mourning for Prince Albert and was obtained locally by combing the beaches or digging mines into the cliff faces. Between 1870 and 1872 over 1,000 men and boys were employed in extracting and carving the jet, but the trade declined after the import of jet from the Continent. Though there has been some revival of interest in recent times, and pieces of jet can be found on the beach, today there is only one shop engaged in producing jet jewellery.

Two creative geniuses
Frank Meadow Sutcliffe, who was born in Leeds in 1853, came to live in Whitby when he was about 17. He recorded the town and its people in photographs which have become recognised as masterpieces in atmospheric re-creation. The writer Bram Stoker stayed at Whitby in the late 1890s while writing his novel *Dracula* and the book was clearly influenced by local features. After being shipwrecked off Whitby, Count Dracula takes the form of a large dog and seeks refuge in the grave of a suicide victim in the graveyard of St Mary's Church. From here he wanders forth at night.

The idea may have come from an actual grave bearing a skull and crossbones, and anyone can immerse themselves in the atmosphere of the book by coming up here on a stormy moonlit night.

A cautionary note
This can be a dangerous coast, especially when it is enveloped by a clinging, cold, damp fog, known locally as a roak, or sea-fret. The holidaymaker must take care, particularly in the more rocky and secluded places. They are not all suitable for bathing and even walking under the cliffs can be dangerous for, apart from falling rock, there is the possibility of being cut off by the tide which must be watched carefully. It is all too easy to be caught unawares when one's attention is held by rock pools teeming with life, or when watching the fascinating range of sea birds.

The times of high tides can be obtained from local coastguards and details are also available in small booklets available from fishing tackle shops, although weather conditions may affect the times.

Railways on the Moors

The success of the Stockton and Darlington Railway, which was opened in 1825, caught the interest of business people in Whitby. With the decline of the traditional industries of whaling, shipbuilding and allied trades and the nearby alum mines proving less prosperous, the town needed to look elsewhere for an income. Development was hindered by the lack of good communication inland and the railway was seen as a lifeline.

Whitby to Pickering

It was thought that a line in the direction of Pickering would help to develop the timber, sandstone and limestone industries in the hinterland and thereby benefit Whitby as the exporting port: such a line was proposed in 1826. At a meeting in 1831 it was decided to ask George Stephenson, the engineer of the Stockton and Darlington Railway, to report on the possibilities of constructing a route from Whitby to Pickering. His report was favourable and, on 6 May 1833, an Act of Parliament authorised a local company to promote a railway between Whitby and Pickering.

A Moorsrail train climbs to Goathland. Right: interesting features on the route of the North Yorkshire Moors Railway. The longest privately-operated railway in the country, it runs for 18 miles

The first sod was cut on 10 September 1833 and on 8 June 1835 a regular service between Whitby and Grosmont was started. In the first three months it carried 6,000 passengers, the third passenger line to be opened in Yorkshire. When the complete line was formally opened on 26 May 1836 it was the fruition of foresight and some wonderful feats of engineering. Trees, and heather bound in sheepskins, were used to create a firm base for the track in boggy areas and the highest point on the railway, 500ft, had to be surmounted by creating a 1-in-15 incline from Beck Hole to Goathland Bank Top. For the first 11 years of its existence the passenger coaches and the goods wagons were pulled by horses along the 24-mile track except up this incline. Here the coaches were hauled up by a rope using a self-balancing system of water-filled tanks. Later this was replaced by a steam-winding system.

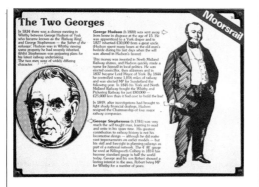

Both George Stephenson and George Hudson were associated with the Whitby to Pickering line

George Hudson, the Railway King, had shown great interest in this railway almost from the start and he had certainly met Stephenson in Whitby. When the Whitby to Pickering company got into financial difficulties, Hudson's York and North Midland Railway bought the line in 1845. Hudson, concerned that the line was isolated, linked it to his York to Scarborough line by building a branch line from Rillington to Pickering which opened in 1845. Hudson then set about converting the Whitby to Pickering line to steam and the first locomotive pulled into Whitby in 1847. However, the incline still presented a danger and negotiating it was very time-consuming. The problem was eventually overcome by blasting a line along the Eller Beck Valley between Beck Hole and Goathland and the new section was opened on 1 July 1865.

The Whitby to Pickering line was now part of the growing trunk railway system and with it came greater prosperity. Now it was easier to transport raw materials both within and out of the area as well as giving even wider distribution to goods imported through Whitby. With passengers able to come from farther afield Whitby was also able to promote itself as a holiday resort.

The Esk Valley and coast lines
In 1865 the Whitby to Pickering line was connected to the railway running through the Esk Valley to Middlesbrough. Travelling by train direct to Scarborough from Pickering became possible in 1882 and three years later the coast line between Scarborough and Whitby was opened. At Whitby it joined the Whitby to Loftus line, which had been opened in 1883, and there linked with lines to Saltburn and Middlesbrough. So by the end of the century the North York Moors was served by

a network of railways of which the Whitby to Pickering line was an integral part.

In 1872 the abandoned incline route between Beck Hole and Goathland was used by a Leeds firm to test an engine it was building for use in Brazil's coffee belt. The line also came into use again when, in 1908, an autocar service was operated especially for tourists during the summer. This proved popular but closed with the outbreak of World War I and was never reopened.

Between the two wars all the North York Moors lines were popular as they were among the most scenic routes in the country. The coast line ran for most of its length within sight of the sea.

Closures
Alas this line did not survive the enforced closures in the decades after World War II. British Rail, as the system had become after nationalisation, was already bringing in cuts and closures to facilitate economies and the Beeching Report in 1963 caused the axe to fall more sharply.

In 1950 the Pickering to Scarborough line closed, followed by the Pickering to York line via Kirkbymoorside in 1953. The beautiful coast line between Whitby and Loftus was also closed in 1958 and the Beeching Report proposed the closure of all lines serving the National Park. The furore was tremendous, especially from the people of Whitby who saw this plan as a move which would set the town back 100 years. However a compromise was struck and the line from Whitby to Middlesbrough along the Esk Valley was left open, although in 1965 the line from Whitby to Scarborough was closed, as was the Grosmont to Pickering section of the Whitby to Pickering line.

Restoration of the Grosmont to Pickering line
The much-loved scenic routes had gone. But as the Esk Valley line had had champions so there were those who sprang to the defence of the Grosmont

Cottage on the original 1836 1-in-15 incline between Beck Hole and Goathland on the Whitby to Pickering line. Below: disaster at the foot of the gradient which was too steep for either horse or locomotive

Moorsrail near its 550ft summit at Ellerbeck. Farther south is the entrance to remote Newtondale

to Pickering line. Alas, there could be no salvation for the railway along the coast. The undertaking to save this was formidable. It seemed this was so too with the Grosmont to Pickering line at first and even the small body of enthusiasts must have been daunted when attempts by several local councils to re-open and subsidise the route collapsed.

However, in 1967 the North Yorkshire Moors Railway Preservation Society was formed and after negotiations with British Rail it purchased the line from Grosmont to Eller Beck. Renovation work began on 2 February 1969 an engine operated on the line – the first for almost four years.

Talks were also going on behind the scenes. People were beginning to see the potential of restoring the complete railway and carrying passengers. After all, this was a route of exceptional scenic beauty where cliffs soared in some parts to

A 9,000-strong preservation society formed in 1967 saved the Whitby to Pickering line. Here a young volunteer tackles the first stage of restoration work on an old van housed at Goathland

400ft. The dale had no motor road, and its position made it an attraction not only to local people but to day visitors and tourists as well. The North York Moors National Park Committee and the English Tourist Board showed interest and were prepared to help with grants.

The outcome of this was the formation in 1971 of the North York Moors Historical Railway Trust Ltd and the purchasing of the remainder of the line to Pickering. After a great deal of hard work the first public services operated by the Trust began on 22 April 1973 and the line was formally opened by the Duchess of Kent on 1 May.

The scheme was now more than just a line operated by and for railway enthusiasts. It had become an immense tourist attraction and part of a transport system linked with the existing British Rail line through the Esk Valley to Whitby and Middlesbrough. Accordingly, new strategies of operation and promotion came into play.

Moorsrail

The success of the North York Moors Railway, or Moorsrail as it is affectionately known, is evident: over 300,000 passenger journeys are undertaken each year. Both steam and diesel engines operate on the line and engines can be seen being repaired at the Grosmont loco shed. This train journey will fascinate anyone visiting the Park or nearby areas. Undoubtedly, apart from the steam trains themselves, a main attraction is the scenery and there is plenty of information available to help you enjoy it. Walks are marked and there are leaflets which explain the routes. The Historical Railway Trail booklet describes the railway route from Grosmont to Goathland and a return walk follows a section of the original track along the old incline.

The Esk Valley Line today

There are similar delights to be enjoyed along the Esk Valley where most of the tiny stations display a poster showing maps of walks – either circular or to the next station. The railway provides an excellent means of exploring this valley and the picturesque villages of Kildale, Commondale, Castleton, Danby, Lealholm, Glaisdale, Egton Bridge, Grosmont, Sleights and Ruswarp. From Danby station it is a mile to the Moors Centre and Information Centre, run by the National Park Authority, at Danby Lodge. This is an ideal place for an introduction to the Moors for there is an exhibition area and talks with slides and films as well as 13 acres of grounds.

A line to Rosedale

When valuable ironstone was discovered in Rosedale there arose the problem of transportation to Teesside. At first it was moved by road to the railway at Pickering and the Ingleby Mining Company opened a private line in 1858. This ran from their mine near Burton Howe, close to Greenhow Bank (an escarpment on the edge of the Cleveland Hills) to Ingleby where it connected with a new line which gave it access to Stockton. However the mining companies in Rosedale wanted something more direct and they negotiated with the North Eastern Railway to construct a line direct to Rosedale. An Act of Parliament in 1859 authorised the North Eastern to carry out such a project and the private line was incorporated into the new scheme. The incline on this line only ran as far as the Ingleby mines and it now had to continue to the top of the moor at a height of 1,370ft. The maximum gradient was 1-in-5 and wagons were hauled up by steel ropes.

The track kept to the moor top, following the contours in sweeping curves around the head of Farndale. At Blakey Junction it reached the road between Hutton-le-Hole and Castleton where a parapet of the original bridge over the railway can still be seen, though the bridge itself has been filled in. The track of the old line is clearly visible. From the Junction a line ran along the west side of Rosedale to Bank Top, close to the road from Rosedale to Hutton-le-Hole with its notorious 1-in-3 gradient. The completed line was officially opened on 27 March 1861 and on 18 August 1865 a branch line from Blakey Junction, built to serve mines on the east side of Rosedale, came into operation.

In its heyday the railway moved an average of 1,200 tons of iron ore per day and brought goods back on the return journey. This was a boom time for the dale, but life was hard for the miners,

Five bands played at Pickering station when it was opened in 1836. In the heyday of the railways stations vied with one another to be the best kept on the line

especially in winter. The weather could be severe on the moorland heights where the line reached a height of 1,370ft above sea-level. Heavy snowfalls often closed the line and in the winter of 1916/17 the line was closed for five weeks with drifts 30ft deep.

Production of ironstone in Rosedale gradually declined until the mines were eventually shut down in 1926, although the railway remained in use during the dismantling and was not finally closed until 13 June 1929. Most of the railway and mining buildings have since disappeared but some rows of cottages remain and, although the railway track has marked the landscape for ever, it provides an ideal route for exploring the North York Moors.

End of the day at Grosmont. The train journey from here to Pickering takes just over an hour

NORTH YORK MOORS

Gazetteer

*Each entry in this Gazetteer has the atlas
page number on which the place can be
found and its National Grid reference
included under the heading.
An explanation of how to use the National
Grid is given on page 78.*

*Above: Snilesworth Moor on the western side of the
National Park*

Ampleforth Abbey, begun in 1922 and completed in 1961

Ampleforth

Map Ref: 95SE5878

Known for its modern Benedictine Abbey and College, Ampleforth was once called Ampreforde, meaning the ford of the sorrel. The main street stretches almost a mile and contains two fine inns, shops, a post office and two churches. Clearly-marked footpaths lead between yellow limestone cottages with red pantile roofs and brick chimney stacks. The village market used to be held outside the White Swan, and the Ampleforth Sword Dance, once part of a folk-play, has recently been revived here (there is no green).

St Hilda's Church, whose registers go back to 1690, has a Norman font and a 12th-century doorway, as well as a carving of the signs of the zodiac. The nearby Catholic Church of Our Lady and St Benedict contains some early work of the Kilburn woodcarver, Robert Thompson.

In 1802 three Benedictine monks fleeing from France settled here. They started their abbey and monastery a mile from the village while earning a living by teaching. Ampleforth College is now England's premier Roman Catholic public school – the present Cardinal Archbishop of Westminster, Basil Hume OSB, is a former Abbot. The Abbey Church is open to the public and parties may be guided around the buildings by contacting the Abbot.

St Benet's Chapel in the crypt contains the high altar stone from Byland Abbey, and the abbey also contains fine oak carvings by 'Mousey' Thompson. Orchestral concerts are regularly held and the public may join a club and enjoy the facilities of the College's sports centre, opened in 1975.

There are magnificent views from Ampleforth Beacon on the road to Helmsley. Nearby Studford Ring is probably the finest enclosure-type of earthwork in the area. Fifty-four yards in diameter, it is thought to date from the Bronze Age but its purpose is not known.

AA recommends:
Campsite: Golden Square Touring Caravan Park, 3-pennants, *tel.* (04393) 269 (2½m S B1257 between Sproxton and Oswaldkirk)

Beck Hole

Map Ref: 86NZ8202

Deep in a moorland valley, Beck Hole lies about a mile from Goathland and is accessible by car only via very steep, narrow moorland roads.

Robert 'Mousey' Thompson

All over the world a mouse carved from oak seems to crawl up table legs, run along chair arms, sit on ash trays, play on book-ends, or prowl on bowls and cheese boards – identifying the work made in the workshops of Robert Thompson's Craftsmen Limited at Kilburn, a tiny village nestling beneath the south-west corner of the Hambleton Hills.

The business was started by Robert Thompson who was born in Kilburn in the Old Hall in 1876, son of the village carpenter and wheelwright. On leaving school he went to Cleckheaton to be apprenticed to a firm of engineers, but he was homesick for Kilburn and at the age

of 20 persuaded his father to let him return and join him as a carpenter.

Young Thompson had seen the wonderful 15th-century oak carvings in Ripon Cathedral and they inspired in him a desire to emulate the art of the great medieval craftsmen. In his spare time he studied wood, experimented with tools and gradually taught himself to carve.

A turning point in his life came when he met Father Paul Nevill, a monk of nearby Ampleforth Abbey. Father Paul was also the parish priest of Ampleforth village and he wanted someone to make an oak cross for his churchyard. Thompson was recommended to him and on seeing the carver's work Father Paul recognised his talent. After the

Craftsmen still continue the traditions begun by Thompson. Each carver is allowed to interpret the mouse trade mark on his own work

cross orders followed for a refectory table and a chair for Ampleforth College and these – two of Thompson's earliest commissioned works – are still in use.

Gradually, as Thompson's reputation spread, orders started to come in from far and wide and to cope with the demand he trained other men to work alongside him. On one occasion Thompson and one of his carvers were working on a cornice for a screen and the man happened to use the phrase 'poor as a church mouse'. Thompson carved a mouse there and then and it struck him that the mouse would make an appropriate trade mark – signifying industry in quiet places – and it has been used as such ever since. This idea of a signature was not a new one: Grinling Gibbons – 17th-century sculptor and woodcarver – chose a pod of peas.

To start with the mice, always carved as part of the piece and never detracting from the finished object, were depicted with their front legs showing but after a while the form varied. Apart from the mouse, another characteristic of much of the work is the wavy surface formed by the use of an adze – a traditional wood-working tool resembling an axe with an arched blade set at a right angle to the handle. This finish enhances the grain of the wood.

Robert Thompson died in 1955 at the age of 79 but his work is carried on today by his two grandsons; his old home is used as the showroom. The workshop, which employs 36 people, is usually surrounded by stacks of sawn oak being left to season naturally.

However, the journey is worthwhile, for the scenery is dramatic and the hamlet is fascinating. Trains from the North York Moors Railway steam past and there are some lovely walks through woodland and across the windswept moors.

Moorland streams converge here to form the short Murk Esk; one of the streams, the Eller Beck, cascades over Thomason Foss into a deep pool just above Beck Hole and the Murk Esk, its waters often a rich brown colour from the surrounding peat, flows rapidly over a rugged landscape until it joins the River Esk at Grosmont.

It is difficult to believe that between 1858 and 1864, some 200 men worked in the iron-ore mines. But the mines were closed and the area's peace is now undisturbed.

Here quoits is still played. The game continues in many moorland villages but Beck Hole was the focus of the game's revival when, in 1984, BBC television featured the village in a clash between two local teams.

The tiny local pub is Birch Hall Inn whose sign was painted by Algernon Newton, a member of the Royal Academy. Framed in oak, his 'canvas' is sheet metal and his work is protected by glass. Depicting Eller Beck, this is believed to be one of the few inn signs in Yorkshire painted by a member of the Royal Academy.

Bilsdale

Map Ref: 89SE5796

The B1257 from Helmsley to Stokesley sweeps along Bilsdale, a broad valley occupied by a scattering of farms and isolated cottages. After climbing out of Helmsley, the road affords panoramic views from Newgate Bank (where there is room to park and picnic) before hugging the floor of the valley to reach its only village, Chop Gate.

Locally, Chop Gate is pronounced Chop Yat, 'yat' being a dialect word

for gate. Chop may come from 'kaup', the Scandinavian for pedlar or chapman. Beyond Chop Gate, the road climbs to the summit of Clay Bank which, with parking and picnic facilities, affords splendid vistas.

William the Conqueror is said to have marched through Bilsdale after his awful Harrying of the North; it was snowing heavily and he got lost. As he shouted for his army, his language was so frightening that the locals still refer to 'cussing like Willy Norman'.

Legends of witch hares being hunted continued into this century, and the Bilsdale Fox Hounds are probably one of the oldest packs in England. The 17th-century Duke of Buckingham hunted with them, but the local hunting celebrity was Bobby Dawson. He died in 1902 aged 86 after a lifetime of hunting. He could outwit a fox and was reputed to have been at every kill. To the right of the door of the modern Sun Inn in Bilsdale is Bobby's tombstone; the vicar banned it from the churchyard because of its hunting theme.

Nearby is Spout House, the former Sun Inn. This lovely thatched cruck house ceased to be an inn in 1914 and fell into disrepair. Its restoration was authorised by the National Park Committee and it was opened to the public in May 1982. It was in this old pub that Bobby Dawson told his hunting yarns, hence the presence of his memorial.

The landlord of the Sun Inn, which has its own cricket team, has been a William Ainsley for 200 years. The eldest son is always called William and by tradition becomes landlord.

The Bride Stones

Map Ref: 89SE5797

There are several collections of stones known as 'the Bride Stones' on the North York Moors. Some are huge natural pieces of rock

One of the Low Bride Stones, a strange Jurassic rock which 260 million years ago stood at the bottom of the sea

shaped into strange forms by the wind and weather and others appear to have been positioned by man, either as complementary to burial mounds or perhaps in connection with pagan fertility rites.

One group of about 40 stones is located on Nab Ridge, on Nab End Moor in Bilsdale. These may have formed the retaining wall of a burial chamber whose earth cover has gone.

High Bride Stones lie beside the road which climbs out of Grosmont and joins the A169 above Sleights. These stones are the remains of two circles, each some 30ft or 40ft in diameter, and in each circle only three stones still stand. The circles could be associated with some standing stones nearby. Low Bride Stones can be found beside the same road, closer to Grosmont.

On the western edge of Dalby Forest on Grime Moor, just above a stream called Dovedale Griff, there is another group of stones. These huge outcrops of rock, taller than a person, have been fashioned by the elements into some curious shapes. They are now in the care of the National Trust.

A line of stones near Hob on the Hill on Gisborough Moor was known as Bride Stones and there are also the Bride Stones near Silpho, with excellent walks nearby.

Bride Stones must not be confused with the Wainstones, the largest group of rocks in the National Park, which are on an escarpment near Carlton in Cleveland. These are popular with rock-climbers and their name, perhaps meaning 'the stones of lamentation', may come from the Saxon 'wanian' meaning 'to howl'; the wind does create strange noises among these rocks. Alternatively, the name may be a derivation of whinstone, a volcanic rock known locally as blueflint or bluestone. Many ancient graves are made from this and at one time it was used for road building.

Brompton

Map Ref: 93SE9482

This quiet village on the A170 near Scarborough has a special place in aviation history. In 1853, some 50 years before the Wright Brothers flew their aircraft at Kitty Hawk, North Carolina, Brompton's squire Sir George Cayley devised a craft which carried a man in the air.

Cayley's machine was a glider and it flew 50yd across Brompton Dale while carrying his coachman. The coachman shouted to Sir George when the flight ended, 'I wish to give my notice. I was hired to drive, not to fly.' Cayley had flown a glider as early as 1804, and the first known flight by a full-sized scientifically-designed aircraft, albeit without an engine, took place in 1809.

The Cayley family has lived here since Stuart times, and among Sir George's other schemes was the impressive Sea Cut which prevented the River Derwent flooding around Pickering and Malton (see Forge Valley).

Brompton's history is interesting. The castle, now gone, used to be the residence of the Kings of Northumbria and the village was probably the birthplace of John de Brompton, Abbot of Jervaulx Abbey and chronicler of events from the arrival of St Augustine to the time of Richard I.

There was a church at Brompton when Domesday Book was compiled. The present building dates from the 14th century and it was here, on 4 October 1802, that poet William Wordsworth married local girl Mary Hutchinson from Gallows Hill Farm.

There is an enjoyable drive through Sawdon to the Wykeham Forest trail with its viewpoint and picnic site.

Byland Abbey, see Wass

Carlton in Cleveland

Map Ref: 82NZ5004

In spite of its name, Carlton is in North Yorkshire, a few miles from Stokesley. The road from the village to Chop Gate at the head of Bilsdale climbs to almost 1,000ft during the ascent of moor-topped Carlton Bank on the northern edge of the Cleveland Hills. From here there are fine views across Cleveland. The Cleveland Way crosses the summit and the Wainstones, weathered rocks loved by climbers, are nearby. Carlton Bank has a gliding club and at one time had a motor cycle scrambling course.

Sheltering beneath the north-west corner of the moors, Carlton's past links with alum mining are reflected in the name of the stream which flows prettily through the village, Alum Beck. Alum shale is unique to the North York Moors and was extensively mined here between 1600 and 1880 for use in the tanning and cloth industries.

St Botolph's Church, Carlton in Cleveland. Canon Kyle, vicar from 1894, bought and managed a local pub

The church has a chequered history. When vicar George Sangar arrived last century the church was derelict so he worked day and night to build a new one. He not only raised the cash but also did all the labouring. The church was completed in 1881 but sadly a fire destroyed it shortly afterwards. Sangar was charged with setting fire to it for some strange reason, but he was acquitted.

Another curious church, St Botolph's, now occupies the site. Its tower is half in and half out of the nave and there is a quaint two-in-one arch which opens both to the nave and the ringers' gallery.

Well-known vicar Canon John Kyle, who died in 1943, ran three farms and rode with the local hunt.

After weddings at nearby Faceby church, the groom and best man still throw pennies for the children. It was also at Faceby in 1634 that Anthony Lazenby established 'for all time' a dole of 12 loaves. These loaves, gifts for the poor, are purchased with money collected from four farms.

Castleton

Map Ref: 84NZ6808

The sturdy dark stone houses with blue slate roofs are typical of a moorland village and present a picture of durability and reliability. At one time the largest village in Esk Dale, Castleton used to be a centre of industry with a market and busy railway station. Today it is a peaceful place, as a weavers' mill stands empty, the market ended a few years ago and one well-known inn, The Robin Hood and Little John, recently closed. Its sign said, 'Kind gentlemen, and yeomen good, Call in and drink with Robin Hood; If Robin be not at

home, Step in and drink with Little John.'

Once the site of a wooden Norman castle with three moats, Castleton overlooks the River Esk. Information about fishing between April and September can be obtained from the Post Office. There are picturesque views from the road leading over Castleton Rigg to the isolated Lion Inn on Blakey Moor and into Hutton-le-Hole. Another road with good views climbs out of Castleton towards Lockwood Beck reservoir. Lockwood Beck operates a 'Trust the Fisherman' scheme for permits (late March to October) and boats may be hired. The reservoir offers opportunities for bird-watching and nature study too, but no water sports are allowed.

Castleton's surroundings are rich in archaeological remains, especially evidence of the Bronze Age people.

Freeborough Hill, beside the A171, has a curious conical shape and may be named after Freya, the goddess of fertility. The hill, a natural feature with a sandstone cap, was possibly the site of an ancient Anglian court.

AA recommends:
Hotel: Moorlands, 2-star, *tel.* (0257) 60206

Cawthorn Camps

Map Ref: 91SE7789

North of the A170 as it heads through Wrelton and Middleton into Pickering is the tiny hamlet of Cawthorne. It can be approached on very minor roads, through Cropton or Wrelton, or even from Pickering and Newton-on-Rawcliffe.

On a scrub-covered 500ft escarpment which overlooks Cropton Forest are the Roman Cawthorn Camps (the hamlet is spelt with an 'e', the moor and Camps are not). At ground level, the remains are difficult to see among the trees and undergrowth, but they lie just off the side of the lane and only yards inside the National Park. To the north, there are impressive views across the Moors and Cropton Forest. The broad Vale of Pickering lies to the south.

These four Roman Camps were established around AD100 during two separate occupations. One of the camps had a system of turf buildings with streets in between and a Bronze Age round barrow had been enlarged to create a platform for the commander to survey his troops. Excavations have also revealed a few Roman artefacts such as chariot wheels, seats and pottery. An incense stone in Lastingham church probably came from here.

It is believed these were not permanent bases, but temporary camps for soldiers on the march. They straddle the route of the Roman road which ran north from Malton towards the North Yorkshire coast and are possibly the only remains of this type in the world. In order to conserve the remains, the site was purchased by the North York Moors National Park Committee in 1983. At the moment they can be reached by a 600yd trek across the scrubland from the roadside.

Cleveland Hills

Map Ref: 88SE4997

The name Cleveland comes from the Norse 'Klifland', meaning 'land of cliffs' and the term includes the northern and north-western edges of the North York Moors as well as the plain which stretches before them towards the Tees. From their earliest history, towns such as Yarm, Stokesley, Guisborough, Redcar and Middlesbrough have all been within the district of Cleveland, along with many villages.

Until 1974 the district of Cleveland comprising moors, hills, dales and plain, was part of the North Riding of Yorkshire. The name included the moorland area which is still known specifically as the Cleveland Hills. A fine view of these hills is framed by the east window of Guisborough Priory.

It is known that these elevated parts of the moor have been inhabited since the Mesolithic Age: some brief Roman settlements were established and after the Harrying of the North by William the Conqueror, only 11 farmers were left in 120,000 acres of the Cleveland Hills. In the 17th century alum was discovered and jet was also mined, while some areas are now afforested.

The Cleveland Hills are very picturesque and contain many individual moors such as Baysdale Moor, Westerdale Moor, Gisborough Moor, Danby Low Moor, as well as some beautiful dales and delightful villages.

Some of the villages carry the 'Cleveland' suffix such as Carlton in Cleveland and Skelton in Cleveland. The area has given its name to these local place names and the title of the Cleveland Way long-distance walk, as well as to a locally-bred and sturdy breed of horse, the Cleveland Bay. The Cleveland Way crosses not only the Cleveland Hills but also the Hambleton Hills.

In 1974, however, local-government boundary changes created several new counties and among them was one called Cleveland. This absorbed a large portion of the North Riding of Yorkshire and some parts of Durham, and it adopted the name of these lovely hills.

The anomaly now is that there are two areas called Cleveland. One is a bustling new county around Middlesbrough, and the other is a peaceful moorland area replete with dales and hills which lies outside that county. A major part of the Cleveland Hills continues to lie within North Yorkshire and some villages, like Carlton in Cleveland, are also in North Yorkshire. Their name has nothing to do with the new county but stems from their history prior to 1974.

The steep scarp of the Cleveland Hills forms the northern boundary of the National Park. Carlton Bank is a particularly good viewpoint

Memorabilia in Laurence Sterne's home, Shandy Hall, Coxwold

A Literary Genius

I am happy as a prince at Coxwold and wish you could see how in princely manner I live. . . . I sit down alone to venison, fish and wild fowl or a couple of fowls or ducks, with curds and strawberries and cream and all the plenty which a rich valley under the Hamildon Hills can produce; with a clean cloth on my table and a bottle of wine on my right hand, and I drink your health.

I have a hundred hens and chickens about my yard and not a parishioner catches a hare or a rabbit or a trout but he brings it as an offering to me. I am in high spirits; care never enters this cottage.'

So wrote 18th-century comic novelist Laurence Sterne when he was vicar of Coxwold living at Shandy Hall. The house, which stands at the west end of the village a short distance from the church, was built as a cottage around the middle of the 15th century and re-named and rebuilt by Sterne. However, after his death it fell into disrepair until the Laurence Sterne Trust took it over in the 1960s and opened it as a museum of the life and work of this eccentric figure.

Sterne was born in Clonmel, southern Ireland, in 1713 and spent his first years there. He was the son of a soldier who, although coming from a well-to-do family had no inheritance and had run away to join the army.

When he was 10 years old, young Laurence was sent to school at Hipperholme, near Halifax, where he gained a good education. After his father's death in Jamaica in 1731 his mother, still in Ireland, seemed to want to have nothing to do with him. However, his education was continued by favour of a generous cousin who was squire of Elvington in East Yorkshire. At the age of 20 Sterne went to Jesus College, Cambridge, where his great-grandfather, who had been Archbishop of York, had once been a Master. It was here that his life-long battle with tuberculosis began.

After taking holy orders Sterne was ordained in the Church of England and, with the help of another uncle (this one Precentor of York Minster) he became Vicar of Sutton-on-Forest – a few miles north of York – rising sometime later to be a Canon of York Minster. But Laurence was drawn to the social whirl of 18th-century York, with its balls, cock fights, gambling and races and because of disagreements with his uncle over this his chances of progressing in the church were marred. In 1741 he married Elizabeth Lumley, a sweetheart of two years standing, but the marriage was not a happy one and his wife, always unstable, eventually suffered a nervous breakdown. They had one daughter, Lydia. Three years after his marriage Sterne became Vicar of the neighbouring village of Stillington. He loved riding and shooting and a story relates how, on his way to take a service at Stillington, he saw a covey of partridges so returned to Sutton for his gun and left the congregation waiting.

Amateur painter and musician, Sterne had also always been something of a writer but it was not until 1759 when he began *The Life and Opinions of Tristram Shandy* that his genius emerged. The first two volumes were published and at the same time he acquired the Living of Coxwold. The novel was an immediate success and Sterne received high acclaim from all quarters: Sir Joshua Reynolds painted his portrait and he was invited to Windsor Palace.

Prosperity followed. Sterne loved the social whirl and travelled a great deal to London and the Continent, although always returned to Coxwold to write – usually leaving his family behind in France. He had completed volumes three to nine of *Tristram Shandy* by 1766 and wrote *A Sentimental Journey Through France and Italy*, but while in London for its publication in 1768 he contracted influenza which turned to pleurisy and he died on 18 March.

Sterne was buried in the parish of St George's Church, Hanover Square and the story goes that body-snatchers stole the body and sold is for medical dissection but someone recognised Sterne and his corpse was returned to the grave. When the burial ground was sold in 1969 for development the Laurence Sterne Trust received permission to remove Sterne's remains to Coxwold. They now lie outside the south wall of the nave, where his original tombstone stands, in the village this extraordinary man loved so much.

Commondale

Map Ref: 84NZ6610

Until recently Commondale was not a particularly pretty village as it endured almost a century of prosperous industrial activity after the railway opened on 2 October 1865.

A Mr Pratt established a thriving brickworks which also produced tiles, pottery, chimneys and drains. This brought prosperity to Commondale, and the works continued through two world wars. Some local cottages contain bricks bearing the name 'Pratt', and the sewage systems of many towns were created at Commondale. After the brickworks closed in the 1950s, Commondale looked derelict for a while. However, it has now rid itself of its industrial image and with the Sleddale Beck meandering through, and set in a deep, broad valley in the hills, it attracts visitors because of its delightful moorland setting.

Known as Colmondale in medieval times, it was the meeting place of travellers because several moorland tracks converged here, including the Monks' Causeway which led from Whitby to Guisborough Priory.

The villagers wanted a memorial (which would endure for ever) to their men lost in World War I and demanded an edifice of Commondale stone crafted by a Commondale stonemason. The name panels were made by Edward Overy from finest Commondale earthenware and a time-capsule is buried underneath.

Marble tomb of father and son in St Michael's Church, Coxwold

Coxwold

Map Ref: 95SE5377

Rich with places of interest, Coxwold is small, compact and highly attractive. The most southerly village in the National Park, its wide, well-tended green verges, and its range of beautiful stone buildings present a charming rural scene.

At one end of the village stands the literary shrine of Shandy Hall; it was here that the modern English novel was born. It was the home of Laurence Sterne (1713-68), one-time vicar of Coxwold and author of *The Life and Opinions of Tristram Shandy, Gentleman* and *Sentimental Journey*.

Filled with Sterne's books and manuscripts, including the world's largest collection of first editions of Sterne's works, 15th- to 17th-century Shandy Hall draws literary pilgrims from all over the world.

At the other end of Coxwold stands Newburgh Priory, founded in 1145 as an Augustinian Friary and now a beautiful country home. It is said that the body of Oliver Cromwell is entombed here, having been brought here by his daughter Mary, wife of Thomas, the 2nd Viscount Fauconberg of Newburgh. The house, tomb and grounds containing a splendid water garden are open to the public.

Other sights in the village include Coxwold's impressive parish church; Colville Hall; the Fauconberg Arms; an old grammar school dating from 1603; almshouses built during Charles II's reign and a modern pottery where purchases can be made.

AA recommends:
Guesthouse: Baxby Manor, Husthwaite (farmhouse), *tel.* (03476) 572 (2½m SW of Coxwold)

Cropton

Map Ref: 91SE7689

This tiny moorland community lies on the National Park boundary north-west of Pickering. On the edge of the village is the site of its ancient castle with views along Rosedale. Just beyond, where the road leads to Cawthorne, is a vantage point with extensive views across the moors and Cropton Forest. Today there is little evidence of the castle's existence and around AD1200 the site contained a half-timbered manor house; the earthworks and mounds are still known as 'T'Hall Garths'.

Cropton's modern church is built on the site of the castle chapel. There is a striking yew-lined approach to it, and outside is a piece of an old cross. Years ago a drinking cup was placed on this cross for the benefit of travellers and a verse ran, 'On Cropton cross there is a cup, and in that cup there is a sup.'

The wide main street is flanked with attractive stone moorland houses and contains what appears to be a disused animal pound, although it has no entrance. This used to contain the village water supply, pumped from the River Seven below. While on the subject of drink, an unusual feature of the village pub, The New Inn, is that it now makes its own beer.

There are walks and drives in Cropton Forest, with a 150-pitch Forestry Commission caravan and camping site set deep among the trees at Spiers House.

AA recommends:
Campsite: Spiers House Campsite, Forestry Commission, 3-pennants, 2-star, *tel.* (07515) 591
Self Catering: Keldy Castle (cabin), *tel.* (031334) 0303 or 2576

Danby

Map Ref: 84NZ7008

A wealth of information about the North York Moors and the National Park Committee's work is available at the Moors Centre, Danby. There are refreshments too, with a picnic area and car park in delightful surroundings.

Danby, sometimes known as Danby in Cleveland to distinguish it from other places of the same name, is a pleasant village deep in the valley

Right: scything in Danby Dale. Canon Atkinson described the dale as 'the loveliest it has ever been my lot to behold'. Below: the Moors Centre

of the River Esk. In strict moorland terms, Danby should perhaps be known as Danby End, the term 'end' indicating the mouth of a dale. The closed portion of a dale is called the dale head. Danby was immortalised by Canon J C Atkinson (1814-1900), vicar of Danby, in his book *Forty Years in a Moorland Parish*.

Canon Atkinson is buried beside St Hilda's Church in Danby Dale, almost 2 miles from the village.

Higher into this rugged dale is Botton Hall. Since 1955, it has housed a community of mentally and physically handicapped people who maintain themselves and their own 'village' by making high-quality goods. These are on sale from shops at Botton Hall. The 'village' has its own post office, workshops, shops, social centre and coffee bar and help is provided by volunteer staff. The emphasis is on self-sufficiency and the project is one of several established in Britain and overseas by the Camphill Village Trust.

Downstream from Danby is Duck Bridge, an ancient and narrow pack-horse bridge which spans the Esk. Probably built around 1386, the name might be a corruption of Duke's Bridge, for it leads to Danby Castle, perched on the tip of Danby Rigg. The castle was the seat of the Latimers, and Catherine Parr, a wife of Henry VIII, once lived here. The castle is not open to the public although a nice letter to the farmer at the farmhouse, Danby Castle, might open its doors to groups such as school parties. One of its rooms is still used by the ancient Danby Court Leet and Baron which administers rights of way and parking on common land (see page 53).

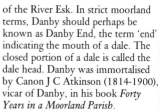

18th-century Ebberston Hall is only three bays wide and one storey high

Ebberston

Map Ref: 92SE8982

Ebberston and neighbouring Allerston are pretty villages on the A170 between Pickering and Scarborough. A local royal mystery involves Bloody Field and Alfred's Cave on the nearby moors. Legend says that in the 7th century, King Aldfrith of Northumbria fought his father, King Oswy, at the Battle of Ebberston. Aldfrith was stabbed and sheltered in a cave, since known as Alfred's or Aldfrith's Cave. Some accounts suggest that Aldfrith survived, others that he died.

The battle may have occurred on the moors above Ebberston and Allerston among the extensive and remarkable early earthworks called Scamridge Dykes. Now with a viewpoint and picnic site, this series of mounds and ditches is a prehistoric settlement of indeterminate age. In the last century 14 skeletons dating from about 1,000BC and an early communal thatched dwelling were discovered.

Ebberston church and Ebberston Hall are out of the village in a wooded dale on the opposite side of the A170. The church, built into a hillside, has Norman portions, while the Hall, built in 1718 and described as a Palladian villa, is of interest. Designed by Colen Campbell, it is open to the public.

AA recommends:
Guesthouse: Foxholm Hotel, *tel.* (0723) 85550 (on B1258)

Egton Bridge

Map Ref: 85NZ8005

Beautifully positioned on the River Esk in a steep-sided valley, Egton Bridge is one of Yorkshire's prettiest villages. Legend says that William the Conqueror's blacksmith left him at York to settle here.

This is one of England's most famous Roman Catholic parishes, known as 'the village missed by the

Reformation'. It is the birthplace of Father Nicholas Postgate, 'Martyr of the Moors', who kept the faith alive when Roman Catholics were persecuted. He was executed in York, aged 82, for baptising a child into the Catholic faith in 1679.

The massive Catholic church of St Hedda dominates the village. Built in 1866, its great roof is ribbed and painted blue with golden stars and there is Belgian terracotta work on the altar. Halfway up the hill towards Egton is the Mass House where Postgate conducted secret Masses and St Hedda's Church contains relics of his ministry. One of the village pubs is called The Postgate.

The Egton Bridge Old Gooseberry Society, formed in 1800, holds a show of giant gooseberries each year on the first Tuesday of August. The world record for the heaviest gooseberry is held by a berry shown here in 1982.

Egton, from 'Egetune' meaning town of oaks, stands on the hill above. Its Horse and Agricultural Society arranges Egton Show in August, one of the largest in the region.

A scene from the life of Jesus, in 19th-century St Hedda's Roman Catholic Church, Egton Bridge

There are some fine walks in the area, particularly through Arncliffe Woods and along the road which hugs the banks of the Esk just out of Egton Bridge, towards Glaisdale. A weir tumbles towards an old mill where a series of stepping stones lead to an island in the river.

Esk Dale

Map Ref: 85NZ7407

Esk Dale is the largest of the dales within the North York Moors National Park and differs from the others because it stretches from west to east.

The River Esk rises at Esklets, a hollow in the moors between Westerdale and Farndale, and then twists and turns under many bridges along the floor of the dale, flowing east until it reaches the North Sea at Whitby. It is a premier salmon river and public fishing for salmon and trout (with the necessary licences) is available along certain stretches. There is boating at Ruswarp.

All the Esk's main tributaries rise in high moorland to the south and flow northwards, to enter the Esk in something akin to herring-bone fashion. The largest tributary is the

Beautiful Esk Dale. The Whitby to Middlesbrough railway line was renamed the Esk Valley Line in 1973

Murk Esk which joins the Esk at Grosmont. This features some spectacular waterfalls, although Sleddale Beck and Baysdale Beck, both joining near its source, are major contributors.

The landscape of Esk Dale is beautiful and dramatic and there are some stunning viewpoints from the surrounding moors which are coated with superb purple heather in autumn. The scenic Whitby to Middlesbrough (BR) railway line, which halts at most villages, is popular with visitors, and steam trains of the private North York Moors Railway join the line at Grosmont.

The roads, particularly those which descend into the villages, are noted for their steep hills and narrow twisting routes. Limber Hill at Glaisdale, for example, has a gradient of 1-in-3 while the lanes into Littlebeck are as steep or even steeper. Like so many others, Lealholm Bank has wonderful views from the summit while the roads along the side of the dale are full of interest. There is a thrilling drive from Key Green near Egton Bridge into Grosmont. Great care is needed when driving in Esk Dale, especially during the summer when farm vehicles are on the move, and many of these roads are not suitable for coaches and caravans.

Esk Dale's villages are unspoilt. Surrounded by a scattering of sturdy farms, many of which offer bed-and-breakfast, they have lovely stone houses, with inns, post offices and shops. There are cricket pitches too and quoits is a popular game.

This is good walking country, with plenty to interest the naturalist, the photographer and the artist.

Fadmoor, see Gillamoor

Farndale

Map Ref: 89SE6697

Farndale is a long, remote valley which reaches deep into the centre of the Moors north of Kirkbymoorside. It contains the hamlets of Church Houses, Low Mill and Lowna, with a scattering of farms and cottages. Some are ancient cruck houses with thatched roofs, and the winding, narrow lanes provide a picturesque circuit. The dale is famed for its wild daffodils. Every spring, around Eastertime, the banks of the gentle River Dove are covered with mile after mile of small yellow daffodils. They are the true wild daffodils native to Britain. Farndale's environment of low-lying damp pastures with sandy loam seems particularly conducive to their growth. Yorkshire folk often call these daffodils 'Lenten Lilies' because they bloom around that season. The flowers, once threatened by plundering visitors, are now protected by law and 2,000 acres of Farndale are designated as a local nature reserve.

Farndale is the setting for several local legends. They include Sarkless Kitty who drowned after a sad love affair; the Farndale Hob whose mischief caused a farmer to move house and the local witch who could turn herself into a black dog.

Poor Kitty loved a wealthy farmer's son but when she became pregnant he abandoned her. Kitty pleaded for a meeting but the young man didn't turn up. A horseman said he had seen Kitty's lover riding in the opposite direction and, in a fit of sorrow, she leapt naked into the flood. Her body was later found near an old ford; ironically it lay beside her beloved who had also perished in the river. He had ridden into Kirkbymoorside to buy Kitty a wedding ring, but had drowned on the way to meet her. The lovers were buried at the roadside but on the anniversary of her death, the ghost of the naked (sarkless) Kitty haunted the area. The river began to claim other victims too until a Quaker couple living nearby secretly exhumed the bodies and re-buried them in a Quaker burial ground; the hauntings and drownings then stopped.

Forge Valley

Map Ref: 93SE9886

Some of the most impressive scenery around Scarborough can be found in Forge Valley, a deep, tree-lined dale with the River Derwent flowing gently along its floor.

Known for its profusion of ash and other deciduous trees, the valley contrasts vividly with the surrounding conifer forests. Its name may come from the establishment of a medieval forge by the monks of Rievaulx Abbey, although there was a foundry here in 1798.

Forge Valley is a National Nature Reserve containing a wealth of wildlife and lies on the route of the Derwent Way, one of the local long-distance walks.

Situated at the northern end of Forge Valley is the hamlet of Everley, and this marks the start of a remarkable early 19th-century drainage scheme. The Derwent used to flood wide areas around Pickering and Malton until Sir George Cayley of Brompton devised a way to prevent this happening by cutting an overflow channel for the Derwent. Known as the Scalby Cut, his waterway slices through the landscape like a canal and was cut by hand between 1800 and 1810. A sluice allows the normal waters to take their course, but floodwater is diverted to the North Sea through Scalby.

Fryup Dales

Map Ref: 85NZ7304

A drive around Little Fryup Dale and Great Fryup Dale makes a pleasant diversion when exploring Esk Dale. Danby Castle stands at the entrance to Little Fryup and from here there is a pleasant journey along Crossley Sides, where bilberries ripen in late August. A pair of narrow roads lead to Great Fryup Dale near Furnace Farm and Wheat Bank and it is fair to say there is little more here than peace and tranquillity, for Fryup is a very scattered community of sturdy houses and farms. High in Great Fryup Dale there is the quaintly named Fryup Street, a tiny lane between a few quiet dwellings.

The eastern road into Great Fryup Dale once had six gates in its first mile. A stone commemorating their removal reads: 'Six gates in next mile a nuisance proved. Helped by kind donors, tenants and others had them removed. USE WELL TIME SAVED'.

Fryup's odd name causes amusement and speculation. It might be derived from Friga, an old English personal name, while the 'up' or 'hop' means a small valley.

The dales meet at Fairy Cross Plain, a name which goes back more than 200 years. 'Cross' refers to the meeting place of two tracks, while 'fairy' is a reminder that this was the legendary haunt of fairies, who were supposed to make butter at night. Fairy rings, formed naturally on the ground by toadstools, were thought to be magical and children would play around them. One old lady gave a graphic account of seeing a little green man here, while another claimed she had found a fairy bairn (a fairy child) in a hayfield.

Fylingdales

Map Ref: 86NZ9003

There is no village of Fylingdales. The name applies to a spacious stretch of moorland and an adjoining coastal area which lies inland near Robin Hood's Bay. The hamlet of Raw, and the village of Fylingthorpe with its views and steep hills can be included, along with many farms and houses and some dramatic and lovely countryside.

Fylingdales Moor rises to almost 1,000ft above sea-level. Crossed by many tracks it lies between the A169 and the A171 and has two remarkable landmarks; one very ancient and the other very modern.

Seventh-century Lilla Cross, one of the country's oldest Christian relics, stands literally in the shadows of the Ballistic Missile Early Warning Station on Fylingdales Moor, built between 1961 and 1962. The latter's three huge white radomes, with the

Fylingdales Ballistic Missile Early Warning Station. Each huge radome is 154 feet high and weighs 100 tons

appearance of gigantic golf balls, are visible from far and near.

The ancient stone cross may be reached by a 2-mile walk across the moor. It commemorates a Christian called Lilla who died in AD626 while protecting Edwin, the heathen King of Northumbria, from an assassin's dagger. Edwin became a Christian as a result and built a church where York Minster now stands.

On a bend in the A169 below the Ballistic Missile Early Warning Station is Ellerbeck, a beauty spot and car parking area which provides views of the North Yorkshire Moors Railway. Those attempting the Lyke Wake Walk are met by support parties here, as it crosses the moor at this point.

AA recommends:
Campsite: Grouse Hill Caravan Park, Flask Bungalow Farm, 3-pennants, *tel.* (0947) 880543
Self Catering: Billira Cottage, *tel.* (0723) 362682

Gillamoor and Fadmoor

Map Ref: 90SE6889

These tiny moorland villages, with less than a mile separating them, are both on the southern edge of the National Park a few miles north of Kirkbymoorside. They are villages through which it is best to stroll, not drive. The influx of visitors to neighbouring and more prominent areas has spilled into these quiet places and each now caters for tourists – if only in a small way – and a walk will reveal many delights.

Gillamoor is perhaps best known for its Surprise View. When leaving the village on the road towards Farndale, there is an abrupt left turn which reveals a magnificent view across the moors, the River Dove and the southerly tip of Farndale. This is one occasion when walking is recommended, because the narrow road and sharp turn makes parking dangerous or even impossible.

Gillamoor contains a three-faced sundial and some fine old houses, one of which used to contain a witch-post. Often made from rowan and decorated with carvings of the cross, these were intended to ward off evil spirits. The church, with a Jacobean altar table, is of interest because it was rebuilt in 1802 by one man, James Smith. The east and north walls have no windows and its sturdy structure was designed to withstand the tough climate of the moors.

Gilling East

Map Ref: 95SE6177

A charming and delightfully compact village in mellow stone, Gilling East is dominated by its castle, approached by a long, steep drive. After long associations with the Fairfax family, it is now owned by Ampleforth College. It dates from the 11th century but, after many alterations and owners, it is now a preparatory school for about 120 boys.

The castle's Great Chamber and impressive gardens are open to the public. The magnificent Elizabethan Great Chamber is used by the boys as their refectory. Completed in 1585, it is noted for its oak panelling, its frieze, the windows and ceiling. The panelling is superb. Large oak panels

Gilling Castle, now a preparatory school for Ampleforth College

Almost hidden by trees, the tiny 17th-century Beggar's Bridge spans the River Esk at Glaisdale

are divided into lozenges and triangles, and inlaid with a variety of patterns. No two are alike. When the College bought the castle in 1929, this panelling was sold separately to Randolph Hearst, the American newspaper magnate. Happily, Ampleforth College managed to re-purchase it in 1952 for restoration to its original position.

The village's history dates back to Norman times when it was known as 'Ghellinges'. The parish church contains portions believed to date from that period. There is some medieval glass in the chancel windows and a fine memorial to Thomas Fairfax.

AA recommends:
Self Catering: Sunset Cottages & Flats, *tel.* (03475) 654

Glaisdale

Map Ref: 85NZ7705

An old guide described the village as having 'many natural charms', and went on, 'It is among meandering streams and wooded vales, and around for miles are the beautiful moors'. This is still a good description

today, for Glaisdale is a sprawling village built on a succession of steep hillsides. There are pleasant walks in the local woods and on the moors.

The path through East Arncliffe Wood to Egton Bridge is delightful. There is an old 'wishing stone' on the way. This is a rock, through the middle of which grew a tree (now dead). Walk around the tree nine times and your wish should come true! Other pleasant walks include the climb up Glaisdale Nab from the ford near the railway station, and the long trek via an ancient 'trod' (paved track), past an imposing school and along the daleside.

Traffic from Egton comes via Limber Hill (gradient 1-in-3) and across the River Esk on a metal bridge. Almost concealed between the metal bridge and a huge railway bridge above is tiny Beggar's Bridge, built in 1619 by Tom Ferris. Tom courted an Egton girl but the swollen river often prevented them meeting. Furthermore, her father thought Tom was too poor. Determined to be a success, Tom went to sea, fought against the Armada and made a fortune. He was made Mayor of Hull and Warden of Trinity House, and returned to build this lovely and graceful pack-horse bridge. He also left a legacy for Glaisdale and Lastingham churches.

Between 1866 and 1876, Glaisdale's iron-ore helped establish Middlesbrough as a major steel town, but there are few signs of its brief industrial role. Charming Glaisdale Dale, running south-west from St Thomas' Church, contained a thriving weaving industry in the 16th and 17th centuries.

Hart Hall Farm is the setting for the tale of the Hart Hall Hob (see page 61), and the Glaisdale and Lealholm Society for the Prosecution of Felons still exists, possibly the only such society still surviving in England.

Goathland

Map Ref: 86NZ8301

One of the most picturesque villages in the North York Moors, Goathland nestles among the heather some 500ft above sea level. Just off the Whitby to Pickering road, and with a station for the North York Moors Railway, it has superb stone houses, excellent hotels and interesting shops. The wide grass verges are shorn to perfection by wandering sheep. Please do not be tempted to feed the sheep, which may even attempt to enter your car in their search for tit-bits. Although they will eat out of visitors' hands, unsuitable or even dangerous food may be given to the annoyance of farmers.

Goathland's name is not linked with goats, but may relate to 'Goda', a Scandinavian settler, or the Swedish 'Goths' or even 'Godeland', meaning God's Land. In 1117, St Mary's Hermitage was established at Godeland. The present church with its interesting font, pulpit and altar stone, is also dedicated to St Mary. Nearby is the old village pound where stray livestock were penned until the owners had paid a fine. It was in use until 1924.

A fine centre for exploration, Goathland is surrounded by extensive moorland, and wooded valleys with lovely waterfalls are within easy reach by foot. One well-known waterfall, 70ft Mallyan Spout, is reached by a footpath which leads from the green beside the Mallyan Spout Hotel. There is a steep but exciting climb down to the waterfall, with Nelly Ayre Foss upstream.

The village is the home of the Goathland Plough Stots, a sword dance team whose displays in the locality have their origins in the settlement in the area by Viking raiders over 1,000 years ago. Close to the village is a camping and caravan site, and Wheeldale Lodge Youth Hostel is nearby. One of the finest remaining portions of a Roman road in Britain, Wade's Causeway crosses Wheeldale Moor near the Youth Hostel.

AA recommends:
Hotels: Goathland Hydro, 2-star, *tel.* (094786) 296
Whitfield House, Darnholm, 1-star, *tel.* (0947) 86215
Guesthouse: Heatherdene Hotel, *tel.* (0947) 86334

Goldsborough and Kettleness

Map Ref: 86NZ8414

Perched near the edge of high cliffs north-west of Whitby, Goldsborough is a lonely, windswept hamlet with a little pub and a history dating back to the Romans who established a chain of defensive signal stations along this stretch of coastline.

This stone at Goldsborough is one of a pair supposedly marking the site of the grave of Wade, a legendary giant but actually a powerful Saxon chief

The site of Goldsborough's Roman station is beside the lane leading down to Kettleness. In the 5th century it was ransacked and its occupants apparently killed as excavations in 1919 revealed skulls, clothing, coins and animal bones, and the bones of a man with a dog at his side. The station had an outer defence consisting of a 12ft-wide ditch. Within this was a 5ft-thick wall, only the foundations of which remain.

Kettleness, half a mile away with open sea views, comprises a few cottages and a coastguard station. Jutting into the North Sea is the 400ft-high Kettleness Point while the Cleveland Way long-distance footpath skirts the cliff top. In 1829 the cliff slipped into the sea, taking with it the entire hamlet of Kettleness. It must have been a gentle slide, however, because the inhabitants had time to reach an alum ship standing off-shore although their homes and the alum works were lost.

In 1857, fossilised ichthyosaurus and plesiosaurus remains were found here and the area has its share of legends and folklore. Near Goldsborough are two standing stones about 100ft apart, each called Wade's Stone. The giant Wade is said to be buried between them. At Kettleness, fairies known as 'bogles' were once said to wash their clothing in Claymoor Well, beating it with bats known as 'bittles'.

Great Ayton

Map Ref: 83NZ5511

Situated on the pretty River Leven with its weirs and flower-bedecked banks, Great Ayton is a village of contrast, its old stone-built cottages mingling with more modern houses. It is affectionately known by the locals as 'Canny Yatton'.

Tucked beneath the northern edge of the North York Moors, it lies just outside the National Park but within the county of North Yorkshire. The A173 runs through the centre and the village's proximity to Middlesbrough means that it is popular with day visitors from Teesside and other parts of the north-east. Its crafts-people, shops, cafés, inns and small businesses are now also welcoming visitors from a wider area, largely thanks to Great Ayton's most famous son, Captain James Cook. His school is now the Captain Cook Museum. Regrettably, the retirement cottage of Cook's parents was removed stone by stone in 1935 and rebuilt in Melbourne, Australia. An obelisk now marks the site.

In 1827 the 50ft Cook Monument was erected on Easby Moor and can

be seen from miles around. The grave of Cook's mother and those of five of his brothers and sisters can be found in Great Ayton's All Saints' churchyard.

The village has two churches, the old All Saints with some Saxon and Norman relics, and the new Christ Church with a tower and a spire. It is also known for its long association with the Society of Friends, or Quakers. Overlooking the High Green is the well-known Friends' School, one of eight Quaker schools in England. Co-educational, its 200 pupils come from all over the world although today not all are Quakers.

Somewhat symbolically, the Cook Heritage Trail, linking five places associated with Cook, begins in front of this school.

AA recommends:
Hotel: Ayton Hall, Low Green, 3-star, country house hotel, 1-rosette, *tel.* (0642) 723595

Grosmont

Map Ref: 86NZ8205

The Romans built a road through Grosmont and a fort to protect it. The village remains strategically placed at the junctions of the Rivers Esk and Murk Esk, and two railways – British Rail's Whitby to Middlesbrough line and the private North York Moors Railway. Approaches by motor vehicle involve narrow roads and steep hills but the views are impressive and the countryside is lovely.

There is little evidence of Grosmont's ancient history. Around 1200, Johanna Fossard founded a priory here. Supported by the French priory of Grandimont, it was known as Grosmont Priory by 1394, but no trace remains.

The village's more recent history involves the railways and the iron-ore industry. During the building of the Whitby to Pickering railway in 1836, a rich ironstone seam was discovered at Grosmont. Extending towards the coast near Skinningrove, it was of the finest quality and a village was built here to house the many miners needed.

The growing village of Great Ayton has the River Leven winding through it and two greens, the High Green and the Low Green

Thus Grosmont helped establish the iron and steel industry on Teesside; 100,000 tons of ore were mined annually and the new railway carried it to Whitby for shipment.

Wade's Causeway

This fine, extraordinarily well-preserved stretch of Roman road was built almost 2,000 years ago. It lies north of Cropton Forest on the edge of Wheeldale Moor, not far from Wheeldale Moor Youth Hostel. Goathland is the nearest village and there are signs to the road from here; it can also be reached from Stape or Egton Bridge. Now in the care of the Department of the Environment, there is no charge for access.

The road represents a remarkable feat of engineering, especially when one recalls that only a century ago some of our own roads were only mud tracks.

Measuring 16ft across and about 1¼ miles in length, it is made up of large, flat stones laid on a bed of gravel and is raised in the centre to facilitate drainage.

Originally built as part of a Roman route which extended from Malton, via the Cawthorn Camps, across the Esk near Grosmont and over to the coast near Goldsborough, the road lay hidden for centuries. Forgotten and neglected on this bleak, boggy moor – 600ft above sea level – it was not rediscovered until 1914. Perhaps the heather which had grown over the stones protected it, but there is no doubt that although stones were removed and feature in existing buildings in the area, the road has survived more or less intact.

It is not difficult to understand why such mystery was attached to the road by our ancestors. They believed it could only have been the work of a giant so the legend about Wade evolved. He lived in nearby Mulgrave Castle with his huge wife

The mine closed in 1871 but for nearly another century the village maintained its industrial tradition with a brickworks.

However, Grosmont no longer has any industries. Its scenic location attracts visitors, but its popularity owes much to the North York Moors Railway whose terminus and locomotive shed is here. The railway uses the beautiful route of George Stephenson's line, built in 1836 as a horse-drawn service. In 1845 George Hudson of York introduced a steam locomotive, but the gradient from Grosmont through Beck Hole to Goathland, which was 1-in-10 in places, was so steep that the coaches were hauled up by rope. A drum, 10ft in diameter, was located at Incline Top near Goathland Station and used a 5½in rope to haul the coaches up the final stretch. Novelist Charles Dickens used that line, which he called 'a quaint old railway' and today steam trains of the North York Moors Railway pass through Ellerbeck and then along the original route through Newton Dale.

One of the legends about the road claims that Wade built it to link his castles at Mulgrave and Pickering

Bell who had to travel to Pickering Castle every day to milk the cows she kept there. Even for giants, this 20-mile trek was arduous so Wade decided to make the journey easier by building a 'footpath'. Bell collected the stones in her apron and Wade laid them. Any that were surplus to requirements were tossed aside – thus accounting for the hillocks which are scattered around the moor. So the road came to be known as Wade's Causeway and although the name comes from a fanciful tale, the true origins of this remarkable construction are well-enough established.

Henry III granted Guisborough Priory a weekly market in the town which grew up around it

Guisborough

Map Ref: 83NZ6115

A fine market town with red-roofed buildings of local stone, Guisborough is situated beneath the tree-lined northern edge of the North York Moors. It used to be the capital town of the Cleveland district of the North Riding of Yorkshire, but since 1974 has been part of the new County of Cleveland.

The town retains its many links with North Yorkshire. Its location makes it a good centre for exploration of both the moors and the coast, while its thriving markets (Thursdays and Saturdays) draw customers from many moorland communities.

The town has much to offer. There is an old market cross with a sundial and a 15th-century church containing the unique Bruce Cenotaph, linking the local Bruce family to the Scottish King Robert the Bruce whose grandfather was buried at Guisborough Priory. Its fine ruins are accessible from the town centre and are noted for the beautiful 56ft arch of the east window framing a view of the Cleveland Hills. The priory, once one of the richest in Yorkshire and the north of England, was founded in 1119 by Robert de Brus for the Augustinian order. A ghost of a Black Monk is supposed to inspect the ruins once a year, at midnight at the first new moon, letting a vanished drawbridge down over an invisible moat.

The beautiful grounds of Gisborough Hall are noted for their huge old trees. One curiosity is that the family name of Lord Gisborough, and indeed Gisborough Moor behind the town, omit the first letter 'u' which appears in the town's name.

Sir Thomas Chaloner of Guisborough introduced alum mining to this area in about 1595. Having recognised the presence of alum on the North York Moors, he travelled to Italy and stole the secrets of how to mine it from the Pope! He is said to have smuggled some of the Pope's experienced workmen into his mines, subsequently being excommunicated.

AA recommends:
Campsite: Tockett's Mill Caravan Park, Skelton Rd, 3-pennants, *tel.* (0287) 35161
Self Catering: Old Font House Cottages, 109-111 Westgate, *tel.* (0287) 32866
Garage: Mackinlay Hyde Motors, 38 Redcar Rd, *tel.* (0287) 32106

Hackness

Map Ref: 93SE9690

It would be difficult to find a more interesting and more beautiful village. Lying deep in the Derwent Valley with its Hall, houses and buildings of mellow stone, and a clear stream rippling beside the road, Hackness is surrounded by leafy woods and lofty moors. The curiously-named villages of Broxa and Silpho are on the hills

Hackness church. The village nestles in the valley of the Lowdales Beck in the Tabular Hills, at the eastern end of the Low Dalby Forest Drive

above, with the steep, winding climb to Silpho affording fine views. Nearby are stones known as the Bride Stones.

The poet William Mason described Hackness as 'A nest of sister vales, o'er hung with hills of varied form and foliage.' Several valleys and streams converge here, such as the romantically-named Whisperdales, while the surrounding hills boast acres of Forestry Commission conifers with splendid walks and a drive open to the public. One valley is so deep that part of it is said never to see the sun between October and March.

Hackness has a history too. A monastery was founded here in AD680 by nuns from St Hilda's abbey at Whitby, and the foundations of the present church of St Peter, with heavy oak pews, were laid in about 1050. It has a 13th-century tower, a 15th-century spire and a magnificent font with a tall oak cover carved in 1480. There is a Saxon cross too, made around AD720 to commemorate an abbess of Hackness. Hackness Hall, built in 1791 by Carr of York is the seat of Lord Derwent. Unfortunately it is not open to the public.

Sculptor Matthew Noble, who exhibited many works at the Royal Academy and carved some of London's best-known statues, was born here and is buried at the nearby village of Brompton.

AA recommends:
Hotel: Hackness Grange Country Hotel, 3-star, country house hotel *tel.* (0723) 369966

Hambleton Hills

Map Ref: 94SE5186

The Hambleton Hills form the western edge of the North York Moors, roughly from the area around Sutton Bank and north to the moorland peak called Black Hambleton. To the west, the villages and hamlets of these hills look across the Vale of York towards the Pennines; to the east and running along the ridge of moorland behind is the route of the old Hambleton Drove Road which now forms part of the Cleveland Way long-distance footpath. The foothills between the path and the boundary of the National Park contain several small, remote villages and there are some on the moors too. They include Thimbleby, Nether Silton, Over Silton, Kepwick, Cowesby, Kirby Knowle, Boltby and Thirlby, with Felixkirk lying below and Old Byland and Cold Kirby on the plain above.

Standing on the moor near Thimbleby is the Hanging Stone – a huge mass of rock 931ft above sea-level, and Nun House – a farm built on the site of a former nunnery. Arthur Mee, in his *King's England* series, said Over Silton was 'a place of far horizons'. The small church of St Mary contains the tiniest of fonts and some Norman stonework.

At Nether Silton, a tall stone pillar in a field near an old manor house presents a puzzle. Facing across the Vale of Mowbray, it bears this sequence of letters:

HTGOMHS
TBBWOTGWWG
TWOTEWAHH
ATCLABWHEY
AD1765
AWPSAYAA

They are thought to be the first letters of the following words: 'Here the grand old manor house stood; the black beams were oak, the great walls were good; the walls of the east wing are hidden here; a thatched cottage like a barn was here erected year AD1765; a wide porch spans a yard and alcove.'

Boltby is a charming place in idyllic surroundings. Strong stone houses crowd beside a rippling stream while Felixkirk's church is one of the few dedicated to St Felix. It has Norman portions and the top of the tower is 400 years old.

Old Byland is a grey-stone village high on the plateau above Sutton Bank. Known by this name since 1541, it was to a site nearby that monks came in 1143 to establish an abbey. But the bells of Rievaulx disturbed them, and eventually they moved into the valley near Wass and founded Byland Abbey.

Cold Kirby is windswept on its lonely site. Dialstone Farm was one of four inns on the ancient drovers' road and there is a fine view of this old track from here.

Harwood Dale

Map Ref: 93SE9695

Deep among the pine forests, this small village lies inland from the A171 between Whitby and Scarborough. Harwood Dale is both the name of the village and the valley in which it stands. The forest to the north is called Harwood Dale Forest while to the south is Broxa Forest, with Langdale Forest over to the west.

The present church of St Margaret was built in 1862 close to the village, but a mile north-west, just off the road, is the ruin of the earlier St Margaret's. This was built in 1643 by Sir Thomas Posthumus Hoby and Lady Hoby of Hackness Hall.

There is a fine view towards the sea from the top of Reasty Bank which climbs onto Broxa Moor. There is a car park too, and the beginning of a nature trail and forest walk. The Silpho Forest Trail is a short 2-mile walk past a Bronze Age burial mound. The demanding Reasty to Allerston Forest Walk covers 16 miles. As it is not circular, careful planning is needed. Forestry Commission leaflets are available for both these walks. The Derwent Way skirts this forest along the banks of the Derwent between Langdale End and High Langdale End.

The moors around Harwood Dale, whether afforested or not, are noted for the number of standing stones, stone circles, howes and tumuli they contain.

On Standing Stones Rigg, about 1½ miles from the village and about ¼ mile south-west of the A171, is a circle 32ft in diameter. It originally comprised 24 standing stones, each some 2ft to 4ft high and a burial chamber was probably sited in the centre. Four stones from the centre can be seen in Scarborough Museum.

AA recommends:
Campsite: Edgemoor, Silpho, Venture Site, *tel.* (0723) 82300

Hawnby

Map Ref: 89SE5489

After John Wesley crossed Snilesworth Moor in July 1757 he

Right: stained-glass window in Hawnby church. Below: sheltered by a distinctive limestone hill, or 'nab', the lovely village of Hawnby in upper Rye Dale presents a tranquil scene. Lonely moorland lies beyond the hill

wrote, 'I rode through one of the pleasantest parts of England to Hawnby.' His route from Osmotherley took him through lonely farmyards, up and down steep hills and across tumbling moorland streams with fords, all spiced with heather and breathtaking views.

Today that route is surfaced for modern traffic, although coaches are banned, but it has plenty of moorland picnic areas and parking spaces.

Known as a stronghold of Methodism, tiny Hawnby with its knot of red-roofed stone cottages clings precariously to a lofty hillside which overlooks the River Rye. The little church of All Saints stands among a tumble of tombstones in the valley beside the River Rye. It claims no treasures, although a church has been here since the 12th century. There is some Norman stonework and an interesting stone cross can be seen near the font.

Arden Hall, seat of the Earls of Mexborough, is hidden among nearby woods and contains part of an ancient nunnery. There is a Nun's Well in the garden and Mary Queen of Scots is said to have spent a night here whilst on her travels.

AA recommends:
Guesthouse: Hawnby Hotel (Inn), *tel.* (04396) 202

Helmsley

Map Ref: 95SE6183

Nestling in a corner of Upper Rye Dale, Helmsley is one of the prettiest of North Yorkshire's country towns. It is a magnet for visitors because roads from Cleveland, Thirsk and York converge upon its market square. With a flowing stream and welcoming shops, restaurants and inns clustered around, plus a market cross and impressive monument to Lord Feversham, Helmsley persuades motorists to stay.

The town's handsome houses and inns are built of local yellow stone with red-pantile roofs, although a Tudor house (Canon's Garth) behind the church, and an extension to the Black Swan Inn are half-timbered. William Wordsworth and his sister, Dorothy, probably stayed at the Black Swan in 1802 on their way to visit Wordsworth's future wife, Mary Hutchinson, near Scarborough. In her diary Dorothy says they 'slept at a very nice inn and were well treated'.

Helmsley boasts a fine, purpose-built youth hostel and there are good sports facilities in the town. Some interesting walks start here, including the long-distance Cleveland Way and Ebor Way. Helmsley also contains the headquarters of the North York Moors National Park Committee, and the Tourist Information Centre is housed in Claridge's Bookshop.

Helmsley Castle, sometimes called Furstan Castle, is close to the market square and dates from 1186. The castle was once inhabited by the Duke of Buckingham, court favourite of James I and Charles I. It was besieged for three months during the Civil War and rendered unusable after its surrender on Cromwell's orders. It was bought by Sir Charles

The attractive stone-built town of Helmsley is particularly busy on Friday, market day

Duncombe in 1689, from whom the Earls of Feversham are descended.

The imposing bulk of the parish church, so often rebuilt that much of its original structure has gone, contains some Norman remains and 11th-century artefacts, while part of the tower dates from the 13th century. The church contains one of 19th-century explorer David Livingstone's letters from Africa.

Duncombe Park, with its 600 acres of parkland and fine mansion built by Vanbrugh, is to become a new attraction for visitors to Helmsley. Ancestral home of the Earls of Feversham, the great house served as a school for girls until 1985. After renovation, the present Lord Feversham hopes to open the gardens in 1987 and the house in 1988.

In 1966 the remains of a 4th-century Roman villa were found at Beadlam, just over a mile from Helmsley.

The town's festival of music and arts is now part of the Ryedale and Helmsley Festival, held each summer.

AA recommends:

Hotels: Black Swan, Market Pl, 3-star, *tel.* (0439) 70466

Feversham Arms, 1 High St, 3-star, *tel.* (0439) 70766

Crown, Market Sq, 2-star, *tel.* (0439) 70297

Feathers, Market Pl, 2-star, *tel.* (0439) 70275

Self Catering: Bank Cottage, Sproxton, *tel.* (04393) 269

Townend Farmhouse (cottage), *tel.* (0439) 71617

Hinderwell and Port Mulgrave

Map Ref: 85NZ7916

Once a major community in this corner of Yorkshire, Hinderwell is now a quiet village less than a mile from the sea.

Its name comes from ancient links with St Hilda, abbess of Whitby. During the last century, it was known as Hilderwell and has been variously called Hylderwell, Hildrewell and Hyndrewell before assuming its present name. As these names suggest, the village churchyard is the location of St Hilda's Well, said to have been blessed by the saint. She maintained a cell here so that she could pray in solitude away from the pressures of Whitby Abbey.

Some delightful countryside and rugged coastal scenery surrounds Hinderwell, and of some interest is the disused, decaying miniature harbour at Port Mulgrave, reached from the village of plain, cliff-top houses by a steep descent. Built last century to cater for the iron-ore boom, it handled 3,000 tons of ore every week and was reached through a mile-long tunnel which emerged from the cliff. The mouth of that tunnel is now sealed.

Hole of Horcum

Map Ref: 92SE8493

The mysterious Hole of Horcum is a huge hollow in Levisham Moor. Large enough to contain two farms and their fields, and to provide the watershed of Levisham Beck, it is little wonder that our primitive ancestors believed it was the work of the devil or a giant.

One legend relates how the giant Wade scooped out the earth to throw at his wife Bell. Another is that the devil picked up a huge handful of earth and cast it across the moors to form 800ft-high Blakey Topping. However, Horcum is disappointingly the work of nature, excavated over thousands of years by the action of springs. It can be admired from the A169 between Pickering and Whitby, and the best place to stop is the car park at the top of the steep and twisting Saltersgate Bank. The rim of this great bowl has become popular with hang gliders, as well as sightseers and hikers. Trains on the North York Moors Railway steam through nearby Newton Dale and these can be seen from vantage points on the neighbouring hills.

Remote and lonely Saltersgate Inn at the foot of the hill was once a coaching halt with a toll-booth and is still sometimes marooned in winter by moorland blizzards. It boasts a peat fire which is supposed to have been kept alight since it was lit in 1801, and at one time was used for making buttered turf cakes. The inn was also the haunt of smugglers and one is said to be buried under the

hearth where the famous peat fire still burns today.

Hovingham

Map Ref: 80SE6675

Hovingham is an attractive, well-kept village with houses and hotels of local stone and a pretty stream. It lies on the Roman road from Boroughbridge to Malton near the wooded edge of the Howardian Hills. Its history goes back a long way and during the construction of Hovingham Hall part of a Roman bath house, two tessellated pavements, some pottery and coins were discovered.

The Hall, built between 1745 and 1755, has a most unusual entrance because the builder, Sir Thomas Worsley, loved horses: an archway leads off the village green into the riding school and stables. The Worsleys are descended from Cromwell and Katherine Worsley of Hovingham is the present Duchess of Kent. The house has another somewhat odd feature, a ballroom on

The Hole of Horcum, a natural hollow, is also known as the Devil's Punchbowl

the upper floor. Its lawn is actually the village cricket field and an annual festival of cricket is held there.

Although the parish church of All Saints was largely rebuilt in 1860, the tower is Anglo-Saxon and there is a Norman window and some stones dating from around AD1,000.

AA recommends:
Hotel: Worsley Arms, 2-star, *tel.* (065382) 234

Castles

Centuries ago, defence of the high plateau of the North Yorkshire Moors with its virtually inaccessible dales was confined to the periphery of the area – as the castles at Helmsley, Pickering, Scarborough and Danby testify.

The extensive remains of Scarborough Castle stand high on the 300ft cliff which separates the north and south bays. With the sea on three sides and just a narrow tongue of land joining it to the town on the fourth, it held a strong position.

It was built in about 1136 by William de Gros on the site of an old Roman signal station and when Henry II took it over the 100ft-high keep was added. This was often put to the test as Scarborough saw a lot of military action. In 1312 unpopular Piers Gaveston, favourite of Edward II, defended it against his enemies but was forced to surrender through starvation. Two hundred years later, during the Pilgrimage of Grace in 1536, Robert Aske and his army lay siege to the castle but Sir Ralph Evers successfully defended it for the king. While Queen Mary held the crown the castle was taken by means of subterfuge. Thomas Stafford and some of his men gained entrance by disguising themselves and although they were able to hold it for a few

Engraving of Scarborough Castle

days, it was soon retaken by the Queen's troops. Throughout the Civil War the castle was constantly under threat. The longest siege lasted a year with the starving Royalist garrison eventually having to surrender.

Neither Helmsley nor Pickering Castles saw the action which beset Scarborough but both are interesting and are fine ruins, the existing castle at Helmsley was built in the 12th century by Walter L'Espec and is remarkable for its defensive earthworks. These consist of two ditches with a double bank which surround the original keep and curtain wall and towers added in the 13th century. The great hall and

buttery were another addition a century later. Parts of the castle pre-date L'Espec's structure. These belong to a castle started by Robert de Roos, Lord of Helmsley between 1186 and 1227.

Pickering Castle, a motte and bailey castle, consists of a keep standing on a high mound (motte) which is surrounded by a ditch, the space between this and the outer walls being known as the bailey. The castle was closely associated with royalty and most of the kings of England visited it when hunting in Pickering Forest. It also served as the administrative centre of the area and was used as a prison after the Civil War, during which it suffered considerable damage.

Overlooking the Esk Valley in the north is Danby Castle, built in the early part of the 14th century by the Latimers. Catherine Parr, Henry VIII's sixth wife, may have lived here for she married John Latimer after the king's death. The castle now forms part of a farmhouse and its buildings and is not open to the public, although a letter to the farmer may make a visit possible for groups such as school parties.

Other castles are known to have been built at Castleton, Cropton, Goathland, Kildale, Roxby, Whorlton and Kirkbymoorside, but in most cases no traces of these remain.

The pretty Hutton Beck flows through Hutton-le-Hole, one of Yorkshire's most attractive villages and the location of the Ryedale Folk Museum

Hutton-le-Hole

Map Ref: 90SE7089

One of the showpieces of the Moors, Hutton-le-Hole's houses, inn and shops surround a spacious and undulating village green divided by a clean moorland stream. Once traversed by fords, there are now tidy bridges and well-kept gardens to uphold Hutton's claim to be one of the prettiest villages in Yorkshire. The grass is beautifully shorn by moorland sheep which freely roam among the sturdy stone cottages.

Near the car park on the road to Lastingham is an old cattle pound, while the tiny church, well-kept as a result of 40 years' fund-raising by the villagers, contains oak furniture by woodcarver Thompson of Kilburn.

A major attraction here is the fascinating Ryedale Folk Museum located in the centre of Hutton-le-Hole. From small beginnings in a cottage, it has expanded out-of-doors to include a completely reconstructed medieval thatched cruck house from Danby, an ancient glassworks, a blacksmith's shop and displays depicting a wide range of local crafts and customs. Children love the witch in her hovel, while indoors there are items – ranging from witch-posts to kitchen utensils – collected from old moorland farms and cottages.

Common land hereabouts is administered by the ancient Spaunton Court Leet and Court Baron with View of Frankpledge, one of the few surviving Courts Leet (see page 53).

AA recommends:
Guesthouse: Barn Guesthouse, *tel.* (07515) 311

Recalling the Past

The Ryedale Folk Museum in Hutton-le-Hole opened in 1964 when the personal collections of bygones belonging to Mr B Frank and Mr R W Crosland were amalgamated for public display in a range of 18th-century farm buildings bequeathed for the purpose by Mr Crosland's sisters. Their niece helped the enterprise with a generous gift of money. Mr Frank was made curator and under his expert guidance, together with the advice of the museum's trustees, the venture has gone from strength to strength.

The exhibits, augmented by a combination of gifts and purchases, chiefly depict the life of the people of the North York Moors and Rye Dale from early times, most particularly during the 17th, 18th and 19th centuries.

Houses and buildings from local villages have also been brought to the 2½-acre site and re-erected with painstaking authenticity. They include the thatched Manor House from Harome, where the lord of the manor lived and held his meetings and courts, dating from about 1600, and the 500-year-old Cruck House from Stangend, Danby. This was a yeoman's cottage, built with the cruck-frame construction typical of the area and a thatched roof. Inside the house there is a witch-post, kept to ward off evil spirits. Made from mountain ash, it has a cross carved into the top as well as various other symbols whoses significance has been lost. There are also small holes; one big enough to hold a small coin, the other – slightly smaller – plugged with sheep's wool. The meaning of these is unknown. The post usually stood by the left-hand side of the fireplace supporting the smoke hood. There is also a stone box in the wall by the fire where salt was stored to keep it dry. This precious commodity, usually in short supply, was essential for preserving food. Spices were often kept in a similar way.

Another cottage, from Harome, is about 200 years old. Here there are two cooking ranges, one designed to burn peat which was obtained from the moors, the other made for the use of coal and wood. A fully equipped period dairy complete with wooden bowls, churns, butter pats and other utensils can be seen here.

Other buildings which recreate the past include a crofter's cottage, an iron foundry, a blacksmith's shop, a saddler's shop and a joiner and wheelwright's shop. All are fully equipped with the traditional furniture, tools and implements appropriate to the various occupants and their trades. One unique reconstruction is the 16th-century glass furnace which was discovered in Rosedale, then carefully excavated and brought to the museum.

The exhibits and buildings of the Ryedale Folk Museum make it easier for the visitor to imagine life as it was on and around the moors in times gone by. With the poor roads and transport the villages were isolated and more or less self-sufficient. Only a limited range of goods could be obtained from the outside world so people engaged in a variety of trades in order that their communities would want for nothing.

Life was hard for the villagers but they had their own entertainments to provide relief from work; dancing to the music of the fiddle and concertina and, in season, enjoying the mummers' play, maypole and morris dancing. There were also games to be played such as quoits and draughts. After a hard day's work they would sit by the fire and tell stories, safe in the knowledge that the witch-post was protecting them from evil spirits.

One of the reconstructed cottages depicting life in the past

Hutton Rudby

Map Ref: 82NZ4606

Strictly speaking, there are two villages here. Rudby lies on one side of the meandering River Leven and Hutton Rudby on the other. They are separated by a wooded glen and linked by an attractive stone bridge.

This is a most attractive area which draws day visitors from Middlesbrough and Teesside. The river winds through the wooded banks and tumbles over a weir as it flows below houses perched on top of the cliffs. There are some pleasant walks in this vicinity; one follows the river bank on the Hutton Rudby side before turning high into the village and on to the spacious wooded green bordered on both sides by rows of pretty cottages.

The church, which sits on the banks of the River Leven at Rudby, dates back to the 13th century and has a good deal of 14th-century stonework. There is some 15th-century stained glass depicting a shield and the pulpit is Elizabethan. Access to the church is through an impressive oak lych gate.

Some nearby villages should not be missed by the visitor to the area. Crathorne is now by-passed by the A19, and contains an old watermill and some delightful white-walled cottages.

Kettleness, see Goldsborough

Kilburn's distinctive White Horse can be seen from the central tower of York Minster, 19 miles away

Kilburn

Map Ref: 94SE5179

Travellers approaching North Yorkshire from the south by road or rail, or even by aircraft, can hardly fail to see the giant shape of the Kilburn White Horse cut from the turf on the side of Roulston Scar, about a mile south of Sutton Bank Top. The only turf-cut figure in the north of England, it is almost 105yd long by 75yd high. Headmaster of the village school, John Hodgson, designed it with his pupils and 33 local volunteers completed the cutting in 1857. Gallons of whitewash were used to paint the original horse but now chalk chippings from the Yorkshire Wolds are used. Natural erosion, the weather and thoughtless people walking across the surface all cause damage, and a registered charity has been formed to maintain the horse. A very steep, narrow road climbs up to the car park and a flight of steps leads up to the horse.

Kilburn village is charming, with pretty gardens and a stream, while stacks of weathering oak provide a clue to the work of the village's famous craftsman – Robert Thompson. He died in 1955 but his old home, a half-timbered house, is now a showroom for fine woodcarving and craftsmanship in oak (see also page 32).

Kildale

Map Ref: 83NZ6009

In ancient times a lake covered the land now occupied by Kildale – a small, quiet village tucked among trees on a plain in the north-west corner of the Moors. Standing on the upper reaches of the River Leven, Kildale continues to be served by the Whitby to Middlesbrough railway line, and the Cleveland Way footpath passes through.

Kildale's past is known to have included Danish settlers; four skeletons with swords, daggers and a battle-axe were found in 1868 during rebuilding of the church. Records also include references to a castle, but little trace of this remains.

In about 1200 a nunnery was founded in Baysdale, a short distance over the hills from Kildale, and in 1312 the Friars of the Holy Cross built a monastery here. However, they were asked to leave by the Archbishop of York because they failed to secure his permission to conduct their services. It is known that a chapel here was dedicated to St Hilda (and not St Kilda as some suggest). Kildale's name probably comes from 'Ketildale', Ketil being a northern name.

The noted Percy family, whose coat of arms can be seen on huge tombstones in St Cuthbert's Church porch, were Lords of the Manor of Kildale. Their mansion has now gone, but Percy Rigg and Percy Cross on the Moors recall their importance.

Kirkbymoorside

Map Ref: 90SE6986

Kirkbymoorside is pleasantly located almost midway between Pickering and Helmsley but is by-passed by the A170. This carries most of the passing traffic but is seen as a mixed blessing as it does tend to isolate the town from casual tourist trade. Even with a small industrial complex on the outskirts, this is a very peaceful market town.

Its position at the southern edge of the North York Moors, and its range of hotels, shops and small restaurants, make Kirkbymoorside a useful centre for touring. There is a thriving market every Wednesday and its community halls are used for art, flower and produce shows, as well as antique fairs and other events. The town's brass band performs regularly.

Kirkbymoorside shows little evidence of its long history. Two castles have come and gone with little to mark their passing, except that the stones of one were used to build the tollbooth in the town centre. The church, almost hidden behind the market place, possesses some Norman masonry, fragments of a Saxon cross, an old Mass dial and some medieval artefacts.

One well-known resident was George Villiers, the 2nd Duke of Buckingham (1628-1687). Rich and powerful, he was said to be one of the most notorious and dazzling courtiers of the time, but died in shame after a life of drunkenness, violence and general misbehaviour. Legend says he lay dying in the worst room of the worst inn in Kirkbymoorside, but this is not so. He died in one of the best houses in the town next door to the King's Head Inn. It was occupied by one of his tenants. There are a number of stories about his demise. One is that he fell from his horse while hunting in Bilsdale, and another says he caught a severe chill and was taken ill while riding. The parish register records his death simply: '1687, George Vilaus, lord dooke of bookingham.' His intestines were buried at Helmsley, and his body taken to London for burial beside his father in Westminster Abbey.

Known locally as 'Kirby', one of the town's problems is how to spell its name. It means 'church-by-the-moor-side' but there are disputes about the presence of the second 'k'!

AA recommends:
Hotel: George & Dragon, Market Pl, 2-star, *tel.* (0751) 31637
Self Catering: Glenmorven, Gillamoor, *tel.* (0751) 75058
Town Farm Cottage, *tel.* (0751) 75058
Garage: CC Specialist Cars, West End, *tel.* (0751) 31867

Kirkdale

Map Ref: 90SE6686

Kirkdale is fascinating. It contains neither village nor hamlet, but there is a tiny 7th-century minster, a cave more than 70,000 years old and a river which disappears underground in the summer.

The little dale can be reached by leaving the A170 between Helmsley and Kirkbymoorside where signposts point to 'St Gregory's Minster', about a mile away. After travelling down steep hills to a wide ford, the sturdy outline of the church can be seen among trees. The first Kirkdale Minster was built around AD654 and dedicated to St Gregory the Great,

An inscription on the Saxon sundial above the south doorway of St Gregory's Minster, Kirkdale, tells how Orm renovated the church in 1060

the first monk to become Pope and the man who sent St Augustine to England.

Above the doorway, carved on a 7ft slab of stone, is a Saxon sundial, the most complete example of its kind in the world. Showing the eight hours of a Saxon day, it bears the longest known inscription from those times. From this we know the church was a ruin before 1066 and that it was rebuilt by Orm, son of Gamal. One name on the sundial is Brand, believed to be the first parish priest to be recorded by name. The church is now used for Anglican services.

Kirkdale Cave, which lies in the wooded cliff above the ford, was discovered in 1821 by a quarryman who came across the sealed entrance by chance. Once inside he found it to be full of old bones and thinking them to be of no value, threw many away. However, fortunately he showed some to a local doctor who recognised their importance. Expert examination revealed that the cave had been the haunt of hyenas and the remains belonged to their prey – animals which had lived some 70,000 years before Christ. They were species which no longer lived wild in the British Isles but proved that this corner of England had once enjoyed a warm, sub-tropical climate. The bones were those of spotted hyena, slender-nosed rhinoceros, woolly rhinoceros, hippopotamus, giant deer, European bison, straight-tusked elephant, mammoth and lion. The remains are now in several museums.

An extensive cave system is believed to exist beneath this area, which probably explains the occasional disappearance of the Hodge Beck, which flows through a gorge on one side of the graveyard. Legend has it that a goose once walked two miles underground from Kirkdale Cave into Kirkbymoorside.

Lastingham

Map Ref: 90SE7290

One of the most attractive and interesting villages on the moors, Lastingham's place in the history of Christian England is assured. Today tourists, pilgrims and experts are drawn to its fine church, but they also enjoy the natural charm of this welcoming spot. Venerable Bede's comment in AD700 that it was 'among steep and solitary hills' is still true today.

It was here in AD654 that Cedd, a monk from Lindisfarne, was given land upon which to found a monastery. Unfortunately, he died of the plague before it was finished, but his younger brother, Chad, succeeded him as Abbot of Lastingham (later becoming Bishop of York and then of Lichfield) and the monastery flourished. The brothers became saints whose feast day is 2 March.

However, the Danes destroyed the monastery in AD866, and it lay in ruins until 1078, when Stephen, Abbot of Whitby, asked William the Conqueror if he could restore it. William consented and Stephen began by building a crypt as a shrine for St Cedd. However, Stephen moved to York in 1086 to establish St Mary's Abbey so the monastery was never completed.

The crypt, with chancel, nave and two side aisles, is a complete church in its own right and is used for special services; it is entered through St Mary's Parish Church. Apart from some levelling of the floor and some plasterwork, it has not been changed since 1068 and contains a wealth of interesting stonework, including an altar. St Mary's has a bier dating to before the Reformation.

Stepping stones across the River Esk: one of the attractions of Lealholm

Lastingham is very small, but a walk around it will reveal several well-heads, one of which is dedicated to St Cedd, as well as an hotel, a restaurant, a post office-cum-shop and a cosy village inn. Near the summit of the hill leading towards Appleton-le-Moors is Lidsty Cross, erected in 1897 to commemorate Queen Victoria's Diamond Jubilee. Elizabeth II's Coronation seat beside it provides a welcome rest with superb views.

AA recommends:

Hotel: Lastingham Grange, 2-star, country house hotel, *tel.* (07515) 345

St Mary's Church in Lastingham partly dates from the 11th century, when work began to replace a monastery destroyed by the Danes in AD866

Lealholm

Map Ref: 85NZ7607

Over the past 20 years or so Lealholm has blossomed from being one of the quieter villages of Esk Dale into a busy Mecca for tourists, complete with toilets, a car park, garden centre and shops.

This is due to several factors: a splendid and spacious village green beside the River Esk with lovely cottages, shops, tea-rooms and an inn; stepping-stones across the river nearby; and lovely views from the surrounding moors. The vista from the top of Lealholm Bank and the adjoining lanes is particularly impressive. A foreign writer said of Lealholm, 'Elsewhere, you have to go in search of beautiful views; here, they come and offer themselves to be looked at.'

Steep and winding hills drop into Lealholm from all sides, and of especial interest to naturalists (although privately owned) is Crunkley Gill, a deep and dramatic ravine which extends upstream from the village. It is said to be the biggest rock-garden in England, for it is rich with trees, ferns, flowers and rare plants. They grow on the banks of the River Esk as it tumbles over rocks and boulders in this delightful gorge. There is no public access to the ravine.

The Whitby to Middlesbrough railway line, with a halt at Lealholm, runs along the northern side of the valley and half-way up Lealholm Bank are two churches. The modern Catholic church stands on a hillside site, while the red-roofed Anglican church has a very small tower, only 6ft wide at the base.

Levisham and Lockton

Map Ref: 92SE8390

A pair of tiny villages high on the moors north of Pickering, Levisham and Lockton were once known as 'the twin towns of the moors'. With their remote farms, sturdy stone cottages and neat appearance, they are more like hamlets than towns. As the proverbial crow flies, they are less than a mile apart.

That mile, however, involves a deep and spectacular valley with winding hills and a route said by one traveller to be 'a breakneck descent and two distressing climbs'. Levisham Beck, which rises in the Hole of Horcum, flows along this valley and at its foot there is a bridge with a watermill and a small waterfall.

Almost hidden away near the bridge is the little church of St Mary. This dates from the 11th century and although the church was largely rebuilt in the 19th century there are some Norman remains.

Lockton's church has a squat, 15th-century tower, with a medieval nave and chancel and a 14th-century arch.

Nearby is Killingnoble Scar, so called because it was once the haunt of peregrine falcons kept by James I for hawking. In 1612 the local people were charged with the duty of 'looking after the birds for the King's use'.

At the foot of the Scar a pool called Newton Dale Well was the scene, long ago, of a Midsummer day fair and a blessing the well ceremony. Because of the health-giving properties of the water, a spa complex was proposed for this site, but it never reached fruition.

Two tortuous and scenic miles out of Levisham, deep in Newton Dale, is Levisham Station – now on the North York Moors Railway – beyond which lies Cropton Forest where there are some lovely walks. There are also impressive walks from Levisham along the Beck into the Hole of Horcum or onto Levisham Moor, rich with tumuli and earthworks.

Littlebeck

Map Ref: 86NZ8804

Strong nerves and good brakes are required on the descents into Littlebeck. The lanes are very narrow with sharp bends and extreme gradients from whichever direction it is approached. One route leaves the A169 as it drops down Blue Bank into Sleights near Whitby, and another way is to take one of two small roads leading off the B1416 which climbs out of Ruswarp towards Scarborough.

This entrancing hamlet is set deep in a wooded valley which extends south from Esk Dale. Some delightful houses surround a quiet pool in the stream – also called Little Beck.

One little-known local custom is

Tiny, pretty Levisham faces Lockton across a gorge in the plateau of the Tabular Hills

the annual Rose Queen ceremony, held in August, in which a local girl is crowned Queen and floated on a raft in the stream. It was in this stream that a man called John Reeves drowned himself in 1679 after betraying the 82-year-old Catholic priest, Nicholas Postgate. The pool is now called Devil's Dump.

Beside the B1416 above Littlebeck is a location called Red Gates. From here a track leads to Falling Foss, a lovely 40ft waterfall in a sylvan setting, which is at its most dramatic in times of flood. There is a car park and picnic site nearby.

The surrounding rocks are thick with ferns, mosses and woodland plants and tucked away nearby is the home of George Chubb carved out of solid rock in 1780. It will accommodate about 20 people and even includes stone armchairs.

Higher up the valley is the delightful open area known as Maybeck with walks and sights to treasure, complete with another picnic site and car park.

Loftus

Map Ref: 84NZ7118

Once a North Riding market town, Loftus is now part of the new county of Cleveland, but it does retain some of the aura of a moorland community even though its weekly market has ended. Its history dates back to Roman times and before William the Conqueror's Harrying of the North, when it was laid waste, Loftus was a thriving township. The gradual return of prosperity began with alum mining and continued with the iron-ore industry which established Skinningrove as a major iron- and steel-producing complex.

The town's dependence upon heavy industry, rather than agriculture, has meant that Loftus (spelt as Lofthouse until the last century) has endured many peaks and troughs in its commercial life. Recently the potash mine at Boulby has brought some work to the area and new projects offer some pleasant shopping facilities. There is also a superb sports centre with a swimming pool, squash courts, saunas and now a jacuzzi.

The coast behind Loftus is dramatic. Here the Cleveland Way crosses the cliffs by Hummersea Scar and continues along the coast to Boulby. Boulby Cliff, almost 700ft high, is the highest point on the east coast of England and from here there are excellent views.

A nice walk through Ness Hag Wood beside Kilton Beck leads to Liverton Mill. Of interest is the site of Handale Priory which was built in 1133 some 2 miles south of Loftus, on what is now the boundary of the National Park. Legend says the woods here contained a serpent which ate young maidens but one day a brave fellow called Scaw came by and smote it with his trusty sword, ridding the area of this terror. He married a wealthy maiden whose life had been threatened by the serpent and Handale Priory is supposed to have contained his coffin. A nearby spinney was named Scaw Wood in his honour.

AA recommends:

Hotel: Grinkle Park, 3-star country house hotel, *tel.* (0287) 40515

Low Dalby

Map Ref: 92SE8587

If there is a secret village in North Yorkshire, it is probably Low Dalby. Nestling in a fold in the hills beside rows of conifers, it is now a thriving centre for the tourist boom which has developed locally because of the recreational value of the forests.

The Forestry Commission began planting conifers in the North York Moors in 1920 and there are now some 50,000 acres of Forestry Commission plantations within the National Park. Low Dalby lies within the large Allerston Forest which comprises many smaller plantations, including Dalby Forest. Much of this forest land is open to the public.

Afforestation has made use of poor land which would otherwise lie idle and has created many jobs. Specially constructed forest villages at Low Dalby, Wykeham Moor and Darncombe house Forestry Commission employees and their families.

Since afforestation, the recreational potential of forests has been recognised and encouraged by the Forestry Commission. At Low Dalby, the Commission has established a Forest Visitor Centre. Here, a whole range of information is available, from details about the work of the Commission and its foresters to illustrated guides about the wildlife which is supported here.

There is plenty to see in Dalby Forest, made accessible by a forest drive from Low Dalby to Hackness

To encourage visitors, there is a forest drive, forest trails, camping and caravan sites and forest cabin accommodation for holidaymakers. The recommended walks vary from about a mile up to 6 or 7 miles, and the forests have several picnic sites and view points.

Dalby Forest Drive (with a small toll) emerges at Langdale End near Hackness, and routes through this forest are popular with motor ralliers.

Visitors to this area must take immense care not to start fires.

Courts Leet

Courts Leet date back to feudal times when the administration of certain aspects of the law was vested in the lord of the manor. A manor – also known as a lordship, or hundred – was the name given to the sub-divisions of a county or shire, each of which had its own court. The word Leet first appeared in Domesday Book, meaning a territorial and jurisdictional area in East Anglia. But by the 14th century the term had spread throughout England and referred specifically to courts over which the Sheriff had no jurisdiction: virtually a royal court which the lord administered for his own profit.

Nevertheless, the tenants of each manor had rights to a certain amount of common land – although this usually consisted of land of little use to the lord anyway – and an important function of the Court was to ensure these rights were upheld. Other obligations included the maintenance of roads, ditches and fences, the appointment of local officers, the judgment of petty offences such as trespass, as well as various administrative duties.

However, the Enclosure Acts of the early 19th century saw the steady decline of the Courts as, with the abolition of common land, one of their main purposes disappeared. By 1946 most had ceased to func-

tion and their responsibilities passed to the County Courts. However, some do remain and the North York Moors can claim four of the 38 still in existence throughout England; probably representing the greatest concentration in such a small area in the country. These operate at Spaunton, Danby, Fyling and Whitby Laithes – although the territory of the latter had become so small that its jurisdiction now embraces only grass verges.

The nominal head of the Court Leet is still known as the 'Lord of the Manor' although these days he does not necessarily have to be present at meetings, usually held annually in October, or maybe even every alternate year. In days gone by the Courts met twice a year and all the residents of the district

attended. The administration of the Court is left to the Steward, or 'seneschal'. At present there is one lord of the manor for the Courts Leet of both Fyling and Whitby Laithes, but at Danby there is a bailiff as well as a steward and he supervises proceedings. A jury of 12 attends and any fines are fixed by the 'affeeror'. Encroachment fines relating to common land are really the only power the Courts have today. For example, if the County Council erect a sign, or the Electricity Board puts a pole on common land the Court is entitled to exact a fine.

One other curious piece of legislation operated by the Courts is the issuing of the licence needed to gather sphagnum moss, sought after chiefly by flower arrangers.

Officers and jury of the Spaunton Manor Court Leet in 1908, with representatives from Appleton le Moors, Hutton-le-Hole and Lastingham

Lythe and Sandsend

Map Ref: 86NZ8413

Lythe Bank is a very steep hill which takes the A174 from Lythe down to Sandsend where the road runs literally along the edge of the sea. There are wonderful sea views from the top and a fine sandy beach, devoid of amusement arcades, at Sandsend below.

Lythe, on the hill, is a small village, but there is a nice inn and adequate car parking. Its sturdy, cliff-top church is worth a visit. Founded in Saxon times, it has endured several restorations and has proved strong enough to withstand the fierce North Sea storms. Seven sailors are buried here who died in the sea below during World War I. They have never been identified.

One of Lythe's noted priests was later to become Cardinal, and then Saint, John Fisher. His stand against Henry VIII at the Reformation cost him his life.

In the village there is a tiny blacksmith's shop whose anvil can be seen through the window. Here is practised an old custom known as Firing the Stiddy (anvil); it celebrates

St Oswald's Church, Lythe – built in 1910 on Lythe Bank, less than a mile from the sea

notable events in the family of the Marquis of Normanby of Mulgrave Castle. This fine building (Georgian and later) stands in a wooded ravine adjoining the village. The grounds – sometimes open to the public – contain the ruins of Foss Castle dating back to the Conquest, and there are places with evocative names such as Devil's Bridge, Wizard's Glen, the Waterfall and Eagles' Nest.

Charles Dickens enjoyed a holiday at Mulgrave Castle and it has accommodated many notable people, including members of the Royal family. Legend says that one of the early inhabitants of Foss Castle was the Saxon giant Wade and his wife Bell (see Wade's Causeway).

Like the A174, Mulgrave Woods descend into Sandsend. Once the site of a Roman cement works, this cluster of pretty houses by the sea is aptly named, as they mark the end of 2½ miles of beach stretching from Whitby. However, this is a holiday centre in its own right with hotels, inns, boarding houses and holiday cottages. A superb cliff-top golf course and 2½ miles of fields separates the village from Whitby. Jet was once mined here and there were alum works which closed in 1867. A railway used to cling to the cliffs here too, but this closed in the late 1950s and some of its tunnels, cuttings and embankments form part of the long-distance Cleveland Way walk.

Marton

Map Ref: 82NZ5115

Once a small North Riding village, Marton is now a part of the Teesside conurbation and a thriving suburb of Middlesbrough. The dual carriageways of the A174 slice through rows of houses and carry a constant flow of traffic from Redcar to Thornaby. At Marton, this busy road is crossed by the A172 which takes traffic out of Middlesbrough to Stokesley.

Today, Marton bears little or no resemblance to the rural village it once was, but these changes can never take away the fact that it is the birthplace of Captain James Cook, the great seaman and circumnavigator (see page 24). His birthplace was a small thatched cottage in the grounds of the former Marton Hall (now Stewart Park), a fine park of 110 acres. James was baptised in St Cuthbert's Church, part of which dates from the 12th century, although most of it was rebuilt in about 1847. The present village school was erected to Cook's memory. The cottage of his birth, however, no longer exists because it was demolished, but the Captain Cook Birthplace Museum has been established near the site in Stewart Park, Ladgate Lane, Middlesbrough, and a granite vase marks the actual location of Cook's cottage. The museum contains relics of Cook's life and voyages, as well as weapons from the South Seas and other displays.

AA recommends:
Garage: Minories, Dixons Bank, *tel.* (0642) 317171

Middlesbrough

Map Ref: 80NZ4920

Middlesbrough would never claim to be a holiday resort. The town's rapid industrial development has produced a sprawling conglomeration of streets and housing estates but there is some excellent shopping in the town centre. There are also some splendid buildings, such as the town hall, dating from 1899, which has a magnificent panelled council chamber. The Roman Catholic cathedral, once a focus of interest, has sadly been declared unsafe and a new one is under construction at Coulby Newham. There are many other fine churches in the town and the library contains a treasury of Greek Bibles.

There are some fine parks, gardens and museums here. For example, the Dorman Museum contains displays of local, social and natural history while Stewart Park, in Ladgate Lane, offers two lakes, an aviary and animal enclosure as well as lots of open space. Also in Stewart Park is the Captain Cook Birthplace Museum. Albert Park, with its lawns, flower beds and impressive War Memorial provides an area of calm within the town.

Middlesbrough's famous Transporter Bridge carries cars and people 850feet across the River Tees

Middlesbrough's art gallery features a permanent collection of 20th-century art, and Newham Grange Leisure Farm at Coulby Newham offers a presentation of local farming life, both old and new, which is based on a working farm complete with animals, machinery and farm services. This is open daily during the summer.

Nearby Billingham, with its renowned Forum, is noted for its range of entertainment and has a thriving arts centre. Every August, Middlesbrough hosts the International Eisteddfod which features a fascinating range of cosmopolitan folklore, dancing and music.

The town is famed for its engineering skills, and its bridges span some of the world's most famous waterways including Sydney Harbour, the White Nile, the Thames and the Volta River in Ghana, while its own bridges are worthy of note. Spanning the River Tees at Middlesbrough is the Transporter Bridge opened in 1911, the only working one of its kind in this country. It carries vehicles across the river on a moving platform. Upstream is Newport Bridge opened in 1934, the first vertical lift bridge in England, and the largest of its kind.

Middlesbrough, now the capital town of the new County of Cleveland, is surrounded by beautiful countryside. Seal Sands, a nature sanctuary in Tees Bay, is noted for its many rare sea birds.

AA recommends:
Hotels: Blue Bell Motor Inn, Acklam, 3-star, *tel.* (0642) 593939
Ladbroke Dragonara, Fry St, 3-star, *tel.* (0642) 248133
Marton Hotel & Country Club, Stokesley Rd, Marton, 3-star, *tel.* (0642) 317141 (3m s of A172)
Marton Way, Marton Rd, 3-star, *tel.* (0642) 817651
Guesthouses: Chadwick Private Hotel, 27 Clairville Rd, *tel.* (0642) 245340
Grey House Hotel, 79 Cambridge Rd, *tel.* (0642) 817485
Longlands Hotel, 295 Marton Rd, *tel.* (0642) 244900
Garage: Auto Enterprises, Unit 7, Ayresome Rd, Letita Ind Est, *tel.* (0642) 245254

Mount Grace Priory

Map Ref: 88SE4498

The full name of this spacious and beautiful ruin is 'The House of the Assumption of the Blessed Virgin Mary and St Nicholas of Mount Grace in Ingleby'. Almost everyone calls it Mount Grace Priory and it is to be found just off the western edge of the North York Moors. Open to the public, it is located close to the Cleveland Tontine Inn where the dual carriageway of the A19 meets the A172 from Stokesley.

This is the largest and best-preserved of all the English Carthusian houses and the only one in Yorkshire. It was founded at the end of the 14th century by a nephew of Richard II, Thomas Holland, who was Duke of Surrey and Earl of Kent.

The spacious ruins provide a striking reminder of the austere lives and the strict rule followed by the resident monks. Having taken a vow of silence, each lived alone in a tiny two-storey cell with a fireplace and a ladder to the upper floor. They lived, ate and prayed in these cells, only 22ft square, being allowed out only by permission of the prior. Each of the 15 cells had a small garden separated from the one next door by high walls, and each monk was given his meals through a square hole in the wall, angled so he could not see who brought it.

In 1420, the priory was extended. More cells were built, bringing the total to 20, and a tower and transepts were added to the priory church.

In the woods above, on the route of the Cleveland Way where there are splendid views across the Vale of York towards the Pennines, is the Chapel of Our Lady of Mount Grace. This is becoming an increasingly popular place of pilgrimage for Roman Catholics. Described in 1642 as having four walls but no roof or shelter, it has now been restored. Access is from Osmotherley.

Osmotherley

Map Ref: 88SE4597

The old name for the village was Osmunderly, probably coming from the Old Norse meaning 'Osmund's Ley', a ley being a clearing. There is little likelihood of Osmotherley's origins having anything to do with the tale of a drowning prince (see Roseberry Topping).

One of the chief attractions for visitors to the village is a large area of open National Trust moorland which borders Cod Beck at a point known as the Sheepwash. This is about a mile from the village, on the road towards Swainby, and there is space for car parking. The area is popular with families who can picnic, paddle in the stream and explore the moors. It is adjacent to Cod Beck Reservoir, a quiet, man-made stretch of inland water which is administered by Yorkshire Water.

Just beyond, on the narrow road towards Swainby is a natural gap called Scarth Nick. Shaped like a V, it was carved by meltwater during the Ice Age, and provides beautiful views over Cleveland.

Osmotherley is an attractive mixture of lovely old stone cottages and stylish modern houses in a lofty situation on the edge of the moors. Once it was a small but busy market town and in the centre is a heavily carved market cross. Next to it is a squat stone table standing on short stone legs. This is probably an old market stall.

John Wesley, the 18th-century founder of Methodism, once stood upon this table to deliver a sermon and one of the first Methodist chapels in the moors was built in a cobbled alley in the village. It bears the date 1754 above the door.

The Anglican church has a 15th-century tower and porch, a long nave with medieval walls, Norman foundations and a Norman font. The foundations of a Saxon apse were found during renovations in 1892.

The Catholic Lady Chapel (see Mount Grace Priory) is nearby and Mass is also said in the Old Hall.

There are fine walks in the surrounding countryside. The Lyke Wake Walk begins nearby and the Cleveland Way passes through. A famous 300-year-old drovers' inn called The Chequers Inn was situated on the road to Hawnby, 800ft above sea level. Now a farmhouse, it has a sign which says, 'Be not in haste; Step in and taste – Ale tomorrow for nothing.' In 1960 this sign vanished, but was found at Northallerton and replaced in 1984.

AA recommends:
Campsite: Cote Ghyll Caravan Park, I-pennant, *tel.* (060983) 425
Garage: Clack Lane (Tim Swales) Clack Lane Ends, *tel.* (060983) 263

Pickering

Map Ref: 91SE7983

Pickering is known as the 'Gateway to the Moors' and its position on the crossroads of the Malton to Whitby and the Helmsley to Scarborough roads amply justifies this title. A thriving market town, it is the focal point of a large rural area.

Monday is market day when the town centre is busy with open-air trading at colourful stalls. At the bottom of the gently-sloping market place, once the village green, is the terminus of the North York Moors Railway, and an olde-worlde atmosphere is created as steam engines hiss and whistle only yards from the market stalls.

Top: the Vale of Pickering. Above: St Edmund, King and Martyr, pierced by arrows. One of several 15th-century wall paintings in Pickering's church of St Peter and St Paul

Overlooking the market place, with its wide range of shops, inns and small business premises, is the huge parish church of St Peter and St Paul whose walls bear a unique gallery of 15th-century paintings. Discovered in 1851, they were promptly concealed beneath whitewash because the vicar thought they would encourage idolatry. Happily, they were rediscovered in 1878. They depict scenes from the Bible, from history and from legend, ranging from St George slaying the dragon to the martyrdom of St Thomas à Becket.

The Beck Isle Museum of Rural Life is housed in the building where Marshall planned England's first agricultural institute. Beside the river in the town centre, it houses a fascinating collection of artefacts of

Walking the Moors

The North York Moors area provides some superb walking country, with something to offer all tastes and capabilities. There are so many paths and tracks that the walker can choose between the difficult and not so difficult, the long or the short. He can walk for hours across open moorland, plan his walk through attractive villages and green valleys, or follow a route close to the sea.

Public rights of way are clearly signposted and are marked on Ordnance Survey maps. A public footpath can be used by anyone on foot but a bridleway can also be used by horse riders. Bridleways can be used by pedal cyclists as well, subject to local authority orders and byelaws, but the cyclist must give way to walkers and horses. Apart from the usual signs marking footpaths and bridleways at roadsides, the National Park Authority marks footpaths with yellow arrows and bridleways with blue arrows. When planning a walk along the shore it is essential to check the times of the tides.

Some well-known long distance walks are entirely or partially within the National Park (see page 76).

One of the best ways of exploring and learning about a particular area is to join a guided walk. Information about these walks can be obtained at the National Park Office in Helmsley or at any information centre.

Walking is one of the most popular pastimes in the North York Moors

At some of the stations along the Esk Valley railway walks are mapped out so that you can follow a route to the next station or complete a circular tour.

Whatever type of walk is embarked upon comfortable and waterproof clothing and footwear should be worn. The weather in the valleys can be very different from that on the moors and is liable to change quickly. It is a good idea to take something to drink and eat as it may be difficult to find refreshment on the way.

Wherever you go always follow The Country Code:
Keep to paths, especially across farmland.
Guard against all risks of fire.
Fasten all gates.
Avoid damaging hedges, fences and walls.
Protect wildlife, wild plants and trees.
Safeguard water supplies.
Keep dogs under proper control.
Leave no litter.
Respect the life of the countryside.

---

rural life. These include a cottage kitchen, cobbler's shop, dairy, barber's and even a Victorian pub bar.

Almost opposite is Beckside Crafts Centre, an example of the new enterprises which are flourishing in the town. A few minutes' walk away is the Kirk Theatre, formerly a Methodist chapel but now a venue for concerts and other events, and along the road past the Railway Station is the Moorland Trout Farm and Lake. Open seven days a week from March to November, visitors can hire everything they need to catch beautiful trout. There is also a shop and a small restaurant.

Almost concealed high above the town is Pickering Castle which probably dates back to the Conquest. It is claimed that every English king who reigned between 1100 and 1400 stayed here to hunt in nearby Blansby Park, and some parts of the old Royal Forest of Pickering still belong to Her Majesty the Queen.

Just outside the town, on the road to Malton, is Flamingoland Zoo and a large nursery and garden centre.

AA recommends:
Hotels: Forest & Vale, 2 Hungate, Malton Rd, 2-star, *tel.* (0751) 72722
White Swan, Market Place, 2-star, *tel.* (0751) 72288

Restaurant: Blacksmiths Arms, Aislaby, 1-fork, *tel.* (0751) 72182
(2m NW on A170)
Campsite: Wayside Caravan Park, Wrelton, 3-pennants, *tel.* (0751) 72608
(2½m W on A170)
Self Catering: 92 Westgate (cottage), *tel.* (0751) 73904
Guesthouse: Cottage Leas Country, Middleton, *tel.* (0751) 72129

Port Mulgrave,
see Hinderwell

Ravenscar

Map Ref: 87NZ9801

The southern tip of the large bay which contains the village of Robin Hood's Bay is called South Cheek or Old Peak. Originally, it was simply the Peak, but confusion with the Peak District of Derbyshire led to the adoption of the South Cheek name. The face of the cliff known as Old Peak was altered forever by alum quarries, worked between 1640 and 1862.

Now the area is better known as Ravenscar. There is a small community of houses, an information centre, tea rooms and the huge Raven Hall Hotel with mock battlements and a dramatic cliff-side golf course.

Overgrown roads are the only evidence of a plan in the 1890s to turn the area into a holiday resort. Beach walks and cliff treks are a feature of this area, while the Cleveland Way passes through the village. Ravenscar is also the finishing point of the challenging 40-mile Lyke Wake Walk from Osmotherley.

Walks along the rocky beach are dangerous due to the fast-rising tide and should be undertaken only as the tide is ebbing; even then, limited time is available. Bathing is dangerous too, but the splendour of this coastline is unrivalled. The cliffs rise to 585ft and tradition says the Danes hoisted a flag bearing a raven's image. In the 3rd and 4th centuries there was a Roman fort here.

The scramble down the South Cheek cliff below the hotel to the boulder-strewn beach is worth the effort, and the area provides splendid views of Robin Hood's Bay.

Some 2 miles to the south is Beast Cliff, rich with springs, where sailors would fill their casks at the Watersplash, a cliff waterfall. The isolated nature of this area makes it popular with naturalists and hikers.

AA recommends:
Hotel: Raven Hall, 2-star, *tel.* (0723) 870353
Guesthouse: Smugglers Rock Country, *tel.* (0723) 870044

Rievaulx

Map Ref: 95SE5785

In his *King's England* series, Arthur Mee described Rievaulx Abbey as being 'among the rarest treasures of our countryside' while St Aelred, one of its abbots, wrote that Rievaulx provided 'a marvellous freedom from the tumult of the world'. Dorothy Wordsworth, sister of 19th-century poet William Wordsworth, said she could have 'stayed in this solemn spot until evening, without a thought of moving'. Turner painted the abbey and today's visitors are entranced by its serene splendour.

Pronounced 'Reevo', it was founded in 1132. The first Cistercian house in Yorkshire, it became the mother church of the Order in England.

The most imposing of the Cistercian houses, it has the earliest Cistercian nave in Britain (1140). The aisles of the chancel and the triforium were not completed until 1240.

During the building the monks lived in rough shelters. They floated huge stones from local quarries along the River Rye, dug canals and dammed the river to provide deep water at the point of work on the abbey walls.

As the abbey grew, trade developed. Its interests included fishing, agriculture and the woollen industry and within 50 years it owned more than 6,000 acres of land and over 14,000 sheep. The abbey had 140 monks and employed 240 lay brothers and 260 hired workmen.

At the Reformation the walls were razed to the ground and many local buildings are constructed with material taken from them. Lead from the roof was buried and nearly 400 years later it was found and used in the restoration of the Five Sisters Window at York Minster.

The abbey is now in the care of the Historic Buildings and Monuments Commission, better known as English Heritage, and attracts some 200,000 visitors each year.

Looking down upon the abbey is Rievaulx Terrace, a beautiful example of landscape gardening completed in 1758. With a lawn ½ mile long, there are two classical temples and superb views. Entrance is from the Helmsley to Stokesley road but there is a nice walk from Helmsley to Rievaulx following part of the Cleveland Way.

Tiny Rievaulx village, perched on a wooded hillside, has some pretty thatched cottages. One was occupied by ancestors of Lord Wilson of Rievaulx, previously Sir Harold Wilson who was Labour Prime Minister for two terms (1964 to 1970 and 1974 to 1976).

AA recommends:
Guesthouse: Middle Heads (farmhouse), *tel.* (04396) 251

Robin Hood's Bay

Map Ref: 87NZ9505

Whether Robin Hood is fact or fiction, there is no hard evidence to link him with the quaint seaside village which bears his name. It was not until Henry VIII's time that it became known as Robbyn Huddes Bay and its other names have included Bay Town and Robin Hood's Town.

The Bay has a rich heritage of legends, tales of smugglers and the lore of fisherfolk. Its houses, shops and other premises sit literally on the edge of the sea beneath a cliff. Older houses crowd along the shoreline and cliff top, and many have been washed into the waves.

Surprisingly, in spite of being so tightly packed, the village is still developing. New rooms, utility spaces and extensions are still being added to this bewildering cluster of red-tiled cottages. Many almost seem to sit on top of one another, overhanging the little King's Beck which flows between the cottages into the sea.

The fine long beach with rocky outcrops is popular with geologists and fossil collectors, but visitors are warned of the dangerous fast-rising tides which can cut off the unwary in minutes. At high tide the sea runs up the village street and one story tells of a ship's bowsprit smashing the window of an inn.

Main picture: shales and clays surrounding sandstone-capped Roseberry Topping have been worn away, leaving this distinctive cone. Jet, alum-shale, coal and ironstone have all been mined here. Insets: the Ionic Temple at Rievaulx Terrace (right) with its painted ceiling by Giovanni Borgnis (left)

The car park is at the hill top, which means a steep walk down to the village and a breathless climb back again. However, there are many places to stop en route, including cafés with lovely sea views.

Robin Hood's Bay features as Bramblewick in Leo Walmsley's book *Three Rivers*, later filmed as *The Turn of the Tide*. He lived in King Street between 1894 and 1913.

AA recommends:
Hotel: Grosvenor, Station Rd, 1-star, *tel.* (0947) 880320
Guesthouse: Croft, Fylingthorpe (farmhouse), *tel.* (0947) 880231

Roseberry Topping

Map Ref: 83NZ5712

The boundary between the counties of North Yorkshire and Cleveland runs across the cone-shaped summit of this conspicuous landmark. However, it lies entirely within the North York Moors National Park and it was purchased by the National Trust in 1985.

There is a car park with a picnic site and the convenience of a local inn at the nearby little village of Newton-under-Roseberry.

Roseberry Topping resembles a small mountain. A shade over 1,000ft, it dominates the surrounding area and offers a short but stiff climb to those who wish to tackle its slopes. The reward is the magnificent view from the summit.

The word 'topping' is used for peaks in the North York Moors; it comes from the Danish 'toppen' meaning peak, or summit. This peak has also been called Odinsburg, however, after Odin, the Norse god of creation.

It is linked to a legend which tells how the mother of baby Prince Oswy of Northumbria dreamt he would drown on a certain day. She asked his maid to take him to the top of Roseberry Topping, away from any water but the maid fell asleep and the child wandered off, only to be found lying face down in a spring on the hillside. His mother died from grief and the legend says they are buried side-by-side at Osmotherley, so called because Os-by-his-mother-lay.

Local people watch the summit of Roseberry Topping for signs of bad weather. A verse says, 'When Roseberry Topping wears a cap, Cleveland must beware a clap'. In other words, mist on the hill means bad weather.

Rosedale

Map Ref: 91SE7295

Rosedale is a long and pleasant valley which extends from the centre of the moors to the south-east. The River Seven, fed by moorland streams, flows along the dale and to the east are the conifers of Cropton Forest. All around are the splendid moors with some very steep hills, remarkable scenery and outstanding views.

Huge rhododendron bushes brighten the route from Lastingham and deer are known to leap out in front of passing cars. Off this road, about ¾ mile into Cropton Forest, is a Forest Office and Spiers House caravan and camping site with splendid walks and drives. There are other camping and caravan sites around the village of Rosedale Abbey as this area is becoming increasingly popular with visitors.

Rosedale Abbey is the largest community in the dale. The priory was founded here in 1158 but was dismantled during the Reformation. A short tower and staircase near St Lawrence's Church are all that remain, and a curious round sundial, which may have belonged to it, adorns a nearby building.

Another of Rosedale's vanished landmarks is its famous chimney, which has given its name to Chimney Bank – a twisting climb, with gradients of 1-in-3 – leading past the White Horse Farm Hotel on to the moor. At the summit there used to be a 100ft-tall chimney, a relic of last century's iron-ore boom in Rosedale. Visible for miles, it was declared unsafe and demolished in 1972.

Memories and reminders of that short but intensive burst of industry remain in the dale. Huge quantities of iron-ore were found and the first mine opened in 1851, yielding three million tons between 1856 and 1885. Other mines followed, transforming this peaceful valley into a bustling industrial complex. The population rose from 500 to 5,000, but by the 1920s the boom was declining and the mines closed after the General Strike of 1926.

The route of a remarkable railway, used to move the ore around the rim of the dale, makes a memorable footpath, but almost all other evidence of the mining boom has now disappeared.

AA recommends:
Hotels: Milburn Arms, Rosedale Abbey, 2-star, *tel.* (07515) 312
White Horse Farm, Rosedale Abbey, 2-star, *tel.* (07515) 239
Self Catering: 1 School Row Cottages, Rosedale East, Pickering, *tel.* (0765) 89605

View across Runswick Bay to Runswick Bay village, popular with holidaymakers, fossil-collectors and artists

Runswick Bay

Map Ref: 85NZ8016

One of North Yorkshire's delightful fishing villages, Runswick Bay is a collection of pretty red-roofed cottages which cling to the cliff in a most remarkable way. It is only a mile or so from the A174 Whitby to Guisborough coast road and is easily by-passed.

Its evident attractions draw tourists and this has resulted in shops, hotels, restaurants, holiday cottages and a car park at the bottom of a very steep hill.

There is a fine, sandy beach which stretches around the bay in which Runswick reclines, and in common with all these bays, visitors must beware of the fast-rising tides. Nonetheless, the sheltered waters do attract pleasure craft and there is usually a line of fishing cobles on the shore near the car park to serve as a reminder that a fishing industry continues to operate from these shores. The lifeboat, always standing by, is a reminder of the prevailing danger of the sea. In 1901 the village women launched the heavy lifeboat themselves to save their fishermen husbands whose cobles had been caught in a storm.

Rye Dale

Map Ref: 95SE5982

One of Yorkshire's more gentle dales, Rye Dale emerges from the moors near Helmsley then broadens into a wide valley as it extends towards Malton. It has given its name to Ryedale District, the largest local authority area in England. This is based upon Malton and extends far beyond the boundaries of the dale after which it is named.

The Rye rises on Snilesworth Moor in the Cleveland Hills, flows through wooded countryside near Hawnby and past the historic ruins of Rievaulx Abbey until it reaches Helmsley via Duncombe Park. This part of its journey takes it through very picturesque scenery.

The river then meanders leisurely across low-lying land as it is joined by rivers flowing from the moors and other becks and streams. North of Malton, the Rye enters the River Derwent at Rye Mouth. The Derwent's long route takes it into the Ouse south of Selby and then the Humber.

The lanes of lower Rye Dale meander like the river to link a patchwork of tiny villages and hamlets. If they lack the splendour of the moors and dales, they offer instead tranquillity and a good deal of interest.

Harome has a delightful thatched inn while the quiet streets of Nunnington overlook its splendid Hall which contains a remarkable collection of miniature rooms. Built on the site of a nunnery, this fine 17th-century manor is maintained by the National Trust and is open to the public. The church, dating from the 13th century, is worth a visit and there are good views from Caulkleys Bank.

Stonegrave's tiny Minster was founded in AD727 and contains a fascinating Saxon cross. Nearby Stonegrave House, home of the late Sir Herbert Read, the poet, art historian and author, is occasionally open to the public for the benefit of the Red Cross.

Oswaldkirk's ancient church, with Norman walls and Saxon foundations, has links with antiquarian Roger Dodsworth whose work is in the Bodleian Library. He was born here in 1585 and baptised in this church. Dedicated to St Oswald, this is one of the few villages named after the patron saint of its parish church. The modern Catholic church is a complete contrast.

Middleton church, near Pickering, has a Saxon doorway, some Norman features, and contains marvellous old crosses, while Slingsby has a 17th-century castle which was never completed or occupied. The villages of Barton-le-Street and Appleton-le-Street are reminders that a Roman road ('stratum') passed this way into Malton ('Derventio').

Kirby Misperton, between Pickering and Malton, is the home of Flamingoland with a popular zoo and pleasure park.

One of three 10th-century Anglo-Danish crosses in St Andrew's Church, Middleton, near Pickering

Malton, with its Roman history and museum, is peaceful now that the A64 by-passes it. It is a welcoming market town (market day is on Saturday), with a wide range of shops and hotels. Heavily dependent upon agriculture, its cattle market on Tuesdays and Fridays is the third largest in Britain. Norton, separated from Malton by the River Derwent, is known for its racing stables.

AA recommends:
Hotels: Green Man, Market St, Malton, 2-star, *tel.* (0653) 2662
(5m E of Castle Howard)
Talbot, Yorkersgate, Malton, *tel.* (0653) 4031
(5m E of Castle Howard)
Wentworth Arms, Town St, Old Malton, *tel.* (0653) 2618
(5m E of Castle Howard)

Sandsend, see Lythe

Scalby

Map Ref: 93TA0190

Scalby was once a village in its own right but is now a suburb of Scarborough with a large complex of seaside entertainment at Scalby Mills. This used to be the site of an old mill but there is now a giant fun park with shops, cafés, bars and paddling pools.

Nonetheless, reminders of Scalby's rural past remain. Inland is the church of St Lawrence with some late 12th- and 13th-century stonework and a 17th-century tower. Another link with the past is the Derwent Sea Cut. This artificial river was cut by hand between 1800 and 1810 to relieve flooding by the River Derwent. The channel reaches the coast at Scalby, near Scarborough, and is also known as the Scalby Cut (see Brompton).

While Scalby is separated from

Scarborough by the North Cliff golf course, it is linked by a walk along the North Bay Promenade and by the miniature railway line which runs to Scalby Mills from Northstead Manor Gardens.

Scalby's development, directly linked to Scarborough's success as a holiday resort, has occurred since World War II, but its scenery and sheltered position on the coast of Scarborough's North Bay make it an ideal holiday base. There is a youth hostel and a touring caravan park and the Cleveland Way passes through the area. The countryside attracts naturalists and geologists and there are pleasant walks through Raincliffe Woods and into the hills behind Scalby where the National Park boundary meets the village. The woods are a continuation of the Forge Valley woodlands and towards the east, on the edge of Scarborough, is a small natural lake, Throxenby Mere.

Folklore

Hobs, or hobgoblins, were Yorkshire's equivalent to the Irish leprechaun or the Norwegian troll. They usually preferred to work on farms and in dairies and although they sometimes drank the cream or stopped the butter forming, they were essentially friendly, helpful little people.

Hobs were adept at avoiding prying eyes and resented anyone who used unfair means to catch them at work. They apparently had an aversion to clothes (although modesty prevailed at certain times) and considered them a hindrance as they bustled about their work. It seemed that the mere suggestion of clothes could turn them into nasty, vindictive and dangerous creatures.

Most villages had their own hob at some time but many of the stories have been forgotten and except for the occasional name – Hob of the Hasty Bank, Hob of Bransdale, Dale Town Hob of Hawnby, Hob of Studford, Hob of Egton High Moor, or a landmark or farm – Hob Holes, Hob Cave, Hob Hill, Hob Green, Hob Thrush Grange, the majority have disappeared into oblivion. However, there are three stories associated with the area which have remained prominent in Yorkshire folklore. These concern the hobs of Glaisdale Hart Hall, Runswick Bay and Farndale.

The hob of Glaisdale Hart Hall worked hard on agricultural tasks around the farm at night and was always on the look-out for extra work. One evening the opportunity arose. A farm wagon, loaded with hay, got stuck in a field and all efforts by the farmer and his men to free it failed. They considered unloading the hay but night fell so they abandoned the idea. There was no alternative but to leave the wagon where it was and take a chance on the hay getting soaked by rain.

Once the men were out of the way the hob set to work and when the farmer came down the next morning he found that the hay had all been safely stacked.

After this one of the farm hands was determined to see the hob and so when he next heard the sound of him threshing the corn inside the barn, he peeped through a crack in the wall. Surprised to see the little fellow almost naked, he persuaded the staff at Hart Hall to make the hob some clothes, which they did, and left out as a thank-offering. However, the hob was not at all pleased with the gift because he realised he had been spied on and he left the Hall for ever.

The hob at Hob Holes on the coast at Runswick Bay was supposed to have the power to cure whooping cough. He used to be called on by mothers who took their stricken children into his cave, uttering the words 'Hob Hole Hob, ma bairn's getten t'kink cough; tak' it off, tak' it off'. Whether it was the sea air or the hob's power is in question, but it usually seemed to work.

A troll or hob, an ugly dwarf-like little man with long hair. Illustrated by Florence Harrison in The Fairy Ring

Bob o' Hurst of Farndale was another happy, hard-working little hob who took it upon himself to replace a farm worker called Ralph, who was killed in a blizzard on the moors. The hob always worked speedily and efficiently around the farm at night – and the grateful farmer left him cream with bread and butter each evening. Several years later Bob o' Hurst was still working there when the farmer's grandson inherited the property and he in turn continued to supply the hob with cream and food.

However, the grandson remarried and the hob turned to mischief when his mean new wife left skimmed milk instead of cream. The hob made the farmer's life so unbearable, with all sorts of things going wrong, that he eventually decided to move.

On the way to their new farm the couple met a neighbour who said 'Ah see thoo's flittin'. A voice piped up from the back of the cart, 'Aye we's flittin'. There sat the hob. The farmer defeated, sighed, 'Well, if thoo's theer, flittin' with us, we may as well gan yam (home) ageean!'

Scaling Reservoir

Map Ref: 85NZ7412

Scaling Reservoir is the largest area of inland water within the North York Moors, and as it dates from about 1957, is a comparatively modern man-made lake. It is not very deep, about 30ft at most, and in the 1976 drought this fell to a mere 15ft – many large trout dying as a result. However, the reservoir has matured into a beautiful moorland lake, rich in many forms of wildlife, especially birds which favour reservoirs and inland waterways.

One peculiarity is that the county boundary between North Yorkshire and Cleveland runs north to south through the centre of the reservoir, but the lake lies within the National Park. Administered by Northumbrian Water, it offers water sports and fishing with worm or fly, as well as facilities for observing birds and other wildlife.

A parking area and picnic site has been provided and there are some excellent walks around the hamlet of Scaling and upon the surrounding moors. There is a picturesque drive through Roxby Woods down to the coast or into Staithes.

Main picture: Scarborough Bay and the old town. Insets: amusements on the beach, the ruins of Scarborough Castle and the harbour

Scaling Reservoir at the foot of Roxby High Moor is the only place in the Moors where sailing is possible

Scarborough

Map Ref: 81TA0488

The Victorians described Scarborough as 'the Queen of Watering Places' and it is England's oldest holiday resort.

There is something for nearly everyone; almost every taste and age group is catered for. It has two bays with golden sands separated by a castle-topped headland; there are modern theatres and cinemas; magnificent hotels and simple boarding houses; restaurants and shops, a busy harbour; noisy amusement arcades and quiet tea dances. There is the colourful bustle of the sea front, the gracious splendour of the Spa and the calm dignity of parks and gardens.

Add to this a quaint old market in the town centre, some very modern shops and a surrounding landscape which is beautiful by any standards and the result is a place to which visitors can return time and time again, yet always find something new.

The town's history is ancient. The remains of very early man were found near Scarborough in 1949 and Bronze Age relics have been found at the castle. The Romans had a signalling station there and in AD966 the Vikings used the natural harbour. It was the Viking leader, Thorgils Skardi, who ordered this settlement to be made, and who gave his name to the town, 'Skardiburgh'.

Invaders made use of nature's fortress behind the harbour, and on that site, in 1136, William le Gros began to construct the present castle. Piers Gaveston, favourite of Edward II, surrendered here to the Earl of Pembroke in 1312 and was executed the same year. Robert Aske, leader of the Pilgrimage of Grace, laid siege to it in 1536. Sir Thomas Stafford seized it in a revolt against 'Bloody' Queen Mary in 1557 only to lose it and his cause a few days later. The Parliamentarians took it in 1645 after a hard battle in which nearby St Mary's Church suffered serious damage. Three centuries later the castle came under attack once more when German cruisers bombarded the town in 1914.

Scarborough's modern appeal

owes much to a Mrs Farrow. In 1620 she noticed that some spring water was different from the usual, with an acid taste, and soon its health-giving reputation attracted visitors from afar. In 1660 a Dr Wittie of Scarborough strongly recommended the beneficial properties of sea bathing which brought people to the town. Scarborough's success as a spa, or watering place and resort, had started and in 1698 the first Spaw House was built.

Here the people could drink the water, but it was the Victorians who made the town the Queen of Watering Places. They built the present Spa (dropping the letter 'w'), a magnificent complex of buildings restored in 1981, welcomed the railway, constructed a promenade, built hotels, shops and theatres, landscaped the gardens and brought style to the Yorkshire coast.

The Theatre in the Round hosts the world premieres of plays by local playwright Alan Ayckbourn. There is an Open Air Theatre, a Royal Opera House and a Floral Hall with top entertainers. The Spa Complex offers dances from gentle waltzes to discos, while the seafront competes with amusements and bingo. On several afternoons in the summer there is a realistic mock battle with warships and aircraft in Peasholm Park, and for children there is the magic of Kinderland's playpark, with the world's longest waterchute nearby at Waterscene.

AA recommends:

Hotels: For a large selection of hotels, see the *AA Hotels and Restaurants In Britain* guide.

Campsites: Scalby Manor Caravan & Camping Site, 4-pennants, *tel.* (0723) 366212 Burniston Road Caravan Site, 3-pennants, *tel.* (0723) 366212

Scalby Close Camping, Scalby Close Filling Station, Burniston Rd, *tel.* (0723) 365908

Self Catering: For a large selection of self-catering establishments, see the *AA Holiday Homes, Cottages and Apartments In Britain* guide.

Guesthouses: For a large selection of guesthouses, see the *AA Guesthouses, Farmhouses & Inns In Britain* guide.

Garage: West Ayton Service Station, Pickering Rd, West Ayton, *tel.* (0723) 862880

Sleights

Map Ref: 86NZ8607

In Whitby's more prosperous days the wealthy built their grand houses at Sleights where the River Esk moves at a leisurely pace in a cosy hollow of Esk Dale, away from the bleakness of the moors.

It is by no means a tourist's village but is a good centre in which to stay for sightseeing and touring other areas. Buses and trains serve Sleights and the main A169 passes through.

Sleights means 'flat land near water'. Modern Sleights is built on a hillside but the road from the village runs through Briggswath to Ruswarp beside the Esk, where there is boating. A striking bridge carries the A169 across the Esk above Sleights Station and provides marvellous views along the valley. Going through Sleights towards Pickering, this road climbs Blue Bank, the first road to be surfaced in the district. In 1759 it first linked Whitby to Saltersgate and by 1788 there was a twice-weekly cart service to Pickering and York. The car park at the summit of Blue Bank gives incredible views of Whitby and the sea.

About 1½ miles upstream is a ruined chapel associated with Whitby's ancient custom of Planting the Penny Hedge, known as the Horngarth Ceremony. In 1159 three hunters drove a boar into the chapel which was the home of a hermit who protected the animal. The hunters beat the monk who subsequently died, but before dying he imposed a penance on those men.

At sunrise on the Eve of the Ascension every year they had to collect short staves from a wood on Eskdaleside, the cost of which had not to exceed one penny. They then had to go to Whitby and at 9am set their staves in the harbour mud, weaving them in the form of a small barrier to withstand three tides. If it failed, the lands of those men would be forfeited to the abbot of Whitby Abbey, or his successors. That ceremony is still conducted at Whitby annually.

At Sleights Lane End, near the junction of the A171 and A169, there is a commemorative plaque which records the first enemy aircraft shot down in England during World War II. It was a Heinkel bomber which fell nearby on 3 February 1940. The British pilot was Peter Townsend, later Group Captain Peter Townsend, known for his romance with HRH The Princess Margaret.

Staithes

Map Ref: 85NZ7818

There are two parts to Staithes. The modern village stands beside the A174 as it runs along the coast to Whitby, but old Staithes is concealed below the cliffs. Coaches are forbidden to descend the steep hill into the old part and access by cars is restricted. There is a car park at the hill top.

This is an 'olde worlde' fishing community with old cottages apparently piled one on top of the other in a glorious jumble as they crowd around the tiny harbour. Narrow alleys and steep steps divide the buildings and there is no room for gardens, so it seems as if the houses huddle together as protection against the sea.

Indeed, houses have been swept away. In 1953, the Cod and Lobster Inn, which stands on the edge of the waves, was severely damaged and on a past occasion 13 houses were claimed by the sea. Staithes is constantly threatened by it as the nearby lifeboat house testifies.

Tourists are catered for here, but there are no amusement arcades, dodgems or bingo halls and the village has managed to retain its own vital character. Indeed, it is a haven for resident artists and the curious and traditional Staithes bonnets can still be seen. The village's connection with Captain Cook, one of the world's greatest seamen, however, gives it extra interest. He was apprenticed to a grocer and draper on the seafront at the age of 17.

There is one oddity about Staithes. It has no Anglican parish church, although there is a Catholic one. The reason may be that in its early days it was merely a landing place, a 'staithe', for nearby Seaton, now part of Hinderwell.

On a Wing and a Prayer

The site of the Yorkshire Gliding Club at Sutton Bank is packed with visitors most weekends, craning their necks to watch gliders cavorting in the sky. It is an ideal spot for gliding, for thanks to geological changes during the Ice Age, the hills were cut away by glaciers, leaving steep-sided cliff faces, which help to provide the 'up-draught' necessary to keep the sleek, high-performance machines aloft. The gliders make use of the 10-mile ridge on the site to maintain their altitude for long periods as they meander from one end of the ridge to the other. On good days – that is when the weather permits – the gliders encounter the right conditions which allow them to take advantage of wind currents and cloud formations to soar on the lift of thermals. Often reaching 5,000ft from a cable launch powered by a winch, the experienced gliders can stay up for as long as they want or can even fly away from the site, often landing in a farmer's field many miles away. There are also flights launched with the help of 'tug' aircraft. The club altitude record stands at 30,200ft.

Visitors are welcome, and at weekends short trial flights can be made for a fee. The club holds residential courses from April to September and these provide an unusual holiday. There is always the chance of 'going solo', and a social life is there to be enjoyed at the end of the day in the circular club house.

Waiting to soar on the thermals . . .

Stokesley

Map Ref: 82NZ5208

Stokesley is a small North Yorkshire market town with a market every Friday. Lying so close to Middlesbrough, it has a great deal of affinity with Teesside and yet it stands on a plain just beyond the north-western edge of the moors. It serves both the moors and Teesside.

The A172 now by-passes Stokesley and this has removed from its main street the former large volume of heavy vehicles and through-traffic, thus allowing the town to become more leisurely and attractive. It might have also taken away some of the trade which is so important for a small town.

Stokesley does not lay claim to any particular beauty or history yet the area behind the main street, along the River Leven, is pretty with its little bridges and flowered grassy banks and it cannot be denied that Stokesley is a gracious town with some lovely old houses and buildings. Efforts are now in hand to make these an asset to the town.

The church has some medieval portions, including a 600-year-old door, but it was largely rebuilt in the 18th century. It stands in a corner near a large open area known as the Plain. This provides ample parking space for shoppers and visitors, except on Fridays when the produce market is held there. A thriving and growing livestock market is also held every Tuesday at the Auction Mart in Station Road.

One event which brings many people to Stokesley is the mammoth Stokesley Show, organised by the town's Agricultural Society. Held on the Saturday following the third Thursday in September, it occupies the Show Field on the edge of the town. This is its permanent home, the field having been purchased by the Society in 1955. The show boasts attendances of around 20,000 with visitors coming to see a huge range of livestock and agricultural and horticultural products and equipment, as well as the demonstration of associated crafts, skills and trades.

On the Wednesday preceeding the show and for the following four days, the town is taken over by Stokesley Fair. Noisy fairground vehicles and stalls literally bring the town to a halt. Apart from these four days, Stokesley is a quiet, unassuming town and a convenient base for exploring the northern edge of the moors.

Sutton Bank

Map Ref: 94SE5182

There can be little doubt that the top of the escarpment known as Sutton Bank affords the finest view in Yorkshire, if not in England. The view stretches from the Pennines in the west, into Cleveland in the north and across to York in the south.

There is a large car park, a telescope and a guide to the points in sight, and the National Park Information Centre is situated here too, with books and information about the area, as well as a picnic area, refreshments and toilets. Information is available on the Sutton Bank Nature Trails and the White Horse Walk. Both start from here and last about two hours.

The A170 crosses Sutton Bank about 6 miles from Thirsk and climbs to the summit of Whitestonecliff over a distance of a mile, with gradients of 1-in-5, 1-in-4 and 1-in-5 again. It holds no terrors for local drivers, but strangers have problems climbing it. Caravans have been forbidden to use it since 1984.

There is a wealth of interest here. Nearby was a noted racecourse where the annual Black Hambleton Races were staged, and there are still racing stables here. Soaring gliders from the Yorkshire Gliding Club fill the sky when the conditions are right because the cliffs funnel the prevailing westerly winds into strong up-currents. The airfield lies but a few minutes' walk from the car park along the cliff top. Visitors are asked not to walk on the airfield, but should use the footpath. Bilberries grow here too and make lovely pies!

Another winding footpath, part of the nature trail, descends the steep slopes to Lake Gormire. This pretty lake, ⅓-mile in circumference, can be seen from the summit and is remarkable because there are no streams flowing in or out of it. It is a natural lake rich with wildlife and probably dates from glacial times. One legend says it is bottomless, while another claims it hides a complete village.

The Cleveland Way passes along the summit, and the old Hambleton Drovers' Road used by cattle en route from Scotland to Malton and York also passed this way.

Swainby

Map Ref: 82NZ4702

Although Swainby has all the appearances of a modern village, it dates back to the 14th century, and possibly earlier. When nearby Whorlton was attacked by a plague, the people moved away and settled here, but it is probable that this was already a community.

Signs of its ancient history were obliterated when it became a mining village during the last century.

Main picture: view from Sutton Bank

Houses were built and some are still known as Miners' Cottages. The miners used donkeys for carrying their belongings and grazed them on nearby Live Moor. Those who lived in the neighbouring district came into Swainby to spend their money, a fact still marked by the Miners' Arms.

Swainby, with its fine parish church, occupies a flat area beneath the moors. Behind the village is Scarth Nick, a gap in the hills where a steep, twisting climb leads onto the moors near Osmotherley where there is good walking country. The route of the Cleveland Way footpath crosses Scarth Nick and the start of the Lyke Wake Walk is also nearby. An old drovers' road climbed onto the moors from Swainby via Scarth Nick.

Leading into the moors behind Swainby is Scugdale, a quiet valley with a hamlet called Huthwaite. This tiny dale, less than 3 miles long, has produced two remarkable people.

One was Elizabeth Harland who died in 1812, having lived until she was 105, and the other was a giant of a man, Henry Cooper. By 1890 he was 8ft 6in tall, and the world's tallest living man. He worked as a farm labourer before joining Barnum and Bailey's Circus, married a tall woman from the circus, and died aged 32.

Thirsk

Map Ref: 94SE4282

Thirsk and the surrounding countryside have become known as Herriot Country thanks to the books of James Herriot, and the television series. The town is visited by those seeking the famous veterinary surgeon, his premises, and the countryside which inspired his books.

But there is a good deal more in Thirsk. It is a busy town in two parts, the old and the new. The new has a fine cobbled market place surrounded by stores, restaurants, antique shops and some fine coaching inns. There are delightful alleys leading to a variety of craft shops and small business premises. The Clock Tower, erected in 1896, is a focal point and stands near the Bull Ring. This cobbled area is used as a coach park but bulls were tethered here prior to being baited well into the 18th century.

The old part of Thirsk is centred around St James' Green which was once the market place. In the 11th century a castle stood near Cod Beck, which flows prettily through the town, but that has long since gone.

The parish church of St Mary is magnificent. Known as 'the Cathedral of the North' because of its splendour, the tower was started in 1410 and it took 50 years to complete the church. There is an impressive roof and some delicate tracery in the battlements which furnish the walls, and one of its bells came from Fountains Abbey. The altar stone is from Byland Abbey.

In Kirkgate, on the approach to the church, is the town museum. It was once the home of Thomas Lord, born in 1775, founder of Lord's Cricket Ground in London. Thirsk Racecourse was opened in 1854.

AA recommends:
Hotels: Golden Fleece, Market Pl, 2-star, *tel.* (0845) 23108
Three Tuns, Market Pl, 2-star, *tel.* (0845) 23124
Sheppards, Church Farm, Front St, Sowerby, 1-star, *tel.* (0845) 23655
Campsite: Thirsk (TRAX) Caravan Club Site, Thirsk Racecourse, *tel* (0845) 25266

Right: inn sign, Golden Fleece, Thirsk

This delightful thatched cottage overlooking Thornton Beck in Thornton Dale is justifiably one of Yorkshire's most-photographed houses

Thornton Dale

Map Ref: 92SE8383

The boundary of the National Park dips near Pickering to include this attractive village. Even though the A170 runs through the centre, Thornton Dale has retained its charm and is a Mecca for visitors.

As long ago as 1907 it was voted the most beautiful village in Yorkshire, a title which may still apply. Its shops, inns, cafés and a lovely forge all provide excuses for staying, and there are lovely walks beside the bubbling streams and through the village lanes. There is a spacious car park in the grounds of the hall, a fine Tudor building which is now a residential home (but with a public bar).

Just off the A170, beside the bridge which crosses the stream near the parish church of All Saints, is one of the most photographed homes in Britain. So beautifully proportioned is this fine, thatched cottage that it appears on calendars, chocolate boxes and magazine covers, as well as advertisements. The frontage is usually bright with flowers and it makes an unforgettable picture.

Roxby Castle used to stand a mile or so along the road to Pickering. This was home of the Cholmleys. Sir Richard Cholmley was known as the 'Great Black Knight of the North' at the time of Elizabeth I and is buried in the parish church. Also buried there is Matthew Grimes who died in 1875 aged 96. He stood guard over Napoleon at St Helena and helped carry the emperor to his grave.

Other features of the village include a 600-year-old market cross and a set of stocks on the green; 12 almshouses completed in 1670 and an old grammar school founded in 1657. There are pleasant walks through Ellerburn towards Dalby Forest.

Thornton Dale is often called Thornton-le-Dale and there are still arguments about its correct name.

AA recommends:
Hotel: New Inn, Pickering Rd, 1-star, *tel.* (0751) 74226

Ugthorpe

Map Ref: 85NZ7911

In its remote situation on the moors above Whitby, Ugthorpe is more a place of pilgrimage than a tourist attraction. It is a small village with an old windmill and some sturdy stone houses and farms.

The village is perhaps best known for its adherence to the Roman Catholic faith. It was one of the few villages to maintain a resident Catholic priest throughout the Reformation when Catholics were being persecuted. Priests' hiding places have been found in some of Ugthorpe's old buildings, including an oak-panelled Elizabethan farmhouse which was once the hall. A chimney in a stable contained a priest hole.

Ugthorpe's part in the survival of the ancient faith came about because during the Reformation priests who had been trained and ordained overseas were secretly brought back by sea. They came ashore near Whitby and were then smuggled into 'safe houses' at Ugthorpe before taking up appointments in the north.

Father Nicholas Postgate, martyred at York in 1679, lived at the Hermitage which is near Ugthorpe and ministered locally in his disguise as a gardener. The present Catholic Church of St Anne was opened in 1857 by Cardinal Wiseman, the first Archbishop of Westminster. The much smaller Anglican Christ Church which stands opposite was opened in the same year.

AA recommends:
Campsite: Burnt House Caravan Park, 3-pennants, *tel.* (0947) 840448

Upsall

Map Ref: 94SE4587

This tiny place, tucked among leafy lanes on the wooded slopes of the Hambleton Hills, has had three castles. One is ruined, one was burnt to the ground in 1918 and the other is still used as a home. Near the entrance to the latter is a fine forge built in 1859 whose entrance is shaped like a giant horseshoe and which bears the words 'Upsall Town'. The roads hereabouts afford marvellous views across to the Pennines and over the Vale of York.

The first castle was built in the 14th century by the Scropes, an ancient Yorkshire noble family, and is known for its 'Crock of Upsall Gold' legend. Finding his castle in ruins, Scrope dreamt that if he stood on London Bridge he would become rich. So he walked the 250 miles to London and stood for hours on the famous bridge. Nothing happened and he began to think he had been fooled. However, a stranger appeared and told Scrope he had had a strange dream; he had dreamt there was a crock of gold under an elderberry tree at Upsall Castle – a place he did not know. Scrope hurried back to Upsall, found the gold and regained his place in society.

The horseshoe-shaped entrance is a clue to the function of this building in Upsall: it is a forge

An unusual 'lion' trough at Wass. The village was partly built from the ruins of nearby Byland Abbey

On the plain below, near Felixkirk, is Nevison House, the supposed home of highwayman William Nevison, nicknamed Swift Nick by Charles II.

Wass

Map Ref: 95SE5579

Peaceful Wass reclines within the most southerly tip of the North York Moors and is reached by narrow, winding lanes between Coxwold and Ampleforth. One route is to turn off the A170 at Tom Smith's Cross, then descend the steep Wass Bank with its wonderful views of Byland Abbey.

Tom Smith's Cross, with parking available, marks the point where several minor roads enter the A170 on the summit of its long descent into Helmsley. Tom Smith was reputedly a highwayman who was gibbetted and the stone base of his gibbet is said to be here.

From Wass there is an exhilarating walk from the crossroads through Elm Hagg Wood to an observatory above Oldstead. Another route leads through the woods and emerges on to a leafy lane just beyond Byland.

The incredible west front of Byland Abbey dominates the locality. This ruined Cistercian church has a 26ft-diameter window dating from the 13th century and the largest nave in England. The size is staggering and cannot be appreciated from the roadside views. It is larger than both Fountains and Rievaulx abbeys and is wonderful to explore.

The monks arrived in 1177 to build this beautiful abbey. It has not featured greatly in national affairs although it did shelter Edward II in 1322 as the English fought the Scots at Scots Corner on the moors above.

A Norman archway still spans the road from Byland Abbey to the pretty countryside around Oldstead.

The Hand of Glory

The remote, isolated situation of the North Yorkshire Moors in the 17th and 18th centuries led to communities where superstitious beliefs were rife. Superstition leads to fear and one of the things people dreaded most was witchcraft. Anyone suspected of having supernatural powers was feared and regarded with awe. Evil spirits were supposed to stalk the land and all manner of customs and objects were invented to ward off these spirits.

However, there were naturally those who were only too ready to capitalise on this fear and turn it to their advantage, and one instrument employed to these ends was the so-called 'Hand of Glory' – a human hand (which had been cured) designed to strike such fear into the hearts of these superstitious folk that they were immobilised while robberies were carried out.

Where the idea came from, or who first used this ghastly object is not known, but it came to be highly prized by robbers and thieves throughout Europe. The Hand of Glory was still being used in Esk Dale until the middle of the 19th century and one found in the dale is now in the Pannett Museum in Whitby.

The easiest way to get hold of a hand was to cut one from a corpse hanging on a gibbet. Once the hand had been obtained it had to be cured and this was done in much the same way as curing a ham. First the

This gruesome cured hand used to hypnotise a robber's victims

blood was drained, then the hand was embalmed and wrapped in a piece of shroud. Salt and pepper and saltpetre were mixed into a solution in which the hand was soaked for two weeks, and finally it was baked hard in the sun.

To complete the charm, a candle was made from a mixture of wax, human fat and Lapland sesame, with a wick composed of human hair from the same dead criminal. This done, the Hand of Glory was ready for use. Before setting out, the burglar placed the lighted candle between the fingers of the hand. He believed this gruesome object had the power to keep his victims asleep, so that he could search for the goods he wanted without being disturbed. If his victims were not already in bed they would be hypnotised by the flickering flame and too scared to move. However, there was more to the robber's ritual. Next he recited:

Let those who rest more deeply sleep,

Let those awake their vigils keep,

O Hand of Glory shed thy light,

Direct us to our spoil tonight.

If he was working with a gang and had entered the house to prepare the way he would continue his incantation with:

Flash out thy blaze, o skeleton hand,

And guide the feet of our trusty band.

Let those who are awake remain awake,

And those who are asleep, keep asleep.

As long as the candle burned the victims would remain powerless and the only way to break the spell was to extinguish the flame with blood or skimmed milk.

The arch on West Cliff is formed by the jawbones of a whale 82ft long

Whitby

Map Ref: 86NZ8911

Whitby's place in the religious, maritime and literary history of England is assured. Surrounded on three sides by the moors and upon the fourth by the North Sea, this picturesque port at the mouth of the River Esk is truly 'twixt moor and sea' but its location makes it somewhat restricted in its communication with other parts of England. Four main roads converge upon the town. Its only rail link is the line from Middlesbrough, although it is hinted the the North York Moors Railway might extend from Grosmont into Whitby.

Nonetheless, the town is full of interest and does attract visitors from all over the world. Its quaint, narrow streets lined with small red-roofed cottages demand exploration, and the British and foreign fishing boats which gather in the harbour are a continuing source of fascination.

Whitby kippers are said to be the best in the country.

Long, sandy beaches and impressive surrounding countryside attract holidaymakers, and the town is rich with history. Whitby Abbey, supreme on its cliff-top site, replaced the original wooden abbey of St Hilda, then known as 'Streonshalh'. This hosted the famous Synod of Whitby in AD664 and the method of determining the date of Easter was decided at this Synod.

The abbey also produced 'England's first poet', Caedmon. He is commemorated by a huge stone cross near the top of Whitby's famous 199 steps. Just beyond is the coastguard station and the strange parish church of St Mary whose interior resembles that of a ship.

Apart from Caedmon, Whitby has inspired many authors, from local girl Mary Linskill to Bram Stoker and his Dracula novel. It is said that Bing Crosby's song *The Bells of St Mary's* was inspired by the parish church, and local songwriter, Eileen Newton, wrote *Somewhere a voice is calling*.

Across the harbour Whitby's old swing bridge opens for passing ships, while higher up the River Esk is a new bridge which carries the road to Scarborough. It was opened in 1980 and the views from it are superb.

The harbourside is replete with the paraphernalia of holidaymaking such as bingo, amusements, sea-food stalls and assorted gift and souvenir shops, but the fishing industry continues and timber ships unload here. Shipping is part of Whitby's life and it was in a

The River Esk flows towards Whitby, dominated by its cliff-top abbey. Inset: a whaler returns. Between 1753 and 1837 some 577 voyages were made from Whitby – still the main fishing port on this coast

Whitby-built ship that Captain Cook sailed on his voyages of discovery.

Both ship-building and whaling have been part of Whitby's history, and the jet industry boomed here during Queen Victoria's time, employing a tenth of the population.

On the West Cliff are some fine hotels, boarding houses and gardens, and the Spa complex contains a theatre and other facilities for entertainment. The Pannett Art Gallery and Museum, and its surrounding park, offers peace from the surrounding bustle, but car parking is always a problem.

AA recommends:
Hotels: Royal, West Cliff, 2-star, *tel.* (0947) 602234
Saxonville, Ladysmith Ave (off Argyle Rd), 2-star, *tel.* (0947) 602631
Sneaton Hall, Sneaton, 2-star, *tel.* (0947) 605929 (3m S B1416)
White House, Upgang Ln, West Cliff, 1-star, *tel.* (0947) 602098
Campsite: Whitby Holiday Village, Saltwick Bay, 3-pennants, *tel.* (0947) 602664
Self Catering: 2 Mill View, Ruswarp, *tel.* (0947) 810763
Regent House, 7 Royal Crescent, *tel.* (0947) 602103
Rose Nook, 21 Coach Rd, *tel.* (0947) 810763
Southview, 17 Coach Rd, *tel.* (0947) 810763

Guesthouses: For a large selection of guesthouses, see the *AA Guesthouses, Farmhouses & Inns In Britain* guide.
Garage: Geo Harrison, 6 Upgang Ln, *tel.* (0947) 603321

Whorlton

Map Ref: 82NZ4802

Whorlton is one of those tiny places which are full of surprises, for it has a place in Scotland's history. It was here, in Whorlton Castle, that details of a plot to marry Mary Queen of Scots to Lord Darnley were worked out.

The castle, originally surrounded by a moat, was probably built in the 14th century and once belonged to Henry VIII, but its scant remains have been left to the ravages of nature. A magnificent gatehouse bears the coats of arms of the Meynells, Darcys and Greys.

Nearby, approached by a long avenue of yews, is the curious Norman Church of The Holy Cross. Its history runs parallel with that of the castle, for its nave is roofless and the aisles have gone, but something of outstanding interest remains. This is the 15th-century tower complete with bell and an east window in the chancel – still used as a burial chapel. Inside is a curious stone cross and one of the earliest oaken effigies in England. A hollow figure of a man with a dog at his feet in a canopied tomb, it probably dates from 1400.

Whorlton, overlooking the plain below, was important until 1428 when plague reduced its population to 10. The remaining inhabitants all escaped to Swainby.

The trees on the slopes have been planted in such a way that from the air the initials E II R can be picked out in the foliage.

Wykeham

Map Ref: 93SE9683

This village of mellow stone houses justifies a halt, for there are pleasant walks nearby (the Derwent Way passes by) and a most interesting lych gate. The church, which replaced the earlier All Saints, was built in the 19th century and features the delightful oak carving of 'Mousey' Thompson. The remarkable lych gate is in fact the tower of an earlier chapel and stands apart from the main building. This gave rise to a legend that two sisters decided to build a church here, but quarrelled before it was completed. One built the tower and the other built the church at a discreet distance. The story is, however, pure fancy.

The truth is that there was a Cistercian nunnery at Wykeham in

This 14-century tower with 19th-century spire forms a unique lych gate for Wykeham's 19th-century All Saints Church, seen in the background

View from the gatehouse of Whorlton Castle. Only this part and the cellars remain of the 14th-century castle

1153, but it was destroyed by fire. Then, in the 14th century, John de Wykeham founded the chapel of St Mary and St Helen, but it fell into disrepair. In 1855, after the present church was built in 1853, the tower of the ancient chapel was restored and fashioned into this unique lych gate.

Modern Wykeham Abbey is a large house set in parkland and it occupies the site of the ancient nunnery. The seat of Viscount Downe, it is occasionally open to the public.

AA recommends:
Hotel: Downe Arms, 2-star, *tel.* (0723) 862471
Campsite: St Helens Caravan Park, 4-pennants, *tel.* (0723) 862771

Yarm

Map Ref: 80NZ4112

Standing within a horseshoe-shaped loop of the River Tees, Yarm used to be a North Riding market town. Before 1974 the river formed the boundary with County Durham but the local government changes of that year placed Yarm within the new county of Cleveland.

Nonetheless, it retains the aura of a Yorkshire market town, although the weekly market is no longer held. The long, main street with its cobbled verges and range of lovely old inns and Georgian buildings, plus a market hall dating from 1710, help to maintain that image. There is little doubt that Yarm, once a busy town and indeed a port, stepped into the shadows as Middlesbrough and Stockton rapidly developed.

However, Yarm has its place in history. It was here, on 12 February 1820, that five men met in the George and Dragon Inn in the High Street to discuss their request to Parliament to build a railway. The result was the world's first public railway from nearby Stockton to Darlington. Their initiative changed the world's transport system, and that historic meeting is commemorated by a plaque on the wall of the George and Dragon.

Another reminder of Yarm's railway history is the huge 43-arch viaduct which passes over the houses of the town. Built of brick and stone, it is one of the biggest viaducts in England.

The town does contain reminders of its earlier history. Known for its annual fair, which was once a cheese fair, Yarm's name comes from the Danish 'Jarum'. The church is part Norman, and there was a friary here in the 13th century. A chapel where John Wesley preached in 1760 is tucked away down an alley near the market hall.

Yarm's position on the River Tees means it is prone to flooding, but a lowering of the river bed has reduced this danger.

Across the river is Eaglescliffe, with its junction on the Stockton to Darlington railway, and Egglescliffe, an elevated village with a green and views across Yarm.

AA recommends:
Garage: Ship Service Station, Richmond Rd, Low Worsall, *tel.* (0642) 780456

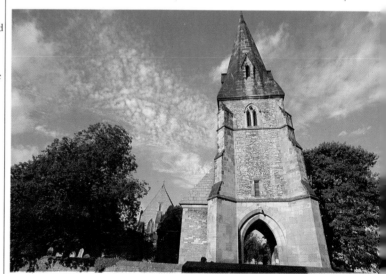

Directory

ABBEYS AND PRIORIES

The historical background to the rich collection of abbeys and priories to be seen on the North York Moors can be found in the article on page 10.

Ampleforth *Abbey and Church*
The modern Roman Catholic monastery and college dates from 1860 to the present day. The Abbey Church is open to the public. *Byland Abbey* 2m W of the village can be found the considerable remains of the Cistercian church and monastic buildings, dating mainly from the late 12th and early 13th centuries. There are remains of a huge circular window and well-preserved glazed tiles are of particular interest. AM. Open all year. Charge.

Guisborough *Priory*
This Augustinian priory was founded in 1119 but the fine remains of the east end of the church date from the 14th century. AM. Open all year. Small charge.

Osmotherley *Mount Grace Priory*
The best-preserved of only nine Carthusian Priories in the country, founded in 1398. Some of the two-storey cells where the monks lived in seclusion are relatively well preserved. The monks met only for service in the church, which also survives. AM and NT. Open all year. Charge.

Rievaulx *Abbey*
Magnificent, well-preserved ruins remain of this Cistercian abbey, one of the largest and finest in England. Dating from 1132, the abbey is an impressive sight, surrounded by wooded hills. AM. Open all year. Charge.

Rosedale Abbey *Priory*
The Cistercian priory gave the village its name, but it was dissolved by Henry VIII in the 16th century and now there are few remains.

Whitby *Abbey*
Impressively situated on the cliff top overlooking the town are the considerable remains of a fine church dating from the 13th century, damaged by shellfire during the 1914-18 war. The abbey was founded in AD657 and in AD664 was the venue for the historic Synod of Whitby. AM. Open all year. Charge.

Below: the River Esk, seen here between Lealholm and Crunkley Hill, contains both salmon and sea trout

Right: much of the lovely Forge Valley is a National Nature Reserve

ANGLING

The North York Moors area offers a wide range of inland fishing locations, as well as the possibility of sea fishing. The River Esk is the principal salmon and sea trout fishery in Yorkshire and there are also the Rivers Rye and Derwent and their tributaries. Lakes and reservoirs include Lake Arden, Bilsdale; Cod Beck Reservoir, Osmotherley; Scaling Dam Reservoir; Lockwood Beck Reservoir; Scarborough Mere.

A rod licence must be obtained to fish any water and to fish a particular water a permit is also needed. Full information may be obtained from: Yorkshire Water, 21 Park Square South, Leeds LS1 2QG. Tel (0532) 440191 or Northumbria Water Tees Division. Tel (0642) 62216.

BICYCLE HIRE

Helmsley Claridges, Church St. *Tel.* (0439) 70401
Pickering Cycle Hire, 127 Westgate. *Tel.* (0751) 75133
Scarborough Len Raine Cycles, 25 Victoria Rd. *Tel.* (0723) 365751

A carved mouse identifies furniture from Robert Thompson's Craftsmen Ltd. Natural seasoning of the oak can vary from two to five years

CRAFT WORKSHOPS

Visitors to the North York Moors can buy items made locally in a wide range of materials: wool, iron, wood, glass and lace, as well as pottery varying from domestic stoneware to fine decorative ware.

Ampleforth The individually-designed rugs and cushions in the *Ampleforth Weaving and Pottery Workshops* are handwoven. Also on sale are mainly reduction-fired earthenware and stoneware items for domestic use. Open all year. Closed Mon, also wkends Oct to Mar. *Tel.* (04393) 503

Brandsby Various woodcarvings and sculptures are on sale at *Acorn Industries*, but they are specialists in all types of traditional furniture made from solid timbers. Each order is designed individually, and customers may submit their own designs. Open daily. Closes 12.15 wkends. *Tel.* (03475) 217

Coxwold A good range of slip-decorated and wood-fired practical stoneware and earthenware is produced by the *Coxwold Pottery*. Open daily Mon to Fri and some wkends. *Tel.* (03476) 344

Helmsley Two miles from Helmsley, in the Main Street at Harome, the *Wold Pottery* produces hand-thrown earthenware slip-decorated in blues, greens, brown and cream. Coffee and wine sets, embossed commemorative pieces and pots empressed with real leaves are all specialities. Closed Sun. *Tel.* (0439) 70805

Kilburn The furniture-making business made famous by Robert Thompson is continued at *Robert Thompson's Craftsmen Ltd.* All furniture is hand-made from naturally-seasoned English oak and bears the well-known 'Mouse' trademark. Carved animals and other small articles are also made. Closed Sun. *Tel.* (03476) 218

Kirkbymoorside All types of wrought-ironwork are made by *Moorside Wrought-iron* at Piercy End, ranging from large items to lamps and door knockers. Open Mon-Fri, wkends by appointment. *Tel.* (0751) 32244

Lealholm A distinctive range of finely-thrown stoneware is produced by the *Forge Pottery*. Items such as planters and vases are decorated with hand-modelled fungi and other applied detail. Hand-modelled cottages and farmsteads also for sale. Open daily. *Tel.* (0947) 87457

Pickering Woollens made from hand-spun yarn, and hessian figures are made at *Cropton Crafts* in Cropton. A wide range of goods made by local amateur and professional craftsmen are also on sale. Open daily May to Oct and Dec. *Tel.* (07515) 607. At Thornton Dale, 2 miles from Pickering, *Yorkshire Woollens* specialises in high quality made-to-measure ladies' garments. Motifs on knitwear are designed to customers' requirements. Hundreds of accessories on show. Open daily. *Tel.* (0751) 72468

Scarborough Visitors to *Valley House Craft Studio* in nearby Ruston can watch or participate in lace-making, lace bobbin-making and embroidery work. Various hand-made items made by other craftsmen.are for sale. Open daily Spring Bank Holiday to end Sept. Also afternoons Mon, Tue, Thur, Oct to Easter. *Tel.* (0723) 862426

Thirsk A small range of traditionally-made contemporary furniture and cabinets is made by *Design in Wood* in Chapel Street. Open Mon to Fri. *Tel.* (0845) 25103. A wide range of domestic furniture in solid English ash, elm and oak is made by *Treske Ltd*, Station Works. Open daily. *Tel.* (0845) 22770

Wykeham Exclusive handwoven fabrics in wool, silk, mohair and other luxury fibres are made by *Ankaret Cresswell*. Emphasis is on the originality of design and short lengths are supplied to garment makers. Open Mon to Fri. *Tel.* (0723) 864406

GOLF

Eaglescliffe and District Golf Club, Eaglescliffe. In a delightful setting with fine views of the Cleveland Hills, this hilly 18-hole course offers pleasant golf to all classes of player. *Tel.* (0642) 780098

Kirkbymoorside Golf Club, Manor Vale. 18-hole parkland course. *Tel.* (0751) 31525

Scarborough North Cliff Golf Club, North Cliff Ave. *Tel.* (0723) 360786

Thirsk and Northallerton Golf Club, Thornton-le-Street, Thirsk. A 9-hole course with good views of the nearby Hambleton Hills. *Tel.* (0845) 22170

Whitby Golf Club, Low Straggleton. This 18-hole seaside course is on the cliff top with good views and a fresh sea breeze. Ravine to cross on course. *Tel.* (0947) 602768

CALENDAR OF EVENTS

May
Helmsley Art Exhibition

June
East Harsley Horse Show
(nr Osmotherley)
Northallerton, North Yorkshire
County Show
Ryedale Folk Museum Mid-Summer
Celebrations

July
Kilburn Feast
Pickering Carnival
Coxwold Fair
Osmotherley Summer Games
Sutton Show
Husthwaite Show
Marton, Cleveland County Show
Kirkbymoorside, Ryedale Show
Sneaton and Hawsker Show
Ryedale Festival

August
Littlebeck Rose Queen Ceremony
Egton Gooseberry Show
Thornton Dale Show
Hinderwell Show
Danby Show
Rosedale Show
Whitby Regatta
Whitby Folk Week

*Maypole dancing at the annual
Ryedale festival which is held in the
grounds of the folk museum at
Hutton-le-Hole*

Egton Show
Burniston Show
Farndale Show
Stokesley, Hutton Rudby Show
Helmsley Flower Show
Chop Gate, Bilsdale Show

September
Lealholm Show
Castleton Show
Stokesley Show
Scarborough Cricket Festival

The exact dates of these of these fairs
and festivals vary slightly from year
to year. There are also several other
events such as fêtes, flower shows,
horse shows and country fairs which
take place throughout the summer.
For full information telephone the
National Park office on (0439)
70657 or any information centre.

OLD CUSTOMS

Blessing the boats, Whitby.
First Sunday in September.
Kiplingcotes Derby. Oldest
horserace in Britain, held since
1519, held through several
parishes from South Dalton.
Third Thursday in March.
Maypole dancing. Hutton-le-
Hole. Third w/end in June.
Penny hedge, Whitby. Hedge
planted on foreshore as penance
for murder of an Esk Dale hermit
in Middle Ages. Eve of
Ascension Day.
Skipping Festival, Scarborough.
Shrove Tuesday.

Table set for dinner at 18th-century Ebberston Hall

INFORMATION CENTRES

The Moors Centre, Danby Open daily Apr-Oct. *Tel.* (0287) 60654

Helmsley *Tel.* (0439) 70401

Hutton-le-Hole *Tel.* (07515) 367

Low Dalby Foresty Commission Interpretive Centre. Forest drive to Hackness starts from here (toll), (Nov-Mar by appointment only). *Tel.* (0751) 60295

Middlesbrough *Tel.* (0642) 245432

Pickering *Tel.* (0751) 73791

Ravenscar National Trust Information Centre. Exhibits relating to local history, wildlife and geology. Open daily Jun-Aug. Weekends only Apr, May, Sep. *Tel.* (0723) 870138

Scarborough *Tel.* (0723) 372261, 373333

Sutton Bank Display on surrounding countryside. Open daily Apr-Oct. *Tel.* (0845) 597426

Thirsk *Tel.* (0845) 22755

Whitby *Tel.* (0947) 602674

PLACES TO VISIT

Besides offering a wide and varied choice of landscapes to explore the area is rich in other places that amply repay a visit. Brief details of the best-known and most impressive follow, though it should be remembered that this list is by no means exhaustive.

Dates, times and similar details relating to such places have a tendency to change, so it is always a good idea to check with a local information centre before making a special trip – particularly to one of the big houses. Dogs are not always welcome in many places open to the public, and certainly should not be let loose in park or farm land.

Bilsdale *Spout House* A renovated and remarkably well-preserved example of a thatched 16th-century cruck-framed house. Small charge.

Coxwold *Shandy Hall* This medieval house is now a museum dedicated to local vicar and writer Laurence Sterne. He lived here between 1760 and his death in 1768, writing *A Sentimental Journey* and *Tristram Shandy.* Open Jun to Sept, Wed & Sun pm. Other times by appointment. Charge.
Newburgh Priory Standing in grounds containing a wild water garden, this large 17th- and 18th-century house has some fine rooms. Open mid-May to end Aug, Wed only, also Sun pm in Aug. Grounds close 6.00. Charge.

Danby *The Moors Centre* An information and countryside interpretation centre in a converted shooting lodge. The grounds contain riverside, meadow, woodland and terraced gardens. Children's play area and brass rubbing centre. Open end Mar to Oct daily, Nov to end Mar, Sun pm.
Botton Village A charitable community of scattered houses and farms where mentally handicapped adults live as normal a life as possible. Visitors may walk round the village, which strives to be self-sufficient. Gift shop with products from the bakery, creamery, sawmill, candle shop, weavery, printing shop and glass workshop. Coffee bar and bookshop.

Ebberston *Ebberston Hall* A small country house built in 1718. Open daily, Easter to 1 Oct. Charge.

Gilling East *Gilling Castle* The Elizabethan great chamber, noted for its panelling, painted glass and ceilings is open to the public. The rest of the 14th-, 16th-, and 18th-century house is now the preparatory school for Ampleforth College. Open weekdays. Garden only, Jul to Sept, Mon to Fri. Small charge.

Great Ayton *Captain Cook Schoolroom Museum* James Cook's father was employed as bailiff by the local lord of the manor who paid for James to begin his education here. Part of the schoolroom now contains maps, books, pictures, etc relating to the explorer's life. Open daily, Easter to Sept pm, Oct, wkends only. Small charge.

Helmsley *Helmsley Castle* Only imposing ruins remain of this 12th- and 13th-century stronghold. The 14th-century domestic buildings contain items of interest. AM. Open all year weekdays, Sun pm.

Hutton-le-Hole *Ryedale Folk Museum* Re-erected buildings on a 2½-acre site contain displays illustrating the origins, superstitions, occupations and crafts of the people of Ryedale from prehistoric times. Open daily end Mar to end Oct. Charge.

Kirby Misperton *Flamingoland Zoo and Holiday Village* The 300-acre zoo contains over 1,000 animals and there are over 30 other attractions in the family funpark. Many other undercover attractions and large lake. Open summer. Charge.

Malton *Castle Howard* One of the greatest houses in Yorkshire, containing art treasures, furniture and ceramics, plus the largest private collection of 18th- to 20th-century costume. Lovely grounds with lake, mausoleum and garden centre. Open Mar to Oct. Charge.

Middlesbrough *Captain Cook Birthplace Museum* Explorer James Cook was born in Marton, 3m south of Middlesbrough, in 1728. This museum was opened 250 years later close to the site of the cottage where he was born. It illustrates Cook's early life as well as voyages of discovery. Situated in spacious, rolling parkland, the museum's other attractions include an aviary of parakeets, a conservatory of tropical plants, and assorted animals and fowl in small paddocks. Open all year. Small charge.
Newham Grange Leisure Farm A working farm illustrating farming life past and present. Wide range of livestock (including rare breeds), old farm machinery, vet's shop, saddlery. Open daily (winter, Sun only).

Horace Walpole said of Castle Howard: 'I have seen gigantic palaces before, but never a sublime one'

Nunnington *Nunnington Hall* A large 16th- to 17th-century house with a magnificent staircase and panelled rooms. The Carlisle Collection of miniature rooms is on display. NT. Open Easter to Oct, Tue to Thur, Sat & Sun pm. Charge.

Ormesby *Ormesby Hall* Interesting plasterwork attributed to John Carr of York, furniture and 18th-century pictures can be seen in this mainly 18th-century mansion. NT. Open end Mar to Oct, Wed, Sat, Sun & Bank Holiday Mon pm. Charge.

Pickering *Beck Isle Museum of Rural Life* This fine Regency building contains a collection of exhibits illustrating the working life, customs and pastimes of the local community during the past 200 years. Open daily Apr to Oct. Charge.
Moorland Trout Farm On Newbridge road near station. Series of large ponds alongside river. Up to 80,000 rainbow and brown trout reared for consumption or restocking rivers. Rods and tackle for hire.
North York Moors Railway, 'Moorsrail' An 18-mile privately-owned line runs from here to Grosmont, through the heart of the National Park. Newtondale Halt is ideal for access to forest and walks. A regular steam and diesel service operates throughout the season. *Tel.* (0751) 73535 (talking timetable).

Nunnington Hall in Rye Dale has the atmosphere of a family home. Inset left: bedroom. Inset right: the Carlisle collection of 22 miniature rooms decorated in different styles includes this Palladian hall

Pickering Castle A large 12th-century keep on an impressive motte (mound). AM. Open all year. Charge.

Ravenscar *Staintondale Shire Horses* East Side Farm has working shire horses and a collection of implements, carts and wagons. Open May to Sept, Sun, Tue, Wed, Fri. Charge.

Rievaulx *Rievaulx Terrace* Laid out in the 18th century, the grass terrace extends for ½ mile. At intervals there are dramatic views of the 13th-century abbey and at either end there are 18th-century garden temples. Open all year. Charge.

Robin Hood's Bay *Museum* A small museum with exhibits on local fossils, shipping and local history. Open mid-May to Sept, pm only. Small charge.

Scarborough *Scarborough Castle* Built about 1135 in a seemingly impregnable position on a headland between the North and South Bays, the castle had a four-storey keep added in 1155 by Henry II. Now only this part remains, the rest having been destroyed by the Roundheads in the Civil War after the Royalists were besieged for a year. AM. Open all year. Charge. *The Crescent Art Gallery, Rotunda and Woodend Museum* The Rotunda contains a museum of regional archaeology. Woodend Museum contains natural history exhibits. Open all year.

Skinningrove *Tom Leonard Mining Museum* Many relics of the Cleveland ironstone industry can be seen in this museum, sited at the former Loftus Ironstone Mines.

An Iron Age settlement and Roman signal station occupied the headland where Scarborough Castle now stands

Thirsk *Osgodby Hall* Situated 5 miles east of Thirsk, off the A170, this small but elegantly-proportioned Jacobean manor house retains several interesting features. These include a walled forecourt, 17th-century staircase and oak panelling. Open Easter to end Sept, Wed & Bank Hol Mon pm. Charge.

Whitby *Whitby Museum and Art Gallery* The wide range of exhibits in the museum include many relating to Captain Cook. Open all year. Charge.

Whorlton *Whorlton Castle* 14th-century castle with magnificent gate house. Open all year.

RIDING AND TREKKING
There are riding establishments at the following places. Many offer rides completely off the road, over moorland or through forests. Most cater for both novice and experienced riders, with rides ranging from an hour to day-long treks. Ring the following stables for more details.

Boltby *Tel.* (0845) 537375
Carlton-in-Cleveland *Tel.* (0642) 701027
Cropton *Tel.* (075 15) 509, 384, 228
Hawnby *Tel.* (043 96) 225, 252
Helmsley *Tel.* (0439) 70355
Irton *Tel.* (0723) 863466
Loftus *Tel.* (0287) 40616
Over Silton *Tel.* (060 983) 344
Pickering *Tel.* (0751) 72982
Ravenscar *Tel.* (0723) 870470
Robin Hood's Bay *Tel.* (0947) 880249
Rosedale *Tel.* (075 15) 619
Saltburn *Tel.* (0287) 22157
Scarborough *Tel.* (0723) 351695
Skelton *Tel.* (0287) 50303
Sleights *Tel.* (0947) 810450
Snainton *Tel.* (0723) 85218
Stainsacre *Tel.* (0947) 604466
Suffield *Tel.* (0723) 362703
Thornton Dale *Tel.* (0751) 74297
Ugthorpe *Tel.* (0947) 840086

An exhilarating ride on the moors above Ravenscar and Robin Hood's Bay

SAILING

Dinghy Sailing
Scaling Reservoir
Club Secretary: Mrs J Norman
Tel. (0287) 32522

Rowing and Canoeing
River Esk, Ruswarp, Sleights
Tel. (0947) 810329
Facilities for inland sailing are also
available at Scarborough.

Off-shore Sailing
Facilities for off-shore sailing are
available at several locations along
the coast; enquiries should be made
locally. Advice may also be obtained
from HM Coastguard.
Tel. (0723) 372323 and (0947)
602107

SHOPPING

Market days
Helmsley Friday
Guisborough Thursday, Saturday
Kirkbymoorside Wednesday
Malton Saturday
Northallerton Wednesday, Saturday
Pickering Monday
Scarborough Thursday
Thirsk Monday

Early closing days
Wednesday Great Ayton,
Guisborough, Helmsley, Pickering,
Robin Hood's Bay, Scarborough,
Sleights, Staithes, Stokesley, Thirsk,
Whitby, York.
Thursday Goathland,
Kirkbymoorside, Malton, Ruswarp,
Northallerton.

USEFUL ADDRESSES

North York Moors National Park
The Old Vicarage, Bondgate,
Helmsley, York. *Tel.* (0439) 70657
Youth Hostels Association
Yorkshire Regional Group,
96 Main Street, Bingley,
West Yorkshire BD16 2JH.
Tel. (0274) 567697

**Yorkshire and Humberside
Tourist Board**
312 Tadcaster Road, York YO2
2HF. *Tel.* (0904) 707961

WALKS AND NATURE
TRAILS

Guided walks
Guided walks are available throughout
the summer. Most of these walks (for
which there is no charge) are led by
the National Park Voluntary Ranger
Service. The majority are afternoon
walks covering 3-5 miles and taking
2-3 hours. There are also day walks
starting at 11.00am and covering up
to 12 miles (packed lunch required).
Main starting points are Danby
(Moors Centre); Goathland; Hutton-
le-Hole; Ravenscar; Robin Hood's
Bay; Sutton Bank. Further details can
be obtained from local information
centres or telephone (0439) 70657.
Waymark walks
There are 25 Waymark Walk
leaflets describing short family walks
(up to 5 miles) within the North
York Moors National Park. These
are available from local information
centres, shops, cafés or by post from
the National Park office at
Helmsley.
A selection of trails
Bridestones Moor Nature Trail
This starts at the car park 3 miles
north-east of Low Dalby. Two-mile
walk through the Nature Reserve
owned by the National Trust and
managed jointly with the Yorkshire
Wildlife Trust. **Goathland Rail
Trail** A 2-hour walk follows the 3½-
mile track bed of George
Stephenson's original railway from
Goathland to Grosmont. The steam
train along the present route can be
taken to return to Goathland. **May
Beck Trail** This 3-hour walk starts
at Maybeck. Turn off the B1416 at
Red Gates. A trail guide (small
charge) is available from the caravan

site. Moorland, forest and traditional
farmland. **Ravenscar Geological
Trail** This short two-part trail visits
the old alum quarries then descends
to the shore. Trail guides on sale at
information centre (small charge).
Sutton Bank Nature Trail A 2-hour
walk down the escarpment edge and
close to Lake Gormire. Trail booklet
(charge) available from Sutton Bank
Information Centre.
Long-distance walks
The **Cleveland Way**, marked with
an acorn symbol, starts at Helmsley
and follows the western and
northern edges of the North York
Moors. After reaching the coast at
Saltburn it follows the magnificent
coastline south to Filey. It is 93
miles long.
The **Lyke Wake Walk**, 40 miles
from Osmotherley to Ravenscar,
crosses the moorland heights and the
watershed between the southern and
northern dales. It is presented as a
challenge to be completed within 24
hours.
The **Esk Valley Walk** follows the
River Esk from source to mouth in
10 short, linking walks.
The **White Rose Walk**, 34 miles,
takes you from the White Horse
near Kilburn to Roseberry Topping
in Cleveland.
The **Derwent Way**, 17 miles,
follows the river from its source in
Fylingdales Moor to West Ayton.
The **Reasty to Allerton Forest
Walk** is 16 miles through Forestry
Commission land.

*Main picture: Wade's Causeway, the
mile-long Roman road on Wheeldale
Moor, makes an unusual walk. Below:
a peaceful path in the Forge Valley*

NORTH YORK MOORS

Atlas

The following pages contain a legend, key map and atlas of the North York Moors, three circular motor tours and 16 planned walks.

North York Moors Legend

TOURIST INFORMATION

⚐ ⚐	Camp Site	⚐	Nature reserve
🚐 🚐	Caravan Site	☆	Other tourist feature
i i	Information Centre	🚂	Preserved railway
P P	Parking Facilities	🏇	Racecourse
🌤 🌤	Viewpoint	⚘	Wildlife park
✗ ✗	Picnic site	🏛	Museum
⌐ ⌐	Golf course or links	⚲	Nature or forest trail
🏰	Castle	ℳ	Ancient monument
🏚	Cave	▨	Places of interest
🏕	Country park	✆ ✆	Telephones : public or motoring organisations
🌺	Garden	PC	Public Convenience
🏛	Historic house	▲	Youth Hostel

 Mountain Rescue Post

◆ ◆ ◆ ◆ Waymarked Path / Long Distance Path / Recreational Path

ORIENTATION

True North
At the centre of the area is 0°24'W of Grid North

Magnetic North
At the centre of the area is about 7°W of Grid North in 1986 decreasing by about ½° in three years

GRID REFERENCE SYSTEM

The map references used in this book are based on the Ordnance Survey National Grid, correct to within 1000 metres. They comprise two letters and four figures, and are preceded by the atlas page number.
Thus the reference for Pickering appears 91 SE 7983

91 is the atlas page number

SE identifies the major (100km) grid square concerned (see diag)

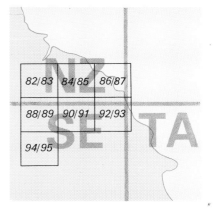

7983 locates the lower left-hand corner of the kilometre grid square in which Pickering appears

79 can be found along the bottom edge of the page, reading W to E

83 can be found along the right hand side of the page, reading S to N

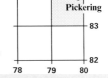

ATLAS 1: 63,360 or 1" to 1 MILE

ROADS & PATHS   Not necessarily rights of way

M1 Ⓢ	Motorway
	Motorway Main road under construction
A 64(T)	Trunk Road
A 168	Main Road
B 1264	Secondary Road
	Single & Dual Carriageway
	Narrow Road with passing places
	Road generally over 4m wide
	Road generally under 4m wide
	Minor Road , Drive or Track
- - - - -	Path
⟫⟫⟩	Gradients: 20% (1 in 5) and steeper
	14% (1 in 7) to 20% (1 in 5)

GENERAL FEATURES

⌁	Radio or TV mast	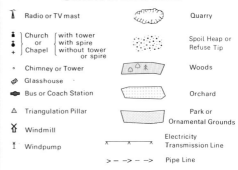	Quarry
⌁ ⌁	Church or Chapel { with tower / with spire / without tower or spire		Spoil Heap or Refuse Tip
∘	Chimney or Tower		Woods
⊘	Glasshouse		
🚌	Bus or Coach Station		Orchard
△	Triangulation Pillar		Park or Ornamental Grounds
☥	Windmill		
⚲	Windpump	⟩—⟩-⟩	Electricity Transmission Line / Pipe Line

RAILWAYS

——————	Multiple or Single Track
┼┼┼┼┼┼	Narrow Gauge Track
⫯⫯⫯	Bridges. Footbridge
▥▥▦	Tunnel. Cutting
┼─a─■─b─┼	Freight Line, Siding or Tramway
	Station (a) principal (b) closed to passengers
╫ LC	Level crossing
	Viaduct . Embankment

WATER FEATURES

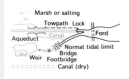

Marsh or salting
Towpath   Lock
Aqueduct   Canal   Ford
Lake   Weir   Normal tidal limit   Bridge   Footbridge
- - - - Canal (dry)

BOUNDARIES

┼─┼─	National	·—·—·—	County
▮	National Park	┼─┼─┼	District
NT	National Trust	NT	always open
		NT	opening restricted

ABBREVIATIONS

P	Post Office
PH	Public House
MP	Mile Post
MS	Mile Stone
LDP	Long Distance Path \
CH	Club House
TH	Town Hall, Guildhall or equivalent
PC	Public Convenience (in rural areas)

ANTIQUITIES

VILLA	Roman	𝕮𝖆𝖘𝖙𝖑𝖊	Non-Roman
⚔	Battlefield (with date)		
☆	Tumulus		
✛	Site of Antiquity		

PUBLIC RIGHTS OF WAY

··········	Footpath	—·—·—·—	Road used as a Public Path
- - - - -	Bridleway	·+·+·+·+·	By-way open to all traffic

Public rights of way indicated by these symbols have been derived from Definitive Maps as amended by later enactments or instruments held by Ordnance Survey on 1st February 1984 and are shown subject to the limitations imposed by the scale of mapping.
Later information may be obtained from the appropriate County Council.

The representation in this atlas of any other road track or path is no evidence of the existence of a right of way.

Danger Area   MOD Ranges in the area. Danger! Observe warning notices

HEIGHTS & ROCK FEATURES

outcrop   cliff   500   250   scree

Contours are at 50 feet vertical interval

To convert feet to metres multiply by 0·3048

Heights shown close to a triangulation pillar refer to the station height at ground level and not necessarily to the summit ,

TOURS 1:250,000 or ¼" to 1 MILE

ROADS
Not necessarily rights of way

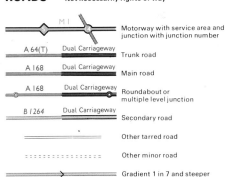

M I — Motorway with service area and junction with junction number

A 64(T) Dual Carriageway — Trunk road

A 168 Dual Carriageway — Main road

A 168 Dual Carriageway — Roundabout or multiple level junction

B 1264 Dual Carriageway — Secondary road

Other tarred road

Other minor road

Gradient 1 in 7 and steeper

RAILWAYS

Road crossing under or over standard gauge track

Level crossing

Station

Narrow gauge track

WATER FEATURES

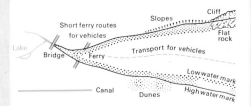

Short ferry routes for vehicles
Slopes
Cliff
Flat rock
Lake
Bridge Ferry
Transport for vehicles
Low water mark
Canal   Dunes   High water mark

ANTIQUITIES

Native fortress

------ Roman road (course of)

Castle • Other antiquities

CANOVIVM • Roman antiquity

GENERAL FEATURES

Buildings

⊕ Civil aerodrome (with custom facilities)

Wood

Radio or TV mast

Lighthouse

Telephones : public or motoring organisations

RELIEF

Feet	Metres	
		.274
		Heights in feet above mean sea level
3000	914	
2000	610	
1400	427	
1000	305	Contours at 200 ft intervals
600	183	
200	61	
0	0	To convert feet to metres multiply by 0.3048

WALKS 1:25,000 or 2½" to 1 MILE

ROADS AND PATHS
Not necessarily rights of way

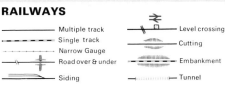

M I — Motorway   .... Path

A 64(T) — Trunk road

A 168 — Main road   } Narrow roads with passing places are annotated

B 1264 — Secondary road

A 168 — Dual carriageway

Road generally over 4m wide

Road generally under 4m wide

Permitted path and bridleway — Paths and bridleways along which landowners have permitted public use but which are not public rights of way. The agreement may be withdrawn.

RAILWAYS

Multiple track   Level crossing

Single track   Cutting

Narrow Gauge   Embankment

Road over & under   Tunnel

Siding

GENERAL FEATURES

Church or Chapel — with tower / with spire / without tower or spire

Electricity transmission line — pylon pole

Gravel pit

NT — National Trust always open

Sand pit

NT — National Trust opening restricted

Chalk pit, clay pit or quarry

Refuse or slag heap

National Park

HEIGHTS AND ROCK FEATURES

Contours are at 10 metres vertical interval

50 ·   Determined   { ground survey
285 ·   by   { air survey

Surface heights are to the nearest metre above mean sea level. Heights shown close to a triangulation pillar refer to the station height at ground level and not necessarily to the summit.

Vertical Face

Loose rock   Boulders   Outcrop   Scree

PUBLIC RIGHTS OF WAY

Public rights of way shown on this Atlas may not be evident on the ground.

Public Paths { Footpath / Bridleway

+ + + + + By-way open to all traffic

Road used as a public path

Public rights of way indicated by these symbols have been derived from Definitive Maps as amended by later enactments or instruments held by Ordnance Survey between 1st October 1982 and 1st March 1985 and are shown subject to the limitations imposed by the scale of mapping.
Later information may be obtained from the appropriate County Council.

The representation on this map of any other road, track or path is no evidence of the existence of a right of way.

WALKS AND TOURS (All Scales)

7 — Start point of walk

→ Route of walk

Line of walk

Alternative route

3 — Start point of tour

→ Route of tour

Featured tour

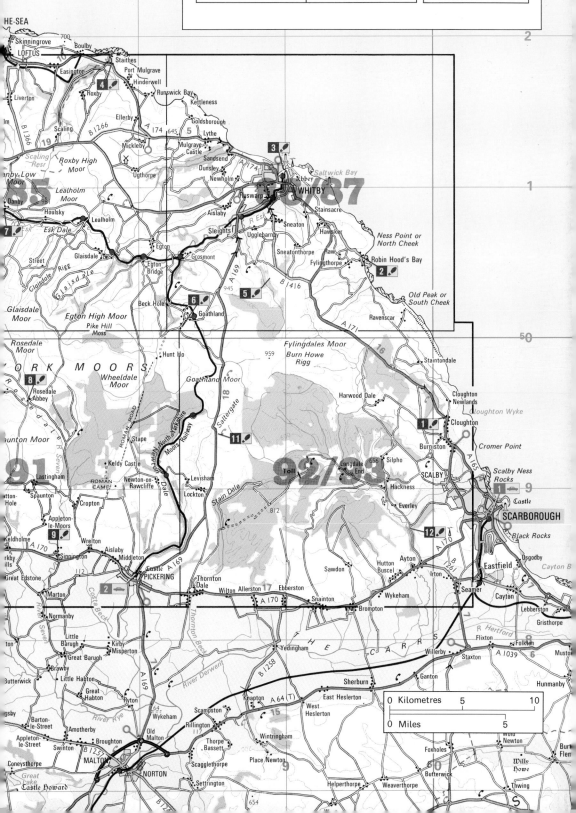

Key to Atlas pages

Distances in miles to PICKERING
Map Ref: 91 SE 7983

Bridlington	31	Leeds	49
Doncaster	70	London	232
Durham	69	Middlesbrough	41
Harrogate	49	Newcastle	78
Hull	44	York	25

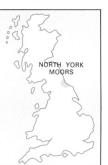

NORTH YORK MOORS

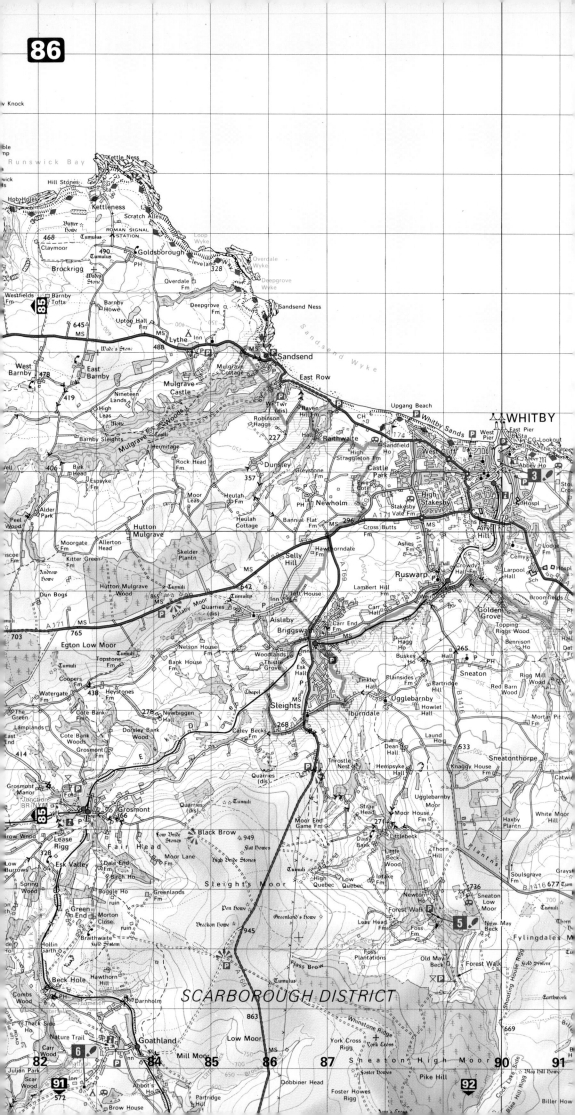

87

17

16

15

14

13

12

11

10

09

08

07

06

05

04

03

02

Saltwick Nab

Saltwick Bay

Black Nab

Cleveland Way

Highgate Howe

Manor House

Moat

Beacon Hill

Stripes Fm

Widdy Field

Russell Hall Fm 304

Gnipe Howe

Maw Wyke Hole

Stainsacre

MS 339

Long Lease

366

26

White Stone Hole

Hawsker Hall Fm

Hawsker Bottoms

dismantled railway

Low Hawsker

High Hawsker

PH

Mitten Hill Fm

Bottom Ho

Homerell Hole

443 444

462

Castle Chamber

MS

555

Smailes

Moor Fm

CG Lookout

Ness Point or North Cheek

Normanby

High Normanby

562

368

Rigg Hall

Raw

2

Robin Hood's Bay

Tumulus

Skerry Hall

PH

Fylingthorpe

723

CG Sta

Earthwork

Tumuli

Latter Gate Hills

Park Gate

Fyling Hall (Sch)

Low Fm

Farsyde Ho

Robin Hood's Bay

Cross Hills

179

Boggle Hole

Moor

Standing Stones

Ramsdale

Tumulus

Oak Wood

Fyling Park

Stoupe Beck Sands

525

Demesne Fm

Park

Stoupe Brow Cottage Fm

157

613 MS

St Ives Fm

Swallow Head

Fyling Old Hall

Cleveland Way

Old Peak or South Cheek

Foulsike Fm

Brock Hall Fm

Kale Croft

Tumuli

604

Hogarth Hill Fm

Oxbank Wood

Thorney Brow

Howdale Fm

Robin Hood's Butts

Tumuli

Raven Hall Hotel

Ravenscar

Blea Wyke Point

Pond Fm

Spring Hill

Brow Moor

Nature Trail

92 538 MS 93 Low Flask Fm 94 96 Howdale Moor 98 99 00

Turf Rigg

570 Flask Inn

Cook Ho

Stony Marl Howes 93

CG Lookout

Wragby Fm

Tumulus

Stony Marl Moor

657

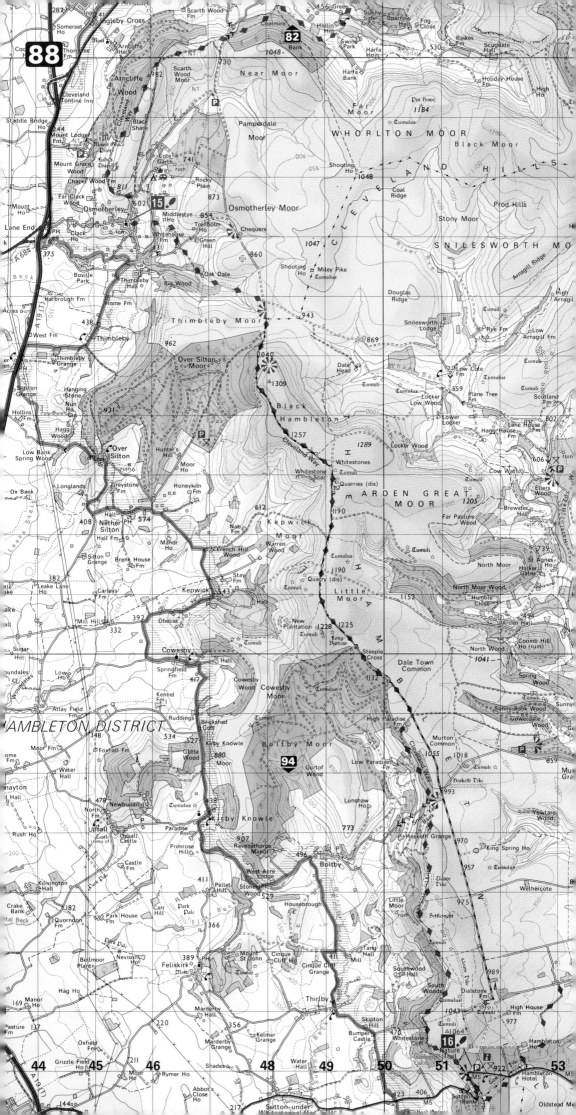

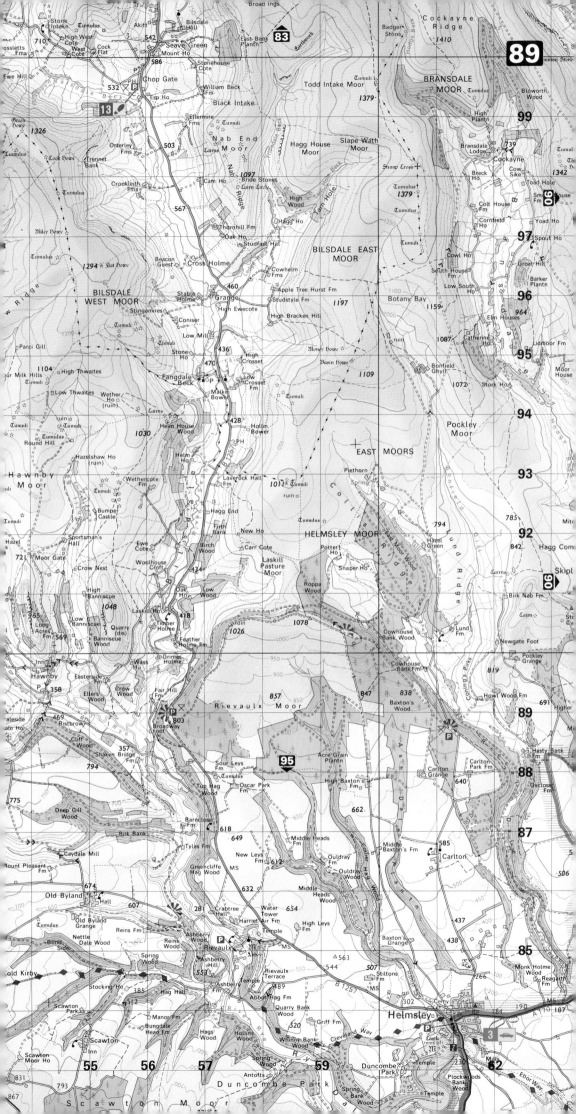

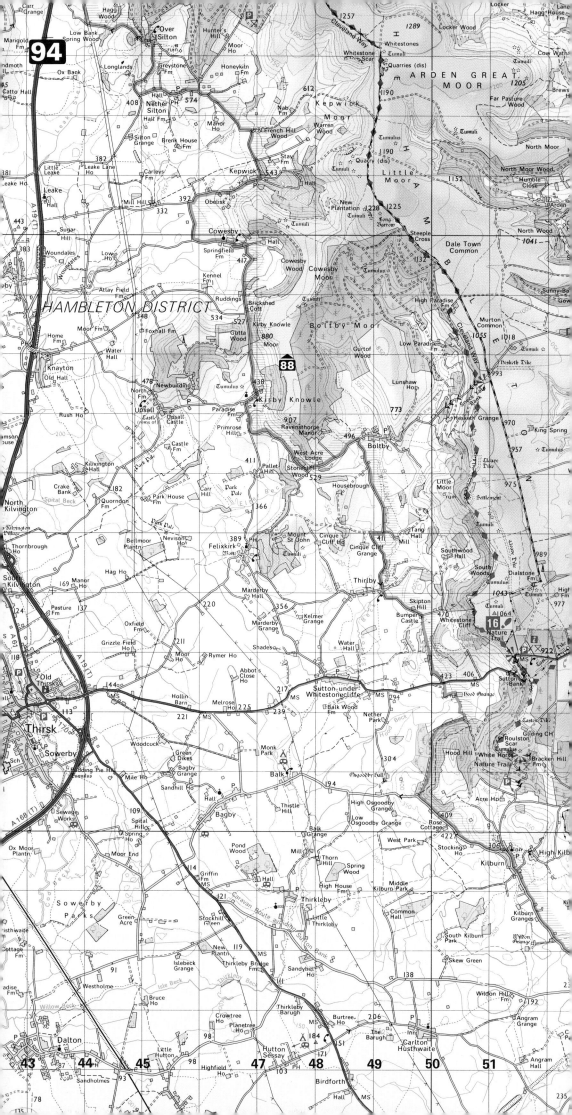

TOUR *1*

The Coast to Dalby Forest

The variety of the North York Moors National Park can be seen in this tour: the coast with its large resort of Scarborough, small fishing villages and the port of Whitby, steeped in seafaring traditions and with a cliff-top abbey; inland, bleak moors, cool forests and picturesque villages.

The drive starts from Scarborough (see page 62), a popular seaside resort with two wide, sweeping, sandy bays and a wide variety of attractions and entertainment facilities.

Follow signs North Bay then Whitby (A171) to leave on the A165. In 1 mile, at the roundabout, keep left and continue to Burniston. Here turn right onto the A171, signposted Whitby. At Cloughton bear left then pass through an afforested area before emerging on the desolate Fylingdales Moor. After 9½ miles turn right onto an unclassified road, signposted Fylingthorpe and Robin Hood's Bay. Descend a steep (1-in-4) hill with hairpin bends and fine views of the sea to reach the village of Fylingthorpe. Keep straight on to Robin Hood's Bay (see page 58). The main thoroughfare is narrow and descends very steeply to the shore. From May to September there is restricted access for motor vehicles. The bay itself has a 3-mile sandy beach.

From the village follow signs Whitby along the B1447 to reach Hawsker. Bear right, and at the end of the village turn right onto the A171. Just over ¼ mile farther turn right again onto an unclassified road, signed Whitby Abbey. There are good coastal views before reaching the fine cliff-top ruins of Whitby Abbey (see page 68). First founded almost 13 centuries ago, most of the present ruins of St Hilda's Abbey are in the Early English style and date from the 13th century. Beside the abbey is the unusual parish church of St Mary. From here 199 steps lead down to the town.

Return for ¼ mile and turn right (no sign). At the foot of the descent turn right and later cross the swing bridge into the town centre of Whitby (see page 68). Red-roofed houses separated by narrow streets cover the steep valley sides on both banks of the River Esk. The harbour still shelters a variety of boats, a reminder of the town's long seafaring past.

Leave by the Teesside road A171 and in 2 miles turn left onto the A169, signposted Pickering. Continue to Sleights (see page 63). Beyond the village the road climbs onto Sleights Moor. Continue for 3 miles. Here a detour can be taken by turning right onto an unclassified road to Goathland (see page 42). A picturesque moorland village, with wide sheep-trimmed grass verges, Goathland has a station for the North York Moors Railway.

Continue with the main drive, following an undulating road over bleak moorland. To the left there are views of the huge 'golf balls' of the Fylingdales Ballistic Missile Early Warning Station (see page 40). *Pass by the lonely Saltergate Inn then ascend.* Pass, on the right, the natural amphitheatre known as the Hole of Horcum (see page 46).

In 4 miles, at the Fox and Rabbit Inn, turn left onto an unclassified road, signposted Thornton Dale. Two miles farther turn left, signed Low Dalby Forest Drive. Shortly join a Forestry Commission road (toll £1). During periods of extremely dry weather the Forest Drive may be closed owing to the high fire risk. One carelessly-discarded match could destroy acres of trees.

If you wish to avoid the toll road continue to the picturesque village of Thornton Dale (see page 66) and turn left onto the A170, signed Scarborough. The main drive can be rejoined at Snainton and passes the hamlet of Low Dalby (see page 53). Here there is a visitor centre. *Turn left at the centre and continue on the forest drive.* This passes through beautiful woodland scenery in the Dalby Forest. *After 5 miles, at a fire tower, turn left then in 2 miles leave the forest drive. In ¾ mile at a T-junction turn right, signposted Scarborough. Pass the Moorcock Inn in the hamlet of Langdale End, then in 1 mile turn sharp right signposted Troutsdale and Snainton. Proceed along an undulating and winding road through Troutsdale.* This is in a picturesque setting amid wooded hills.

After 4 miles leave the valley, keeping left on the ascent. At Snainton turn left onto the A170, signposted Scarborough, and pass through Brompton (see page 34). Continue to West Ayton, then cross the River Derwent and turn left onto an unclassified road, signed Forge Valley. The road follows the river through the Forge Valley with thick wooded slopes on either side.

In 1¾ miles turn right, signed Lady Edith's Drive. A short detour can be made by keeping forward at this junction for a nearby picnic site and viewpoint. Continue with the main drive along a pleasant byroad through the Raincliffe Woods. Two miles farther pass a pond on the right, then in another mile at a T-junction turn right to re-enter Scarborough.

A delightful courtyard tucked away in attractive Robin Hood's Bay

Whitby still has a fishing fleet numbering about 45 boats

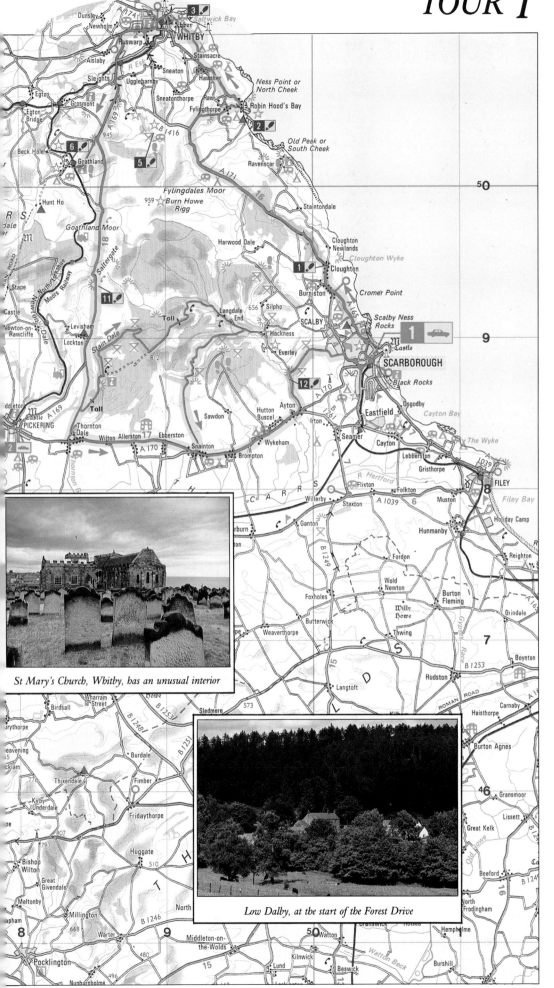

St Mary's Church, Whitby, has an unusual interior

Low Dalby, at the start of the Forest Drive

TOUR *2* ^{55 MILES}
Moorland and Dales

Exhilarating high moorland with superb views contrasts with green dales and pretty villages. Places well worth stopping to visit include the moorland village of Goathland with its nearby waterfalls; the loco shed of the North York Moors Railway at Grosmont; the Moors Centre at Danby and the attractive village of Hutton-le-Hole with its fascinating Ryedale Folk Museum.

The drive starts from Pickering (see page 56), a busy market town on the northern edge of the Vale of Pickering. The now-ruined castle was used as a hunting lodge by English kings between 1100 and 1400. Also of interest are the Beck Isle Museum of Rural Life and the southern terminus of the North York Moors Railway.

Follow the Whitby road A169, gradually climbing towards the moors. After 4¾ miles pass a turning on the left to Lockton. A detour can be made to visit the attractive hilltop villages of Lockton and Levisham (see page 52), on the edge of the Tabular Hills, before descending to the steep valley of Newton Dale. Continue the main tour, climbing to 920ft on Lockton Low Moor and passing on the left the Hole of Horcum, a spectacular natural hollow popular with hang-gliders (see page 46).

Descend to the Saltergate Inn. Continue on the A169 for 2¾ miles before turning left onto an unclassified road, signed Goathland. The three huge white 'golf balls' which can be seen to the right of the A169 are the fibreglass radomes (protective coverings for radar equipment) of the Fylingdales Ballistic Missile Early Warning Radar Station.

Cross Goathland Moor before descending to Goathland. Bear right and pass the Mallyan Hotel to enter the village (see page 42). The village has a station for the North York Moors Railway and there are several attractive waterfalls nearby. Mallyan Spout, 70ft, can be reached by a footpath which starts near the Mallyan Hotel.

Follow signs for Whitby and cross the railway. Climb steeply onto the moors and after 2 miles turn left onto the A169. In another ¼ mile turn left again onto an unclassified road, signed Grosmont and Egton. The road crosses Sleights Moor. Later there are fine views to the right along Esk Dale.

Descend steeply into Grosmont (see page 43). This village developed in the 19th century to house miners for the local iron-mining industry. The northern terminus of the North York Moors Railway is here.

Proceed over the level crossing and River Esk then ascend steeply (1-in-4) to Egton (see page 38). In the village bear right and at the Wheatsheaf Inn turn left, signed Glaisdale. Continue with the Castleton road and in 1 mile bear right. In another ¾ mile, at the T-junction, turn right for Lealholm. Recross the River Esk then turn left, signed Danby. Continue through Esk Dale for 3½ miles to reach the Moors Centre (see page 73). This is a visitor centre for the North York Moors National Park.

Keep left to reach the village of Danby (see page 37). Of interest in the village are the remains of 14th-century Danby Castle and the high-arched Duck Bridge over the River Esk, built in 1386.

Go over the staggered crossroads and continue to Castleton (see page 34). Follow the Rosedale signs and in ½ mile bear left to climb along the 1,000ft-high Castleton Rigg. After 4 miles turn left, still signposted Rosedale. On the left pass a small medieval white cross, known as Fat Betty. The top part rests directly on the base, the shaft having disappeared.

Cross the plateau of Rosedale Moor for 4 miles and then descend into Rosedale (see page 59), before turning left for Rosedale Abbey. This quiet village became a busy mining centre after the discovery of ironstone in 1856. Next to the church are the scant remains of the 12th-century Cistercian nunnery after which the village was named.

At the end of the village turn right and ascend Rosedale Chimney Bank (1-in-3). This gets its name from a previous landmark, a 100ft-high chimney. A remnant of the iron industry, the chimney was demolished in 1972 for safety reasons but the arches of iron kilns can still be seen on the right. The 1,022ft summit of Rosedale Chimney Bank is a superb viewpoint with magnificent moorland scenery all around.

Cross Spaunton Moor. On the descent there are fine views ahead. After 3 miles, at the T-junction, turn right for Hutton-le-Hole (see page 48). This pretty village contains the Ryedale Folk Museum (see page 48).

Turn left onto the Kirkbymoorside road. In 2¾ miles, at a T-junction, turn left onto the A170, signed Scarborough. Return through the agricultural countryside of the Vale of Pickering, passing through the villages of Wrelton, Aislaby and Middleton to Pickering.

Viking crosses in Middleton church

Remains of Rosedale's 12th-century Cistercian nunnery

The Tabular Hills rise from the Vale of Pickering

Superb views from Rosedale Chimney Bank's 1,022ft summit

TOUR 3 68 MILES

The Cleveland and Hambleton Hills

This drive through hilly country includes three fine viewpoints, at Newgate Bank, Clay Bank and Sutton Bank. It has a particular appeal for those interested in the rich Christian architectural heritage of the Moors area. Stops can be made to visit Rievaulx Abbey, Mount Grace Priory, Byland Abbey and Ampleforth College.

The drive starts from **Helmsley** (see page 46), an attractive stone-built village. Ruined 12th-century Helmsley Castle stands in the grounds of Duncombe Park (now a school).

Follow signs Stokesley to leave by the B1257. Ascend and in 1½ miles turn left onto an unclassified road, signposted Scawton. Descend steeply through thick woodland before turning right by the near side of the river bridge, signed Rievaulx Abbey. Follow the River Rye to Rievaulx (see page 58). Many of the houses in this small village were built with materials from the 12th-century Cistercian abbey, but despite this there are impressive remains of Rievaulx Abbey (see page 70), in a splendid setting.

Continue with the unclassified road and ascend through the woods to the junction with the B1257. To the right is the entrance to Rievaulx Terrace (see page 58). This ½-mile-long grass terrace has 18th-century garden temples at either end and views of the abbey, Ryedale and the Hambleton Hills (see page 44).

To continue with the main drive turn left, signed Stokesley, and rejoin the B1257 which climbs to over 800ft, with fine views from the Newgate Bank Picnic Area. Descend into Bilsdale (see page 33). Here the moors rise to over 1,100ft on both sides of the dale.

Pass through the hamlet of Chop Gate (pronounced 'Chop Yat') to reach the 842ft road summit of Clay Bank. The Forestry Commission car park has panoramic views towards Middlesbrough and Roseberry Topping, a distinctive conical hill (see page 59). To the east is Botton Head (1,489ft), the highest point on the moors.

Descend through a forested area to Great Broughton. Two miles farther, at a roundabout, take the second exit to enter Stokesley (see page 64). Leave by following signs to Thirsk (A172) and in ¾ mile turn right onto the A172. Follow the foot of the Cleveland Hills for 8 miles before branching left to join the A19. In ½ mile a road to the left can be taken to visit Mount Grace Priory (see page 55). This ruined Carthusian priory dates from the 14th century.

Continue with the main drive on the A19 for ½ mile then branch left onto the A684, signposted Northallerton. An important road and rail junction, the market town is situated on rising ground east of the River Wiske, outside the National Park. It is a busy commercial centre for the surrounding area.

Follow signs Thirsk to leave Northallerton by the A168 and continue through agricultural countryside. In 7 miles turn right onto the B1448 to enter Thirsk (see page 65). This old market town astride the Cod Beck has a fine 14th-century church, some interesting historic houses and inns, and a well-known racecourse to the west.

Follow signs Scarborough to leave by the A170 and approach the escarpment of the Hambleton Hills. Beyond Sutton-under-Whitestonecliffe pass a turning, on the right, to Osgodby Hall (see page 75). Begin the steep ascent of Sutton Bank (see page 64) with gradients of 1-in-4 and hairpin bends. The car park at the 950ft summit of Sutton Bank is a fine viewpoint, with extensive views back across the Vale of York to the distant Pennines on a clear day.

In just over ¼ mile turn right onto an unclassified road, signed White Horse Bank. One mile farther begin the descent of White Horse Bank (1-in-4). The huge figure of a horse was cut into the hillside in 1857. *At the foot of the descent keep forward for the village of Kilburn (see page 49).* The village was the home of woodcarver Robert Thompson, 'The Mouseman of Kilburn'. Oak furniture is still hand-made by Robert Thompson's Craftsmen Ltd (see page 32).

Continue with the Coxwold road and in 1½ miles bear right, then at the T-junction turn left. Pass Shandy Hall (see page 73) before entering Coxwold (see page 37). At the crossroads turn left, signed Byland. Alternatively keep forward with the Oulston road to visit Newburgh Priory (see page 73).

Continue with the main drive to Byland Abbey (see page 70). At the village of Wass (see page 67) turn right for Ampleforth (see page 32). At the end of the village bear right signposted Oswaldkirk and pass Roman Catholic Ampleforth College. Reach Oswaldkirk and keep forward, joining the B1363 signposted Helmsley. In ¼ mile turn left onto the B1257. At Sproxton turn right onto the A170, signposted Scarborough, for the return to Helmsley.

Intricate wrought-iron gates at the entrance to Newburgh Priory

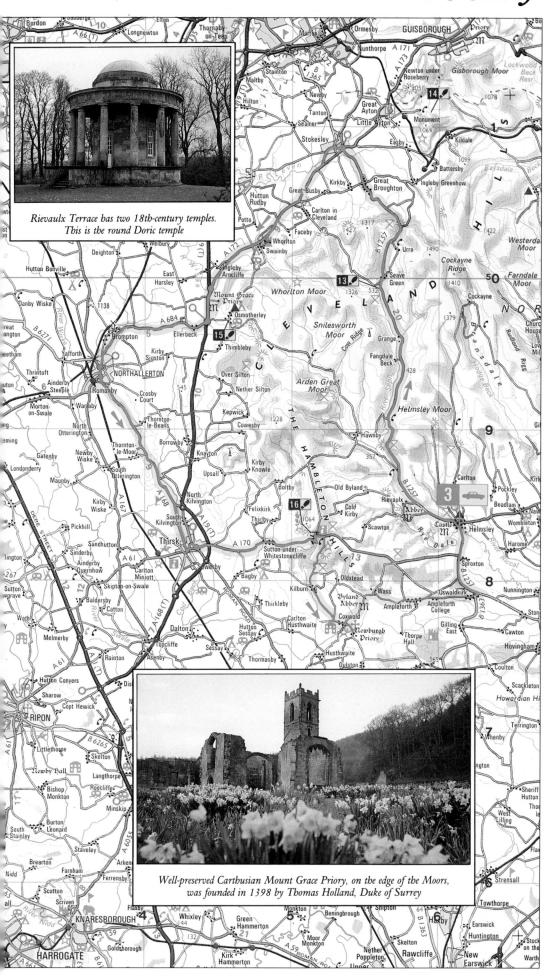

Rievaulx Terrace has two 18th-century temples.
This is the round Doric temple

Well-preserved Carthusian Mount Grace Priory, on the edge of the Moors,
was founded in 1398 by Thomas Holland, Duke of Surrey

WALK 1
Cliff and Shore

Allow 2 to 2½ hours

One of the attractions of this easy walk is the access to the shore at Cloughton and Hayburn Wyke. With children it would be wise to allow extra time to explore the boulder-strewn beaches. The route follows the Cleveland Way coastal footpath and returns along the trackbed of the old Scarborough to Whitby railway.

Where the road to Ravenscar leaves the A171 (TA012947) follow the lane down by the side of Cober Hill and park at the bottom. Go through the gate by the farm and follow the lane down to the cliff top at Salt Pans. The word 'wyke' is of Scandinavian origin and is used at several locations along the Yorkshire coast to denote a narrow inlet sheltered by headlands. To the immediate south of Cloughton Wyke is Hundale Point. Its namesake dale close by is said to be the shortest dale in Yorkshire. The huge slabs of sandstone along the shore often show fine examples of ripplemarks, looking as fresh today as when they were made over 150 million years ago. These sandstones are in fact remnants of a huge river delta which then covered this part of north-east Yorkshire.

Turn left to follow the Cleveland Way cliff path to Hayburn Wyke. The steep climb from Salt Pans gives extensive views southward towards Scarborough, Filey and on a clear day, the distant headland of Flamborough. A broad ledge well below the cliff edge but above sea level is a veritable jungle and a haven for wildlife. This tree-covered, boulder-strewn platform is known locally as the undercliff and is seldom visited by man. Badger, fox and even deer are found here together with many smaller mammals, birds and insects. The plant growth is often luxurious, the trees and boulders giving shelter to a wide range of plants, particularly ferns. *At Hayburn Wyke the path drops down through the woodland bearing right to reach the shore.*

Hayburn Wyke is a delightful and secluded bay with woodland coming right down to the shore and a twin waterfall cascading over a rocky ledge. Much of the woodland here is protected as a local nature reserve and managed by the National Trust and the Yorkshire Wildlife Trust.

Return from the shore by the same route but in only a short distance, where the Cleveland Way turns left, continue straight ahead. At the edge of the wood cross the stile and continue uphill through the field, gradually bearing left to pass between the farm buildings and out in front of the Hayburn Wyke Hotel. Continue a short distance up the road and turn left along the trackbed of the old railway to return to Cloughton.

The trackbed of the old Scarborough to Whitby railway line makes an ideal walking route and was acquired for this purpose by Scarborough Borough Council in 1975. Walkers can now follow the route from the outskirts of Scarborough to the start of the huge brick viaduct over the River Esk at Whitby, a distance of some 20 miles. The route can also be used, as on this walk, for making shorter circular routes linking the coastal footpath. *Leave the railway at the bridge over the trackbed and turn right to the car park.*

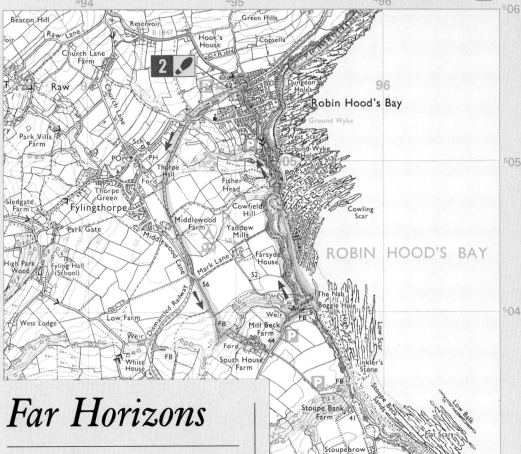

Far Horizons

Allow 2 to 2½ hours

Most visitors approach Robin Hood's Bay by
road, park in the car park and walk down the
hill into the old village. A more exciting and
interesting approach is this walk along the beach
from Boggle Hole. A good way to spend the day
would be to follow this walk in the morning and
spend the afternoon exploring the delights of the
seashore and the old village.

*Start in the station car park (pay and display)
(NZ949055), leaving by the lane at the opposite end to
the main car park entrance. Join the road and turn
right to Fylingthorpe and almost immediately opposite
follow the track bed of the old Scarborough to Whitby
railway line.*

The Scarborough to Whitby railway line was
built by John Waddell of Edinburgh and opened in
1885. In the short distance between Ravenscar and
Robin Hood's Bay the line drops some 400ft and
sweeps inland to avoid, as far as possible, some of
the steep-sided valleys draining into the bay. The
trackbed between the outskirts of Scarborough and
Whitby is now a walkway owned by Scarborough
District Council.

On local maps the word 'park' appears several
times: Park Villa; Fyling Park; Park Gate and High
Park Wood for example. This is a sure indication
that there was once a medieval deer park here
where game was protected either for sport or food.
Earth embankments, originally surmounted by a
fence or pole, are the only evidence of the park
today.

*The bridge over Middlewood Lane has been removed.
Drop down here to the road and continue ahead along
the lane signed 'Unsuitable for Motor Vehicles'. This
lane drops steeply to a ford and footbridge and then
climbs up between the buildings of South House farm to*

join the road. Turn left down the road to Boggle Hole.

Boggle Hole was once a mill, one of several in
the area, and is now a very popular Youth Hostel.
The word 'boggle' is a local name for a hob or
goblin once said to frequent this area. If the tide is
out the great curved scallops of the bay's reefs are
clearly visible. Formed from the oldest rocks in the
area, they are a paradise for fossil hunters and
those interested in the fascinating creatures that live
between the tides can search the rock pools.
Remember, however, that these specialised animals
and plants will not live very long once taken out of
their natural habitat, so don't collect them and
always put back rocks that you turn over. The bird
life of the shore can be equally interesting, with
several species of gull and wader in regular
attendance.

Until quite recently the southerly approach to
'Bay', as the village is known locally, was by a
steep track from Ravenscar. This descended to the
shore at Stoupe Beck and from there followed the
beach to the village, causing problems at high tide.
*If the tide is out you can walk along the shore back to
Robin Hood's Bay. If the tide is in, cross the footbridge
by the Youth Hostel and follow the cliff-top path to the
village.* Explore the village at leisure and perhaps
return again as so many have done before.

Robin Hood's Bay – village and beach

Of Serpents and Saints

Allow 2 to 2½ hours
(for the longer walk a good half day)

This two-in-one walk gives the option of a cliff-top walk from Whitby to Robin Hood's Bay, returning by bus, or a short easy walk never far from Whitby. In either case allow extra time to explore Whitby Abbey, the nearby parish church and some of the hidden alleys and courtyards of the old town. Flat shoes are advisable as much of the cliff walk is along a path lined with narrow wooden planks. Heels could catch in the gaps between the planks. If intending to take the longer route check the bus times in Whitby before you set off.

From the swing bridge in the centre of Whitby (NZ899111) go up Bridge Street and turn left to walk along Church Street and up the famous 199 steps to Whitby Abbey. You may find this takes longer than you expected, such is the wealth of interest on the way. The Tuscan-style old 'town hall' with 16 massive pillars dates from the late 18th century and was used by the Lord of the Manor as a court house and an office for collecting rents and taxes. Among the interesting shops along Church Street are those selling Whitby jet or 'black amber' jewellery. Tradition demands that you count the church steps and if you don't count 199, start again! For many years there was debate as to how many steps ascended the cliff, so in 1877 a stone inscribed with the correct number was set in the wall at the top. Also at the top of the steps is the

Caedmon Memorial, a richly-carved stone cross to the memory of England's first religious poet.

Dating from about 1110, the unique Parish Church of St Mary has a magnificent tiered pulpit with ear trumpets, boxed pews, many with family names and a fine Norman chancel arch almost hidden by the curious Chomley Pew erected in about 1600. Nearby are the imposing ruins of Whitby Abbey, refounded in 1078 to replace the famous earlier foundation of St Hilda, dating from 657. It was St Hilda who gave her name to a local ammonite or 'snakestone'. These flat, coiled fossils are found in rocks below the abbey and, according to tradition, are the headless snakes which St Hilda drove from her abbey. To this day Whitby's crest depicts three coiled 'Hildoceras'.

From the abbey cut through the car park and turn right to take the cliff path in front of the coastguard lookout. From the cliff top the remains of a wreck can be seen, a reminder of the many maritime disasters which have occurred along the coastline. *The path continues along the cliff edge and through a caravan site (signed Cleveland Way). Continue on the site road and cross a stile onto the Cleveland Way again to proceed along the cliff edge. Follow the path to the hilltop just beyond the Fog Horn Station and lighthouse, from where there is a good view down the coast.*

Those walking to Robin Hood's Bay should continue on the coast path. Most of the remainder of the circular route is on tarmac and some may prefer simply to retrace their steps back to Whitby along the cliff path. *If completing the circular route follow the tarmac lane from the lighthouse via Brook House to the road and turn right. Continue, with views ahead of Whitby Abbey. Just past the track to Knowles Farm (on the right) look for a narrow path on the left which goes towards New Gardens. Go through a gate and continue straight ahead, joining a narrow road. Where this bends right, continue straight ahead along a narrow path to join the road. Turn left downhill and right along the harbourside to return to the town centre.*

Coastal Heritage

Allow 2½ to 3 hours

Generally easy, with some steep parts, this walk follows the coast path from Staithes to Port Mulgrave before swinging inland to follow a pleasant wooded valley. As the walk does not return through Staithes, it is probably a good idea to explore the attractive village before setting off on the walk. Warning: part of the cliff path is poorly fenced, making the walk unsuitable for children unless carefully supervised by adults.

Park in the car park at the top of the bank (NZ782184) which is close to the site of the old coastal railway. Follow the road down to Staithes. If you look across the deep valley you can still see the abutments which led to a high viaduct. Boulby Potash Mine is prominent, the only potash mine in the country. From nearly 4,000ft below the surface salts from ancient desert seas are mined to produce much-needed fertiliser.

It is worth lingering in the village to explore the narrow lanes and alleys. The name 'Staithes', locally pronounced 'Steers', means a wharf or jetty.

From the harbourside follow steep Church Street from near the Cod and Lobster Inn, passing the Mission

Church of St Peter the Fisherman on the right. Follow the Cleveland Way (signed) which continues at the top as a path and turn sharp left, past some farm buildings. Continue straight ahead for some distance, crossing two stiles, then go uphill steeply to the cliff edge. It is at this point that children need to be kept close to adults. Immediately after the stile at the top of the hill the cliff path is unfenced. Farther on the path is poorly fenced, although the cliff is less sheer. Looking back from the top of the hill the great cliffs of Boulby can be seen, the highest cliffs on the east coast of England.

Follow the cliff path round to Port Mulgrave (see page 46), a grand title for so small a place. Looking down onto the 'port' from the road a crumbling jetty can be seen, marking one side of a small harbour. A steep path can be taken down to the beach for a closer look. *Pass the Boat House Tea Rooms and join the road at Port Mulgrave. Follow the road to Hinderwell, turning left at the church and crossing the A174. Go down West End Close, turning right into Porrett Lane, which becomes a rough track. Follow this round towards the caravan site. Turn right and where the track turns sharp left continue ahead through gate and through fields. Cross a stile and follow sign down a steep hill to a footbridge over Dales Beck.*

Cross the bridge and turn right parallel to the beck. After a little way start climbing through the wood and then follow the path down a ridge. Where three paths meet take the forward left which bears right and after a short distance leave the wood. After climbing a stile cross scrubland and climb another stile before descending to a caravan site. Follow the caravan site access road to Dalehouse. Turn right up a steep road to reach the main road, then right and left to reach the car park.

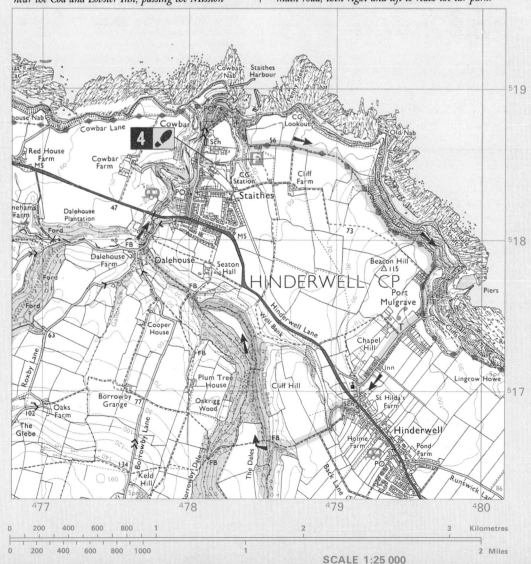

WALK 5
Echoing Woods

Allow 2½ to 3 hours

Waterfalls, woodland, stepping stones and open moor are all ingredients of this easy walk around the delightfully-named Littlebeck Valley.

Turn off the B1416 at Redgates Corner and follow the road signposted Falling Foss and Newton House to a car park (NZ889035). From here walk down the track towards Falling Foss. This track is part of an old coach road from Whitby over the moors towards Hackness and Pickering. The Foss is a very attractive waterfall set in woodlands that were once part of a large private estate. *At Midge Hall double back on the path leading alongside the gorge above the stream.* Midge Hall was the keeper's cottage and at one time had a double-seater outdoor privy which was virtually suspended over the waterfall!

Follow the path downstream to the Hermitage. This folly is carved out of solid sandstone with two stone armchairs on top. From the small balcony in front of the Hermitage the steepness of the valley sides can be fully appreciated. These woodlands are now owned by the Forestry Commission and are managed as a conservation and recreation area. *Go down steeply towards the stream and pass an old alum quarry. Continue to join the road at the secluded hamlet of Littlebeck.*

Turn right up the road, pass the village hall and follow the left fork for a short distance, then turn left off the road along a footpath (signposted). Bear right and cross the top edge of three fields with the hedge on the right. Cross the two stiles and drop down the side of Low Farm. Go through the gate, pass below the farm and continue diagonally down to the right to the track and ford. Follow the track parallel to the stream. Avoid the footbridge (unless the stream is in spate), cross the weir and then the stepping stones. Follow the path through the wood to a second set of stepping stones and continue downstream to a metal footbridge. Cross this and turn sharp right uphill, signposted Dean Hall.

The route now continues on a paved trod or pannierway. There are many of these early routeways, slabs of sandstone laid in lines, in the Whitby area. Often running for many miles, they are probably of medieval date and were in regular use by both foot travellers and the pack ponies which were used for transporting goods of all descriptions. *Turn right where the path joins a track which cuts up to the right between the buildings of Dean Hall and joins the road. Turn right on the road and very shortly veer forward left along the second (unsigned) bridleway towards the old quarry. Keep right at the fork and go up the side of the quarry onto the open moor and then keep right to go through the pine trees with the wall and fields on the right.*

Emerging from the trees, continue ahead across the moor, still keeping the fields on the right. Gradually swing left to pass to the left of the new barn and keep forward on the track to the road. Cross the road, follow the footpath (signposted) towards Thorn Hill, but shortly veer to the left of the buildings to follow a track over the moor to Newton House Lodge. Turn right down the road.

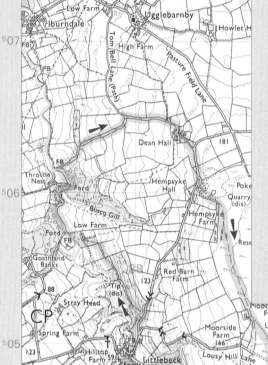

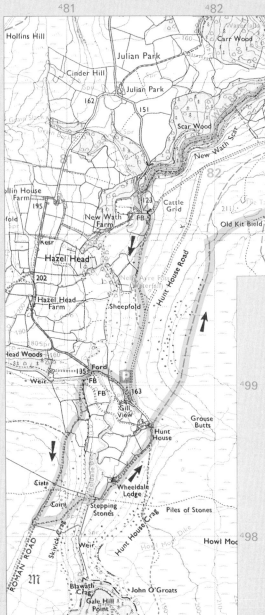

A Roman Road

Allow 2½ to 3 hours

This is a moderate walk but includes a scramble across boulders below the 70ft-high Mallyan Spout waterfall. The walk could develop into an all-day excursion if you have children with you. The steep-sided wooded valley of West Beck is ideal for games or a picnic and part of the walk is along a Roman road. The return route is over open moorland but if the weather is poor it would be advisable to return from **Hunt House** along the road.

The walk starts in Goathland, opposite the church (NZ828007). Follow the footpath down the right hand side of the Mallyan Hotel, signposted Mallyan Spout Waterfall and at the stream turn left upstream signposted Mallyan Spout. On reaching the waterfall there is a scramble over boulders which can be very

slippery. The path passes in front of the fall and continues to meander by the side of the stream. There are more boulders along the way and in places the path is very muddy, even on a hot sunny day.

The North York Moors National Park has the lowest rainfall of any National Park in the country and does not have many waterfalls. Nevertheless, several can be reached from Goathland, Mallyan Spout being the highest. The West Beck is a delightful stream tumbling amongst huge boulders beneath tree-covered hillsides. Woodpeckers are common and you may see the white-fronted dipper.

Reach the road and go straight ahead (left). At the second bend, just before the cattle grid, turn right past the house and follow the path over the moor towards Hunt House. From the lay-by near Hunt House turn right down the track, cross the first footbridge and turn right along the stream bank. Go left uphill, following the track signposted Roman Road. Turn right over the stile at the top and bear left along the wallside to join the Roman road. Follow the road as it climbs gradually to the moor.

Often called Wade's Causeway after the legendary giant who supposedly built it, this is one of the best-preserved sections of Roman road in the country. Built as a military project about AD80 it probably fell into disuse some 40 years later. The road has been traced from near Malton, a Roman town, to the lower slopes of the moors above Pickering. Here, at Cawthorne, are the remains of four Roman military training camps and from here remains of the road become more visible until the route of the road reaches this well-preserved section on Wheeldale Moor. Beyond Wheeldale the road continues to Lease Rigg above Grosmont where it appears to end at another camp site.

Follow in the Romans' footsteps, cross the step stile and continue ahead for about 200yd before doubling back on a path (left) and dropping to the stepping stones over Wheeldale Beck. The route of the Lyke Wake Walk continues straight up the moor but take the more gentle route to the left. This goes past Wheeldale Lodge, a former shooting lodge now used as a Youth Hostel. Follow the track to Hunt House and a few yards along the tarmac road cut forward, right, up the moor. The track climbs gradually, in a straight line, to the rocky outcrop and then follows the edge of the hill towards Goathland. The rocky outcrops are inhabited by adders but these snakes usually disappear before you have a chance to see them. Bear gradually right and pass to the right of a small tarn before going downhill to return to Goathland.

108

WALK 7
Moorland and Dale

Allow 2½ to 3 hours

A breezy moorland walk followed by an easy walk along a country road. Broad views along the Esk Valley and Little Fryup Dale, a high-arched medieval packhorse bridge and a detour to the Moors Centre at Danby are some of the attractions of this moderately easy walk in the heart of the national park.

From the railway station in Danby (NZ708084) turn right to follow the road which crosses the railway and the River Esk. Notice Danby Mill on the upstream side of the river bridge; the mill wheel and machinery have been renovated in recent years. Follow the road into Ainthorpe and turn left up the road to Fryup.

Opposite the Fox and Hounds is the village quoits pitch. This ancient game is increasingly popular in villages throughout the length of the Esk Valley. A pitch 11yd long has a square bed of clay at each end in which is set an iron post or hob. Basically the game involves throwing a bevelled metal ring or quoit from post to post. Great skill and some strength is required and, as with all good games, tactics play an important part. *Just past the tennis court the road bends left. Take the bridleway (signed) to go straight forward up Ainthorpe Rigg and onto the moor.*

Pass through a gate. There are extensive views from the path, which farther on is clearly marked with a line of stone cairns. The North York Moors is very rich in the evidence of early man, particularly from the Bronze Age period of between about 2,000 and 4,000 years ago. Hundreds of burial mounds or tumuli are found on the high moor and in this area extensive field systems have also been discovered.

Reach the edge of the hill, with views over Little Fryup Dale through a gap into Great Fryup Dale. *Where the path forks take the left path down to the road junction and turn left along the road.* Farther on pass Danby Castle, a 14th-century palace-fortress probably built by William le Latimer. Tradition suggests that Henry VIII stayed here but in fact there is no evidence that he ever travelled farther north than York. The building is now part of a farm and not open to the public.

Just past the castle turn sharp right down the road to Duck Bridge. This fine example of a medieval packhorse bridge is one of three remaining in the Esk Valley, the others being at Glaisdale and Westerdale, though the latter was extensively renovated in the 19th century. Duck Bridge was built in about 1386 and has low walls leaning out over the water, typical of this kind of bridge. *Do not cross Duck Bridge but continue following the road as it bears left.*

On the opposite side of the river stands Danby Lodge, now known as the Moors Centre. This was previously a shooting lodge on the estate of Lord Downe but since 1976 has been used as a visitor centre by the North York Moors National Park Authority. A detour to view the exhibition, visit the grounds or enjoy refreshments is well worth while. Cross a stile on the right to follow a public

footpath to the centre, but take care crossing the railway and do not allow children to run on ahead. Admission is free and the centre is open daily from Easter to October.

Once essential for transporting goods across the moors, these paved trods are convenient paths for today's walker

Forgotten Industry

Allow 2½ to 3 hours

A moderately easy walk through rural Rosedale, with its reminders of the forgotten ironstone industry. The middle section of the walk is overgrown in summer and one field can be boggy.

Start at the village green in Rosedale Abbey (SE724959) and take the path between the school and church. Cross the road and take the footpath straight ahead into the caravan site and turn right along the track through the site. Approaching the end of the site pass through a metal gate (footpath signed) to continue the walk over fields. About 15 minutes from the start of the walk the path descends to a footbridge over the River Seven, here little more than a stream. Go across the field to steps over a stone wall and turn right along Daleside Road towards Thorgill.

Just before Thorgill turn right down a track and follow the signs through Low Thorgill Farm. Go through a metal gate from the farmyard. Following direction of yellow arrow on post, cross field and continue over a footbridge across stream. Proceed up the fields towards Hill Cottages. The next part of the route follows an ancient paved way or 'Monks Trod'. Cross another footbridge and continue across two fields, then along a track which bears left. Pass through a gate and continue up to the cottages, a typical row of miners' houses.

Cross the road and follow the track up towards the white house. Turn sharp right before you get to the house, over a stile next to a small red-tiled outhouse and right again immediately, over a fence and onto a rough track. This goes to Clough House, just visible from the road amongst the trees. Continue through a wooden gate and bear left (crossing a fence just before the house). Cross a fence again just after the house (this part of the path is overgrown). Bear left (crossing another fence) into a young conifer plantation. Continue up to the old railway trackbed. Follow this round the head of a steep-sided valley and round the contour towards Knottside, bearing right and keeping on the trackbed, with young conifers on the left. Reach mature conifers and climb over a rough fence, continuing through the wood. Turn left up a track, to cross a wire fence and reach the road.

Cross the road and follow the bridleway (signed) down to the left and then turn right onto a footpath, with the derelict farmhouse and pond on the left. The path goes gradually downhill through rough pasture. Bear right by a hawthorn tree obviously used as shelter by sheep, and continue downhill to a road and stream. Pass through a gate and go right up the road for about 50yd, then bear left on path parallel to and above the stream, crossing the bottom of two fields. Just after leaving the second field, keep the stone wall on the left and continue down to a wooden gate, crossing the stream by a footbridge. Continue through a larger gate and bear slightly uphill, crossing the corner of the field diagonally to a bridlegate.

Go across the next field (boggy and overgrown), parallel to the stream, to reach a gate in the stone wall. In the next field drop down to reach a ladder over the stone wall in the corner of the field. Continue, following a well-marked path parallel to the stream through several more fields, to return to the village, with the old chapel on the right.

SCALE 1:25 000

WALK 9
Riverside
Ramble

Allow 2 to 2½ hours

From the centre of Sinnington this walk goes through pleasant woodland often close to the River Seven. Above Appleton Mill the route climbs steadily to the top edge of the woods and then gradually descends towards the Hall and Sinnington church.

Start at the river bridge at Sinnington (SE745858). Many villages along the southern edge of the moors have names ending with -ton, a sure indication that they were established by invading Angles in the 6th and 7th centuries. Sinnington has been by-passed by the A170 and is now a quiet, pleasant village through which the River Seven flows.

Follow the road to the right past the school, on the

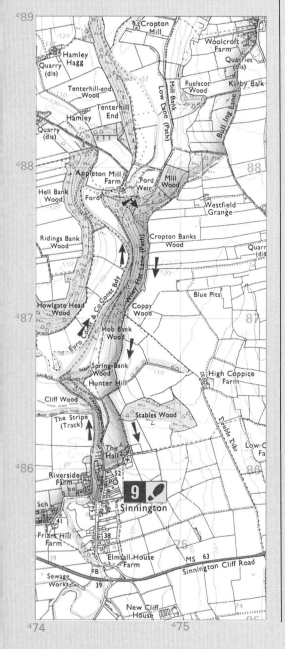

east side of the river, and then bear left down the no through road. Where the road ends continue down the bridleway to the river bank. The bridleway is signposted left but continue straight ahead along the footpath into the woods, gradually climbing and then dropping to a field gate and through a meadow. About three-quarters of the way across the meadow cut up right to the corner of the wood and cross a stile to follow a path through the wood high above the river.

These woodlands are a pleasure to visit at any time of year, but particularly in the spring. Before the leaves are fully open on the trees the ground is a carpet of early spring flowers including primroses, violets, wood sorrel and wood anemone. Later in the season bluebells, woodruff and wild garlic are found. The woods are also home for badgers and a variety of birds.

Descend to the river bank but then follow the right-hand edge of a field, climbing steeply uphill after about 150yd. At a crossroads of paths turn right and continue to climb steadily to the top edge of the wood. Ignore the path to your left and follow the path to the right as it gradually descends. Leaving the wood continue over an open area and bear left along a field-side to a track. Turn right and after about 100yd turn sharp left towards Hall Farm. Join the road where it bends and continue between the buildings, past the church and downhill to return to Sinnington.

The church of All Saints has many original features dating from Saxon and Norman times, although it was restored in 1904. The old Hall nearby has high perpendicular windows. It dates from the 12th century and was built by the de Clere family. In the centre of Sinnington is a maypole, one of only a few remaining in this area. In 1708 the Quakers made attempts to stop the fun and games around the maypole, but not, it seems, with much success. Close by is a low hump-back bridge spanning a dry ditch which may have once been a flood channel or possibly an old mill-leat. The bridge spanning it is medieval but the bridge across the River Seven dates from 1767.

Allow extra time on the walks if with children

Dale of the Daffodils

Allow 2 to 2½ hours

This easy walk through Farndale is particularly popular in spring when thousands of wild daffodils line the path alongside the River Dove. It is however a stroll to be savoured at any season of the year. The return route along field paths down the flank of the valley has pleasant distant views of the dale.

From the small car park at Low Mill (SE673952) take the path (signposted High Mill) which goes down to the footbridge over the River Dove and turn left to follow the path upstream parallel to the river. Tens of thousands of people tramp this famous 'Daffodil Walk' in spring. It is not the only place in Farndale, or indeed in the North York Moors, where the daffodils grow that they come to see, but it is certainly one of the best. Nobody is sure how the daffodils first came to be here, although they have been here for centuries. For most of the year the Dove is a placid river but come the winter snows or autumn rains and it is quickly changed to a racing torrent and the river once powered several mills along its course. It is shaded by alder trees and as the Gaelic word 'ferna' means alder these may have given Farndale its name.

Continue alongside the River Dove for about 50 minutes, passing through several stiles, before reaching the disused buildings of High Mill. Pass between the buildings and follow the track up to Church Houses, passing through a gate. At the end of the track turn right (signed Hutton-le-Hole) onto a tarmac road. Continue, passing the Church of St Mary on the left and gradually climbing to pass Mackeridge House on the right. Just beyond the house turn right on the footpath (signed) by a stone wall. Keep a stone wall on the left and follow the edge of the field for a little way before turning left over a step stile to cross the wall. Keep the hedge to the right before passing through a gate. Cross the field and pass through a second gate before passing to the left of Bragg Farm. Pass through a third gate and continue along the track. After about 200 yd the path cuts down the field (signed footpath) to the buildings of Bitchagreen Farm. Cross the stone wall and keep the farm on the right, passing through a gate, before going slightly up to the left. Cross a stile and pass immediately in front of a small cottage to keep ahead towards Cote Hill, crossing another stile. Keep the new barn on the left and go down to the right-hand field gate and then straight down the edge of the field, passing through a gate and passing a gate opening on the left.

Bear left over a stile and continue down a field and through a gate. Continue along the track towards High Wold House (there may be ropes across the track). In the farmyard turn right through a field gate (signpost) and go down the field, crossing a stile and bearing left at the bottom to cross the stream and follow the trod (paved path) down to the River Dove and Low Mill.

WALK *11*
A Dramatic Landscape

Allow 3½ to 4 hours

This walk is particularly attractive in late August or early September when the distant moorland is a haze of purple and mauve and the scent of heather is on the wind. For part of the walk the route follows the edge of the steep gorge of Newton Dale where the steam trains passing far below look like toys. Take care along the edge of Yewtree Scar where the cliffs fall sheer to the valley below.

Park in the car park at Saltergate (SE853937) and follow the main road to the hairpin bend on Saltergate Bank. From here there is a good view northwards towards the Fylingdales Early Warning Station. In the foreground is the ancient Saltergate Inn, situated on the old road from Robin Hood's Bay. Fish were brought here for salting before onward transit to inland towns. *Turn left over the step stile and follow the path down into the Hole of Horcum. Continue down the valley passing to the right of the old*

farm buildings. *Continue along the path through the middle of the fields avoiding any routes which climb uphill. Where the valley narrows keep the fence and wall on the left and continue down to the confluence of two streams. Cross both streams and turn sharp right up Dundale Griff, signposted footpath.* The word griff is used in this area to denote a very steep-sided little valley, often with cliffs along its flanks. Another common local word is rigg, used to describe a long narrow hill or ridge.

On coming onto the open moors, bear right across the moors. Shortly pass Dundale Pond on your right, probably built in medieval days as a watering hole for animals, *and continue up the dry valley, gradually bearing up to the left. At the corner of the walled field strike off on the path straight across the moor to reach the edge of the escarpment overlooking Newton Dale, then cut down to the right towards the ruins of Skelton Tower. Continue along the path, bearing to the right and following the edge of the dale northwards to Yewtree Scar. Leave the broad track where it swings away from the edge of the valley and follow the path along the cliff top.* **Take care if with children.**

At the north end of Yewtree Scar continue with the path as it bends right, away from Newton Dale. Go along the field side to the edge of a tributary valley and then almost immediately bear right again to cross the moor and climb up towards the hairpin bend of Saltergate Bank. Climb up towards the road, keeping the fence line on the left, then follow the road back to the car park.

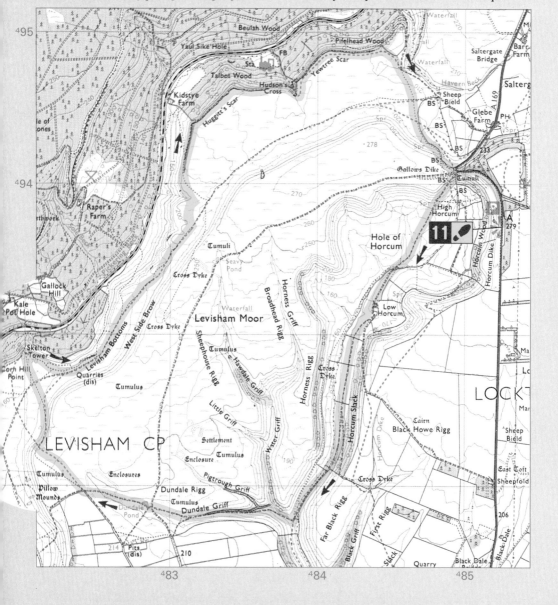

Dawn Chorus

Allow 2 to 2½ hours

This is an easy walk along river-bank and woodland paths through the steep-sided Forge Valley, much of which is now designated as a National Nature Reserve. Start this walk at dawn on a fine June morning and you will have ample recompense for a very early rise.

Park at one of the two small car parks (SE983874) on the road out of West Ayton towards the north end of Forge Valley and walk a short distance downstream to cross one of two footbridges over the River Derwent. The path now follows the river bank downstream. Close to the bridges is the site of the old forge and cottages from which the valley takes its name. In medieval times Forge Valley would have been an important through-route for travellers between the Vale of Pickering in the south and Hackness and Whitby to the north. A forge was as important to early travellers as a petrol station is to us today, and with abundant limestone, wood for charcoal and an ample water supply this was an ideal site.

The woodlands here have been described as one of the best remaining examples of mixed woodland in north-east England and are now designated as a National Nature Reserve. A wide variety of trees, including oak, lime, wych elm and birch are complemented by a rich ground flora of wood anemone, primrose, bluebell, woodruff, orchids and many other species. In late spring parts of the woodland are almost covered with the broad green leaves and white flower heads of ramsons or wild garlic. Look for the yellow globes of marsh marigold and yellow flag (iris) growing in the river.

Where the path enters a field continue straight ahead keeping the fence on your right. Over to the left is a small weir built by the water authority to measure flow rates in the Derwent. A little downstream, although out of sight, are sink holes in the bed of the river through which some of the water percolates. After travelling underground for some miles the water is trapped in the limestone and is then tapped to supply Scarborough with its water.

Forge Valley was named after the forge which existed here between the 11th and the 19th centuries

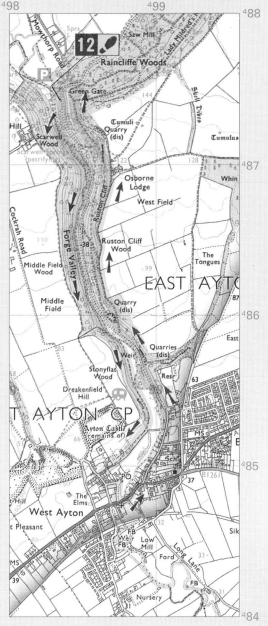

The path merges into a rough track which bends gradually right uphill to pass close to the ruins of Ayton Castle, dating from about 1400. Continue ahead to join the road, turning left downhill then quickly left and right to the road bridge on the A170. Cross the bridge and turn left on the road to Hackness. Follow the road as it drops back into Forge Valley and about 300yd beyond the weir (having passed one bridleway) cross the road to follow the signposted bridleway which cuts steeply uphill bearing right of the road. Near the top of the wood where the path divides, take the left fork to follow the path along the top edge of the woods with fields on the right.

The richness of the birdlife in Forge Valley is perhaps best experienced on one of those still, warm and slightly misty June mornings just as dawn is breaking. For those who have experienced the full flood of the dawn chorus echoing along this ancient wooded gorge, the memory will last a lifetime.

Pass the back of Osborne Lodge Farm and within a short distance start dropping downhill. Continue on this path which gradually swings round to join the road near Green Gate. Turn left along the road to return to your car.

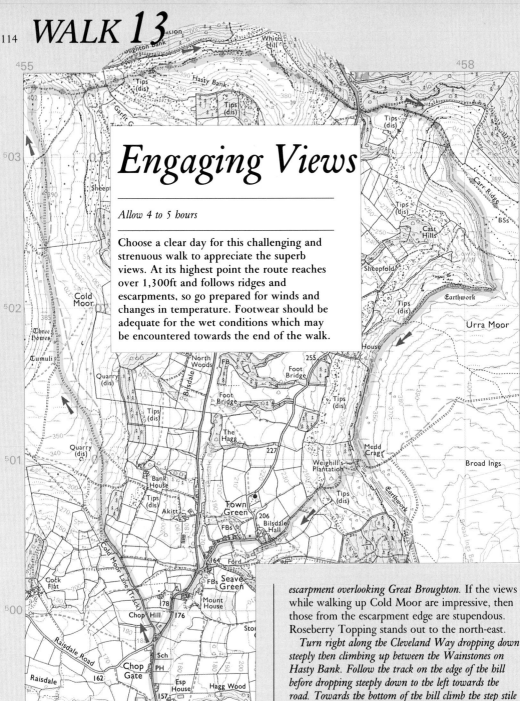

Engaging Views

Allow 4 to 5 hours

Choose a clear day for this challenging and strenuous walk to appreciate the superb views. At its highest point the route reaches over 1,300ft and follows ridges and escarpments, so go prepared for winds and changes in temperature. Footwear should be adequate for the wet conditions which may be encountered towards the end of the walk.

Start your walk from the car park at Chop Gate (SE559994) pronounced 'Chop Yat', and walk up the road into the village. Turn left on the road to Carlton and almost immediately right up a track by the Wesleyan Chapel. Chop Gate is a hamlet rather than a village. The name derives from Chapmans' Gate – chapman being an old name for a pedlar or travelling salesman, and gate being an old word for a road crossing. *Follow the path through the gate up to the moor and leaving the stone wall on your left, climb up the ridge. At the first cairn the path bends slightly to the right to follow the edge of the hill overlooking Bilsdale.*

The views as you walk along the ridge of Cold Moor are impressive. To the left the land falls gradually down into the remote head of Raisdale while on the right the head of Bilsdale unfolds. *The path now joins a broad track. Follow this straight over Cold Moor to join the Cleveland Way at the*

escarpment overlooking Great Broughton. If the views while walking up Cold Moor are impressive, then those from the escarpment edge are stupendous. Roseberry Topping stands out to the north-east.

Turn right along the Cleveland Way dropping down steeply then climbing up between the Wainstones on Hasty Bank. Follow the track on the edge of the hill before dropping steeply down to the left towards the road. Towards the bottom of the hill climb the step stile and turn immediately right down the wall side, avoiding the more obvious forest track.

Climbing up amongst the Wainstones can be an exciting experience and a stop may be made if rock climbers are searching for more difficult routes. Take care along the top of Hasty Bank; the path passes close to the edge of old stone quarries.

Cross the B1257 and continue along the Cleveland Way, which climbs the hill opposite. Keep the wall on the left and when you reach the second bridlegate across your path pass through and then bear right along the edge of the hill, leaving the Cleveland Way on the left. The path now becomes indistinct but follows the prominent earthwork (ridge and ditch) around the contour of the hill to Medd Crag.

This earthwork is one of hundreds to be found throughout the North York Moors. They may have been cattle enclosures, territorial boundaries or defensive works.

At the old quarry near Medd Crag turn right downhill with the old barn on your right. Continue on an obvious track which bends downhill to Bilsdale Hall, where you turn left down a tarmac lane to Seave Green and the B1257. Turn left along the main road to return to Chop Gate.

Moorland Matterhorn

Allow 2½ to 3 hours

Roseberry Topping is perhaps the most prominent landmark in the North York Moors. Although only 1,057ft high the craggy south-west face draws the gaze upwards to emphasise the height. This moderate walk, which begins at Gribdale Gate car park, follows the escarpment to Roseberry Topping and then drops to Airy Holme Farm before returning to Gribdale Gate.

Start at the car park at Gribdale Gate (NZ593110) which can be reached on a narrow road from Great Ayton (follow signs for station). Approaching from Great Ayton, park in the first car park at the top of the hill. Cross the cattle grid and turn left up the hill, following the Cleveland Way. The path levels out at the top of the hill to follow the edge of the escarpment. The moorland on the right is the location of an important archaeological site excavated during the 1950s and now known to be a complex burial site dating from the New Stone Age and Bronze Age.

Keep the stone wall (conifer plantation boundary) on the left and go through the bridlegate in the wall which crosses the path just above Little Roseberry. Drop downhill before climbing the flank of Roseberry Topping. If you decide not to climb Roseberry Topping turn left through a field gate on the level ground before the hill and follow the track towards Airy Holme Farm.

The view from the summit of Roseberry is well worth the climb. Immediately below is the village of Newton under Roseberry, which a 19th-century historian described as a 'small, dirty insignificant village', quite a contrast to what we see today. In the distance is the industrial complex of Middlesbrough. It is difficult to realise that when the young James (later Captain) Cook looked out over this same area less than 300 years ago, there was only a handful of farms along the banks of the meandering River Tees. Due east, beyond Guisborough, the sea is clearly visible. The lower slopes of Roseberry Topping have for centuries been worked for the alum and ironstone they contained. In fact it was early mining activity which led to the collapse of the hillside giving the hill the dramatic rock face we admire today. Looking down towards Airy Holme Farm you can still see evidence of old workings and the trackbeds of railways built to take the ironstone to lower levels.

From the summit drop down the steep south-east slope, towards the Cook Monument high on distant Easby Moor. Pass through a bridlegate and down towards the old mines. Turn right along the track towards Airy Holme Farm, turning left to pass in front of the farm and join the tarmac road. As a boy Cook went to school at nearby Great Ayton and lived with his family at Airy Holme Farm before later moving to Staithes and then Whitby before setting off on his travels.

Continue down to the cross roads at Dikes Lane and turn left up the road to reach Gribdale Terrace. These houses were built to accommodate the ironstone miners who worked the rich ores in the vicinity.

The road bends sharp left here but follow the track straight ahead with the Terrace on the left and continue straight up the fields to return to Gribdale Gate.

WALK 15
The Drovers'
Walk

Allow 3 to 3½ hours

A gradual climb from Osmotherley brings you
to a high point overlooking the A19 and A172,
with panoramas of the distant Pennines. The
drone of traffic is left behind as the path
descends to Sheepwash, a favourite picnic place.
The route of an ancient cattle-droving road is
then followed before the path curls back to
Osmotherley.

*Leave the centre of Osmotherley (SE457973) and
follow the Swainby road uphill, turning left into
Ruebury Lane on the outskirts of the village. The route
is following the Cleveland Way. Follow the track,
gradually bearing right. Pass on the right of Chapel
Wood Farm and continue across the fields.* Hidden by
the trees down on the left are the ruins of Mount
Grace Priory. Founded in 1398 this is one of only
nine Carthusian priories founded in England and is
the best preserved. The monks lived in virtual
isolation in individual cells, one of which has been
reconstructed at Mount Grace.

*Enter the conifer plantation and take the path
forward right, gradually climbing to the hill top. Go
through scrub woodland and past the TV station. There
are occasional tantalising views down through the trees
on the left. Passing through two bridlegates onto the
open moor, follow the right hand of the two paths,
gradually veering away from the conifers.* From here
there are distant views towards Live Moor and
Carlton Moor, the onward route of the Cleveland
Way.

*Approaching Scarth Nick leave the Cleveland Way
and follow the obvious path sharp right down to the
road and follow this to Sheepwash,* a popular picnic and
parking spot by Crabdale Beck. *Cross the footbridge and
follow the broad track uphill.* This is the line of the
old Hambleton Drove Road along which cattle and
sheep from Scotland and the northern counties
were driven to markets in London and the south.
Drove roads were in use for several centuries
before the development of a railway network in
the early 19th century made them obsolete. This
road followed the high ground of the moors to
Sutton Bank, from where it dropped across the
Vale of Pickering towards York.

*Continue along the track which becomes a tarmac
road. Just before a junction turn right onto a path with
a field on the right and moor on the left. Go through
the right hand of two facing field gates and continue
through the field with the wall on the left. Turn left
along the track, going downhill to re-join the Cleveland
Way at a good farm road. Turn sharp right, pass on
the right of White House Farm and go downhill to
cross the footbridge and follow the path uphill through
the woods. Cross the field towards the church and return
to Osmotherley.*

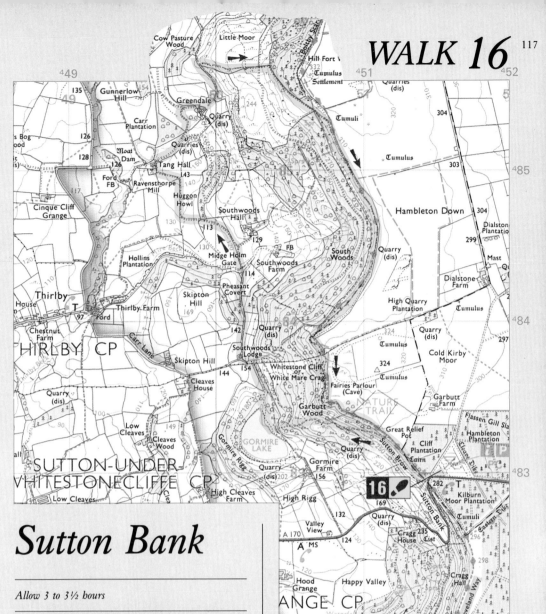

Sutton Bank

Allow 3 to 3½ hours

The view from Sutton Bank, where this walk commences, has been described as the finest in England. Certainly few would deny that on a clear day it is one of the best. The route down towards Lake Gormire is steep but not difficult and the path back along the top of the escarpment gives ever-changing views of the scene below.

Start from the Information Centre at Sutton Bank (SE515831). Walk to the edge of the escarpment and turn right along the Cleveland Way.

From the path there is a view down to Lake Gormire, one of the few lakes in Yorkshire and the only one in the North York Moors National Park. Reputed to be 'bottomless', it is in fact fairly shallow. The lake was formed by glacial action but a legend holds that the devil leapt from Whitestone Cliff on a white horse and disappeared into a hole in the ground. This filled with water to form the lake. Another local legend tells how a white mare with her rider plunged from the same cliff into the lake. Pass the lake at midnight and you might hear the rider grooming his horse! In the distance the Pennines can be seen, while to the south the cliffs of Roulston Scar provide a good take-off platform for gliders from the Yorkshire Gliding Club.

Follow the path of the Sutton Bank Nature Trail along to where a narrow path (marked number 3) branches off down to the left. This route passes through pleasant woodland which provides cover for a wide range of birds, animals and insects.

Garbutt Wood is managed by the Yorkshire Wildlife Trust as a nature reserve.

Continue down to the edge of Lake Gormire, passing on the way a standing stone. Turn right along the lake side, heading away from the lake, and just beyond the end of the board-walk turn left to Southwoods Lodge and then right, through a gate and along a broad bridleway. Approaching Southwoods Hall walk straight over the cross-road and continue up the tarmac road to where it bears right towards the Hall. Continue through trees and through a field gate, gradually turning left downhill, then go through a gateway and up a grassy track.

At the top of the rise turn sharp right along a slightly raised route where the old hedge has been removed. Go through a field gate and then turn forward left to Tang Hall. Keep the farm on the left then turn sharp right over the cattle grid to follow the lane up to Greendale. Approaching Greendale Farm pass through a field gate on the left of the farm entrance and go up the field to a bridlegate on the edge of the wood. Turn left uphill and then right at the first junction of paths.

Pass through a young forestry plantation and then go over a stile into scrubland. Bear forward right to re-enter the forest and continue uphill. Cross the broad forest track and a little way uphill bear right alongside an old wall. Follow this until you emerge on the Cleveland Way at the top of the hill. Continue along the edge of the escarpment to return to Sutton Bank.

Index

Page numbers in bold type
indicate main entries

A

abbeys and priories **70**
Ainthorpe 108
Aislaby 98
Allerston 38
Ampleforth **32**, 100
Ampleforth Abbey 13, 32, **70**
Ampleforth College 32, 41
angling **70**
Arden Hall 12, **45**
Arncliffe Woods 38
Ashberry Pasture 22
Ayton, Great 9, 25, **42**, 115
Ayton, West 96, 113

B

Ballistic Missile Early Warning
    Station 40, 96, 98, 112
Baysdale Convent 12, 49
Baysdale Moor 35
Beast Cliff 57
Beck Hole 27, 28, **32**
Beck Isle Museum of Rural
    Life 56, **74**
bicycle hire **70**
Billingham 55
Bilsdale 12, 18, **33**, 114
Black Hambleton 16, 44
Blakey 15
Blakey Junction 30
Blakey Moor 34
Blakey Rigg 17
Blakey Topping **46**
Blue Bank 63
Boggle Hole 103
Boltby 44, **45**
Botton Hall 37, 73
Boughton, Great 100
Boulby 9, 23, 24, 53, 105
Boulby Cliff 53, 105
Bransdale 7
Bride Stones, The **33**
Brompton 18, **34**, 96
Broughton, Great 114
Broxa 44
Broxa Forest **45**
Burniston 96
Burton Howe 30
Byland Abbey 11, 12, 67, 100

C

Captain Cook Birthplace
    Museum 55, **73**
Carlton Bank 34
Carlton-in-Cleveland 33, **34**
Castle Howard **73**
castles **47**
Castleton 13, 15, 29, 30, **34**, 47,
    98
Castleton Rigg 98
Cawthorn Camps 8, **34**, 43
Cawthorne 34
Chop Gate 18, 33, 100, 114
Church Houses 39
Clay Bank 33, 100

Cleave Dyke 8
Cleveland Hills 9, **35**, 60, 100
Cleveland Way 17, 23, 34, 35,
    44, 46, 49, 54, 55, 57, 61, 65,
    102, 104, 105, 114, 116, 117
Cloughton 96, 102
Cloughton Wyke 102
Cod Beck 56, 65
Cod Beck Reservoir 56
Cold Kirby 44, 45
Cold Moor 114
Commondale 29, **36**
Countryside Commission 23
Courts Leet **53**
Cowesby 44
Coxwold **36**, 37
Crabdale Beck 116
craft workshops **71**
Crescent Art Gallery, Rotunda and
    Woodend Museum **75**
Crook Ness 17
Cropton **37**, 47
Cropton Forest 37, 43, 59
Crunkley Gill 51

D

Dalby 6, 48
Dalby Forest 22, 33, 53, 66
Danby 13, 15, 29, **37**, 53, 98,
    108
Danby Castle 37, 40, 47, 108
Danby Dale 14, 18, 37
Danby Low Moor 35
Darncombe 53
Derwent, River 39, 45, 60, 61,
    113
Derwent Sea Cut 61
Derwent Way 39, 45, 69
Dove, River 39, 111
Duncombe Park 20, 46
Dundale Griff 112

E

Eaglescliffe 69
Easby Moor 42, 115
East Arncliffe Wood 41
Ebberston **38**
Ebberston Hall **73**
Ebor Way 46
Egglescliffe 69
Egton Bridge 29, **38**, 41, 43, 98
Eller Beck 29, 33, 40
Eller Beck Valley 28
Ellerburn 66
Elm Hagg Wood 67
Esk Dale 9, 18, 28, 34, **38**, 51,
    67
Esklets 38
Esk, River 34, 37, 38, 41, 43, 51,
    63, 68, 108
Everley 39

F

Fadmoor **40**, 41
Fairy Cross Plain 40
Falling Foss **52**, 106
Fangdale Beck 18
Farndale 7, 14, 22, 30, 39, 111
Fat Betty 18, 98
Felixkirk 44, 67
Flamingoland Zoo and Holiday
    Village 57, **73**
Forestry Commission, The **53**
Forge Valley 22, **39**, 96, 113
Freeborough Hill 34

Fryup Dales 14, 18, **40**, 108
Fylingdales Moor 8, 18, **40**, 53,
    96, 98
Fylingthorpe 40, 96

G

Garbutt Wood 117
Gillamoor **40**, 41
Gilling Castle 41, 73
Gilling East 41
Gisborough Moor 33, 35, 44
Glaisdale 14, 18, 29, 39, **41**
Glaisdale Moor 6, 16
Goathland 15, 17, 28, 29, **42**, 43,
    96, 98, 107
Goathland Bank Top 27
Goldsborough **42**, 43
golf **71**
Gormire, Lake 18, 65, 117
Gribdale Gate 115
Grosmont 8, 28, 29, 33, **43**, 98
Grosmont Priory 12
Guisborough **35**, 44
Guisborough Priory 8, 12, 44, **70**

H

Hackness 11, **44**
Hambleton Drove Road 16, 44, 65
Hambleton Hills 8, 18, **44**, 66,
    100
Hand of Glory **67**
Harome 48, 60
Harwood Dale **45**
Hasty Bank 114
Hawnby **45**
Hawsker 96
Hayburn Wyke 102
Helmsley 13, 17, 20, **46**, 100
Helmsley Castle 47, **73**
Hinderwell **46**
hobs **61**
Hole of Horcum 46, 52, 96, 98,
    112
Hood Hill 18
Hovingham **46**
Hovingham Hall 47
Howardian Hills 47
Hundale Point 102
Hunt Cliff 22
Huthwaite 65
Hutton-le-Hole 30, **48**, 98
Hutton Rudby 49

I

information centres **73**

K

Keldy 6
Kepwick 44
Kettleness 42, 43
Kilburn 17, 32, **49**, 110
Kilburn White Horse 49
Kildale 29, 47, **49**
Killingnoble Scar 52
Kirby Knowle 44
Kirby Misperton 60
Kirbymoorside 28, 39, 47, **50**
Kirkdale 11, **50**
Kirkham 12

L

Langdale 8
Langdale End 45, 53, 96

Langdale Forest 45
Laskill 13
Lastingham 10, 11, *51*
Lealholm 29, *51*
Lealholm Bank 39, 51
Lease Rigg 8
Leven, River 49
Levisham *52*, 98
Levisham Beck 52
Levisham Dyke 8
Levisham Moor 46, 52
Lilla Cross 18, 40
Littlebeck *52*, 106
Littlebeck Valley 106
Lockton *52*, 98
Lockton Low Moor 98
Lockwood Beck Reservoir 34
Loftus 28, *52*
Low Dalby *53*, 96
Low Mill 39, 111
Lowna 39
Lyke Wake Walk 17, *56*, 57, 65, 107
Lythe and Lythe Bank *54*

M

Mallyan Spout 42, 98, 107
Margery Stone, The 18
Marske 25
Marton 24, *55*
Maw Rigg 8
Maybeck 52
Medd Crag 114
Middlesbrough 28, 35, *55*
Middleton 60, 98
Moorland Trout Farm 57, 74
Moors Centre, The 29, 37, *73*, 98, 108
Moorsrail 29, 39, 74
Mount Grace Priory 12, *55*, 70, 100, 116
Mulgrave Castle 54
Mulgrave Woods 54
Murk Esk 33, 39, 43

N

Nelly Ayre Foss 42
Ness Hag Wood 53
Nether Silton 44, 45
Newburgh Priory 37, *73*, 100
Newgate Bank 33, 100
Newham Grange Leisure Farm 55, 73
Newtondale 7, 18, 19, 98, 112
Newton Dale Well 52
Newton-under-Roseberry *59*, 115
Northallerton 100
North York Moors Crosses Walk 17
North York Moors Historical Railway Trust Ltd 29
North York Moors National Park Committee 9, 35, 37, 46
North York Moors Railway *29*, 39, 74
North Yorkshire and Cleveland Heritage Coast 23
North Yorkshire Moors Railway Preservation Society 29
Norton 61
Nunnington Hall *74*

O

Old Byland 44, 45
Old Ralph 18

Ormesby Hall *74*
Osgodby Hall *75*, 100
Osmotherley 17, *56*, 59, 119
Osmotherley Moor 16
Oswaldkirk 60, 100
Over Silton 45

P

Pannet Art Gallery and Museum 68
Pickering 12, 13, 27, 28, 29, *56*, 98
Pickering Castle 43, 47, *56*, 75
places to visit 73
Port Mulgrave 9, *46*, 105

R

Ravenscar 9, 17, *57*, 102, 103
Raincliffe Woods 61, 96
Raisale 114
Raw 40
Reasty Bank 45
Riccal Dale 14
riding and trekking 75
Rievaulx *58*, 100
Rievaulx Abbey 8, 12, *58*, 70
Rievaulx Terrace *75*, 100
Rillington 28
Robert Thompson's Craftsmen Ltd 32, 71
Robin Hood's Bay 24, 25, *58*, 96, 103, 104
Robin Hood's Bay Museum 75
Roseberry Topping 17, *59*, 115
Rosedale 98, 109
Rosedale Abbey 9, 14, 15, 30, 37, *59*, 98, 109
Rosedale Chimney Bank *59*, 98
Rosedale Moor 98
Rosedale Priory 12, *59*, 70
Roulston Scar 18, 49, 117
Roxby 47
Roxby Woods 62
Rudby 49
Runswick Bay *60*
Ruswarp 29
Rye Dale 14, 18, 46, *60*
Ryedale Folk Museum *48*, 73
Rye, River 45, *58*, 60

S

sailing 76
Saltburn-by-the-Sea 23
Saltergate 112
Saltersgate Bank 46
Saltpans 102
Sandsend 54
Sawdon 34
Scalby 61
Scalby Cut, The 39
Scalby Ness 23
Scaling Reservoir 22, 62
Scamridge Dykes 8, 38
Scarborough 28, *62*, 96
Scarborough Castle 47, *63*, 75
Scarth Nick *56*, 65, 116
Scugdale 65
Seal Sands 55
Seaton 63
Seven, River *59*, 109, 110
Shandy Hall 36, 37, *73*, 100
Sheepwash *56*, 116
Silpho 33, 44, 45
Silpho Forest Trail 45
Sinnington 110

Skinningrove 52
Sleights 29, 33, *63*, 96
Sleights Moor 96, 98
Slingsby 60
Snainton 96
Snilesworth Moor 60
Spaunton 53
Spaunton Moor 98
Speeton Cliffs 23
Spout House 73
Sproxton 100
Staintondale Shire Horses 75
Staithes 24, 25, *63*, 105
Standing Stones Rigg 45
Sterne, Laurence 36
Stokesley 35, *64*, 100
Stonegrave 60
Studford Ring 32
Sutton Bank 18, 22, 44, 49, *64*, 100, 116, 117
Swainby *65*

T

Tabular Hills 7, 8, 18
Tees, River 69
Thimbleby 44
Thirlby 44
Thirsk *65*, 100
Thomason Foss 33
Thornton Dale *66*, 96
Tom Leonard Mining Museum 75
Troutsdale 96

U

Ugthorpe 13, *66*
Upsall *66*

W

Wade's Causeway 8, 42, 43, 107
Wainstones, The 33, 114
walking 57
walks and nature trails 76
Wass *67*, 100
West Beck 107
Westerdale 18
Westerdale Moor 35
Wheeldale Beck 107
Wheeldale Moor 8, 16, 42, 43, 107
Whisperdales 44
Whitby 9, 25, 26, 27, 28, 53, *63*, *68*, 98, 104
Whitby Abbey 10, 11, 24, *68*, 70, 96, 104
Whitby Museum and Art Gallery 75
White Horse Bank 100
White Rose Walk 17
Whitestone Cliff 18
Whorlton 47, 65, *69*
Whorlton Castle *69*, 75
Wrelton 98
Wykeham *69*
Wykeham Forest 34
Wykeham Moor 53

Y

Yarm 35, *69*
Yewtree Scar 112
Yorkshire Gliding Club *64*
Yorkshire Wildlife Trust 22, 117
Young Ralph (Ralph's Cross) 17

Acknowledgements

The publishers would like to thank the many individuals who helped
in the preparation of this book. Special thanks are due to the
North York Moors National Park Authority.

The Automobile Association wishes to thank the following photographers,
organisations and libraries. Many of the photographs reproduced are the copyright
of the AA Picture Library.

M Aldelman 64 Sutton Bank Glider; *R H Hayes* 28 Incline Tragedy; *D A Idle* 27 Train, 28 Incline Cottage Beck Hole,
29 Campton Tank No. 5, 29 Stripper Volunteer, 30 Engine; *The Mansell Collection* 47 Scarborough Castle,
103 Robin Hood's Bay; *Mary Evans Picture Library* Back Cover Scarborough, 12 Rievaulx Abbey, 24 Staithes, 26 Lifeboat,
61 Troll, 67 Hand of Glory, 108 Packhorse; *S & O Mathews* 64/65 Sutton Bank; *C Molyneux* 62 Scarborough Bay,
62 Scarborough Castle, 63 Scarborough Harbour, 75 Scarborough Castle; *Nature Photographs* 16 Red Grouse,
(A K Davies), 19 Heron (P Sterry), 21 Bell Heather (P Sterry), 21 Duke of Burgundy (P Sterry), 21 Great Crested Grebe
(C Carver), 22 Whiskered Bat (S C Bissett); *R Newton* Front Cover Low Bride Stones, 1 Wheeldale Moor,
3 Runswick Bay, 5 Little Fryup Dale, 6 Cropton Forest, 9 Runswick Bay, 10 Whitby Abbey, 11 Byland Abbey,
11 St Mary's Crypt Lastingham, 12 Rievaulx Abbey, 13 Quaker Meeting House Laskill, 14 Wheeldale Moor,
14 Young Ralph's Cross, 15 View from Chimney Bank, 17 Sheep, 17 Old Ralph's Cross, 18 Little Fryup Dale,
23 Staithes, 26 Whitby Jet, 30 Pickering Station, 31 Snilesworth Moor, 32 Ampleforth Abbey,
32 Robert Thompson's Workshop Kilburn, 33 Low Bride Stones, 34 Carlton in Cleveland, 35 Cleveland Hills,
37 Tomb in St Michael's Coxwold, 37 Danby Dale, 37 Moors Centre Danby, 38 Ebberstone Hall, 38 Egton Bridge,
39 Esk Dale, 40 Fylingdales, 41 Castle Gilling East, 42 Wade Stone, 43 Wade's Causeway, 44 Guisborough Priory,
44 Hackness Church, 45 Hawnby Church, 45 Hawnby, 46 Helmsley, 46 Helmsley Market Day, 47 Hole of Horcum,
48 Ryedale Folk Museum, 49 White Horse Kilburn, 50 Saxon Sundial Kirkdale, 51 Lealholm, 51 Lastingham,
53 Dalby Forest, 54 St Oswald's Lythe, 56 Vale of Pickering, 56 Wall Painting Pickering Church,
60 Viking Cross St Andrews Middleton, 62 Scaling Dam, 65 Golden Fleece Hotel Thirsk, 66 Thornton Beck,
67 Upsall Forge, 67 Wass, 68 River Esk, 68 Jaw Bone Whitby, 69 Whorlton Castle, 69 Yarm, 70 Forge Valley,
71 Kilburn, 73 Ebberton Hall, 74 Castle Howard, 76 Wade's Causeway, 76 Forge Valley, 93 Goathland Tor Cross,
96 Robin Hood's Bay, 96 Whitby, 97 St Mary's Whitby, 97 Low Dalby, 98 St Andrew's Middleton,
99 Abbey Ruins Rosedale, 99 View from Chimney Bank, 100 Newburgh Priory; *North York Moors National Park*
9 Carlton Quarry, 52 Levisham, 57 Walkers, 75 Ravenscar and Robin Hood's Bay; *North York Moors Railway*
27 Map & Symbol, 28 George Stephenson; *V Patel* 43 Gt Ayton The Green, 58/9 Roseberry Topping, 68 Whitby;
Ryedale Folk Museum 53 Spauton Manor CT, 72 Ryedale Maypole Dancing; *Shandy Hall* 36 Laurence Sterne Shandy Hall;
W D Spence 16 Shooting Butts, 25 William Scoresby Senior, 25 Whalebone Scrapers, 60 Runswick Bay, 68 Whalers,
99 Tabular Hills; *R Surman* 58 Rievaulx Ionic Temple, 74 Nunnington Hall, 101 Rievaulx, 101 Mount Grace Priory;
H Williams 6/7 Glaisdale Moor; *T Woodcock* 7 Roman Signal Station, 17 Hambledon Hills, 41 Beggars Bridge Glaisdale,
62 Scarborough Bay.

Other Ordnance Survey Maps of the North York Moors

How to get there with Routemaster and Routeplanner Maps

Reach the North York Moors from Lancaster, Newcastle, Lincoln, Peterborough, Chester,
Liverpool and Manchester using Routemaster map sheets 5 and 6. Alternatively use the
Ordnance Survey Great Britain Routeplanner Map which covers the whole country on one
map sheet.

Exploring with Landranger, Tourist and Outdoor Leisure Maps

Landranger Series
1¼ inches to one mile or 1:50,000 scale

These maps cover the whole of Britain and are good
for local motoring and walking. Each contains
tourist information such as parking, picnic places,
viewpoints and rights of way. Sheets covering the
North York Moors are:

- 93 Middlesbrough and Darlington
- 94 Whitby
- 99 Northallerton and Ripon
- 100 Malton and Pickering
- 101 Scarborough and Bridlington

Tourist Map Series
1 inch to one mile or 1:63,360 scale

These maps cover popular holiday areas and are
ideal for discovering the countryside. In addition to
normal map detail ancient monuments, camping and
caravan sites, parking facilities and viewpoints are
marked. Lists of selected places of interest are
included on some sheets and others include useful
guides to the area.

Tourist Map Sheet 2 covers the North York Moors

Outdoor Leisure Map Series
2½ inches to one mile or 1:25,000 scale

These maps cover popular leisure and recreation
areas of the country and include details of Youth
Hostels, camping and caravanning sites, picnic areas,
footpaths and viewpoints.

Outdoor Leisure Map Sheets 26 and 27 cover the
North York Moors

Other titles available in this series are:

Channel Islands
Cornwall
Cotswolds

Ireland
Lake District
New Forest
Northumbria

Peak District
Scottish Highlands
Yorkshire Dales